WALTER A. NETSCH, FAIA: A CRITICAL APPRECIATION AND SOURCEBOOK

WALTER A. NETSCH, FAIA: A CRITICAL APPRECIATION AND SOURCEBOOK

Northwestern University Library | Evanston, Illinois

© 2008 by Northwestern University.

Published 2008 by Northwestern University Press.

ISBN-10: 0-8101-2541-2

ISBN-13: 978-0-8101-2541-4

Library of Congress Cataloging-in-Publication Data

Walter A. Netsch, FAIA: a critical appreciation and sourcebook/
Northwestern University Library; [contributions by Russell T. Clement ... et al.].
   p. cm.
Includes bibliographical references and index.
ISBN-13: 978-0-8101-2541-4 (cloth : alk. paper)
ISBN-10: 0-8101-2541-2 (cloth : alk. paper)
1. Netsch, Walter. 2. Architects—Illinois—Chicago—Biography.
I. Clement, Russell T. II. Netsch, Walter. III. Northwestern University
(Evanston, Ill.). Library.
NA737.N38W35 2008
720.92—dc22

2008010232

To the memory of the original members of the
Northwestern University Library planning committee in 1962:
Clarence L. Ver Steeg, Richard D. Ellman,
David Jolly, Jens Nyholm, Moody E. Prior,
John C. Sanderson Jr., and Robert H. Strotz

—WALTER NETSCH

Contents

Foreword

When I look at the Northwestern University Library, I wonder how it turned out the way it did. Northwestern University had an elegant, classical library designed by a prominent architect, James Gamble Rogers. Rogers had just finished Yale's magnificent Sterling Library, and his Charles Deering Library was another outstanding monument of the period. It was a campus icon. I didn't want to touch that building and was sensitive to its beautiful site and landscaping. The Lakefill project was under way, and we were resolved to keep the lake next to the existing campus. Remodeling or incorporating Deering Library into a larger library was out of the question. We wanted a continuum of what was — a continuum of the past in a modern, functional style.

Beginning in 1962 I met twice a month with the Library Planning Committee, chaired by Clarence Ver Steeg. We were a thoughtful and creative group who started with the overarching question "What is a library today?" We weren't inhibited by the past and elected not to replicate attractive features of the Charles Deering Library, such as its spacious reading room. We discussed how students use libraries, we read books and articles (I even stole a book about library architecture but soon returned it because it was so outdated), we listened to students, librarians, consultants, and faculty members. Before I started drawing, we developed succinct goals about how the building would function. I had previously designed libraries at Grinnell College and the Illinois Institute of Technology, but the Northwestern Library required a different level of programming.

The list of primary objectives grew and grew. Two goals stick in my mind: first, that carrels and classrooms be integrated with the book collections; and second, that the books be easy to find. Computers were coming, and we planned a small central computer facility for a single computer. A Core Library, open 24 hours a day, was a priority. I remember how empty most of the stack floors were in 1970. When I visited a Level 5 stack tower in 2006, I was amazed at how much the collections have grown. However, the fundamental reader-book relationship remains the same. The library is the culmination of the work of the committee and an important Field Theory building. I'm amazed that it was built as programmed and that we avoided getting trapped into using ungainly features such as standard windows and doors.

My career as an architect spans seven decades. I was hired by Skidmore, Owings & Merrill in 1947 as a fluke — I applied only at the urging of a colleague in Morgan Yost's residential architectural practice. Assignments on large-scale SOM projects — in Oak Ridge, Tennessee; Chicago; San Francisco and Monterey in California; Washington, D.C.; and Japan, as well as the Air Force Academy in Colorado Springs — forged my career and standing as an architect. These projects gained worldwide attention, and I was singled out as a promising young architect. The Air Force Academy design was a hard sell, the Cadet Chapel in particular, because some people didn't think it looked like a church. It's the only building I had to redesign. The architecture community supported the second design tremendously at a time when the press and factions in Washington wanted to kill it. Fifty years later appreciation for its design and geometry as a monument to modernity continues to grow. I'm pleased with its recent preservation and the respect with which Academy buildings are being maintained.

Notable projects followed, many appearing in these pages. Most memorable are those that reflect Field Theory, my signature design aesthetic, which was influenced by modern art, patterns in nature, and Japanese and Algerian cultures — historic Japan for its revered past, Algeria for its forward-looking social revolution. Of these I am especially fond of the Miami University Art Museum in Oxford, Ohio — my Louvre. I'm still thinking about new ways for architecture to respond to modern life. At present, I'm completing urban sustainability designs to endure the effects of global warming, called the 2060 Project.

It is fitting that this volume, which charts my ideas and career in my own words and those of others, should be produced by Northwestern University Library. Like the building, this book too is a continuum of the past.

I'm grateful to the many teammates on many projects and for all of the effort on this project. I wish to thank two people in particular. The first is my wife, Dawn Clark Netsch, who shares my moods and quandaries with love and devotion. The second is Russ Clement, who organized a library exhibit of my work and who developed and managed this complex compilation into a book that will be distributed to libraries throughout North America.

Praiseworthy modern architecture is an absorption and synthesis of the society around us — the physical manifestation of the ability and drive to see beyond accepted solutions and aesthetics. The critical difference between good and mediocre architecture is the depth of the design search, with both its joys and sorrows. All of my designs are different. I had a personal desire not to copy but to probe for the excitement of architecture.

Walter Netsch

The idea for a book on Chicago architect Walter Netsch originated with an exhibit, *Walter Netsch and the Northwestern University Library,* held in the University Library in 2006. Matthew Teti, an Art Collection staff member, proposed and helped prepare the exhibit. Matt felt that a large abstract painting, Oli Sihvonen's *The Matrix,* donated by Walter and Dawn Clark Netsch when the library opened, was underappreciated. Beyond an opportunity to redeem the painting's reputation, Matt was interested in brutalist architecture. As head of the Art Collection, I was curious about the radical change of architectural styles from the Charles Deering Library (1932) to Netsch's Northwestern University Library (1970).

A research web site on Walter Netsch's work and career was created to document the 2006 library exhibit and related events: www.library.northwestern.edu/art/walternetsch. While preparing the exhibit, Walter's affability and passion for the arts drew us into his orbit. After the exhibit, Art Collection staff members Lindsay King and Jessica Thomson and I conceived a modest print bibliography and chronology, based upon research for the web site.

Walter ardently supported the idea, which evolved to include essays on his work. Professors and architects who had published before on Walter and had established personal relations with him were contacted. Each was eager to contribute. Their admiration and respect for him are manifest in the essays, which function in part as a festschrift.

Throughout his career Walter was a dynamic theorist and author with a strong pedagogical impulse. (More than one prestigious architecture school courted him to become its dean.) No assessment of Walter's career of the sort we were undertaking would be complete without a selection of his own writings. While the statements included here represent only a sampling of his publications and presentations, they nevertheless reveal the breadth of his intellectual inquiry and thought process. These lectures and articles were prepared and delivered during the most active years of an intense architectural career. For a complete record of his writings, please consult the Bibliography of Primary Sources (pages 131–38).

Updates to the bibliography are posted on the Walter Netsch research web site, maintained by Northwestern University Library's Art Collection. Copies of most of the primary sources cited in the bibliography are available in University Archives, Northwestern University. We urge readers to send corrections and additions to the bibliography and chronology to the Art Collection.

Working in a building designed by Walter Netsch leaves an inescapable impression. Forty years after the library was completed, it continues to radiate his presence. Touring the building with Walter as a guide is an illuminating experience. Much to his satisfaction, after decades of profound changes in research and pedagogy, the library generally "works" in the ways he envisioned.

For two decades, beginning in 1962, Walter was Northwestern University's premier architect. From the sweeping design of the campus Lakefill expansion project, he went on to design seven buildings at Northwestern. He had the good sense and good luck to marry Dawn Clark Netsch, a Northwestern alumna, Northwestern law professor, and trailblazing political activist. In 2004 Walter was named the first Life Member of the Northwestern University Library's Board of Governors. We proudly claim him as our own.

Russell Clement

Acknowledgments

Appreciation is expressed first and foremost to Walter Netsch and Dawn Clark Netsch, who opened their minds, hearts, and home to this endeavor. Walter's engaging personality, his love of design and aesthetics, his enthusiasm for life and work, his open-mindedness and graciousness, and his commitment to leave the world a better place inspire us all.

Matthew Teti, Lindsay King, and Jessica Thomson prepared the 2006 library exhibit Walter Netsch and the Northwestern University Library and identified Netsch-related sources for the bibliography. Lindsay and Jessica created the Netsch research web site, www.library.northwestern.edu/art/walternetsch, and skillfully piloted it through multiple incarnations. Lindsay and Jessica located and scanned images, checked and rechecked citations, sorted and organized files, prepared and edited annotations, and assisted with the chronology and other sections. Lindsay also helped edit the essays. Russell Clement coordinated the exhibit, wrote the biography of Walter, and managed the book project. Lauren Wright, an Art Collection student assistant, aided with citation verification, made copies, and provided notes used in some of the annotations.

Kevin Leonard, associate University Archivist and a long-time Netsch aficionado, provided invaluable assistance with fact checking and locating materials for the exhibit. Debbie Vaughan, director of the Chicago History Museum's Research Center, was an able and genial guide to the museum's Walter Netsch archives. Personnel at institutions with buildings designed by Netsch verified facts, names of buildings, renovations and additions, supplied photos and archival information, and offered encouragement and support. William Jones at the University of Illinois at Chicago; Daniel Meyer, Anne Stephenson, and Ben Dueholm at the University of Chicago; Jeri Vargo and Helen Bergamo at Wells College in Aurora, New York; Don Smith at Grinnell College; and Roger Rainwater at Texas Christian University were particularly helpful.

Sincere appreciation goes to the essayists Robert Bruegmann, Sarah Dunn, Martin Felsen, David Goodman, and Robert Nauman, whose respect for Walter Netsch and enthusiasm for the book were exhilarating. Tom Fredrickson, senior editor, and Vickie Lata, senior designer, who both work in Northwestern University's Department of University Relations, deserve special mention for their exceptional commitment to the project. Tom edited several drafts, fact-checked and corrected errors, clarified passages, coordinated and collaborated on the book's design, and is responsible for a superior final product. Vickie's elegant and sensitive design shows on every page. Profound thanks to Jim Fuhr for speedily and thoroughly indexing the book.

Chronology

Projects for which Walter Netsch was the primary designer are listed by name alone; entries for other projects indicate the scope of his involvement. Dates indicate when Netsch's involvement in a project began.

1920

Walter Andrew Netsch Jr.
born February 23 in Chicago

1934

Attends Hyde Park High School,
Chicago; graduates 1937

1938

Postgraduate year at Leelanau School
for Boys, Glen Arbor, Michigan

1939

Studies at Massachusetts Institute
of Technology, Cambridge,
Massachusetts; graduates 1943

1943

Joins U.S. Army Corps of Engineers;
serves in North Pacific; discharged 1946

1946

Designs for L. Morgan Yost,
Kenilworth, Illinois

1947

Joins Skidmore, Owings & Merrill
(SOM) in Chicago

Designs for SOM in Oak Ridge,
Tennessee

1949

Honorable mention in the *Progressive Architecture* U.S. Junior Chamber of
Commerce Architectural Competition

Joins SOM's Chicago office

Lake Meadows Shopping Center,
Chicago

1950

Del Monte Shopping Center,
Del Monte, California

Recent Buildings by Skidmore, Owings & Merrill exhibition at the Museum of
Modern Art, New York (September 26–
November 5) includes a model of
Del Monte Shopping Center

1951

Joins SOM's San Francisco office

1952

Elmendorf Air Force Base Hospital,
Anchorage, Alaska

1953

Greyhound Service Garage,
San Francisco

Designs military air bases in Okinawa,
Japan (continues through 1954)

1954

Plans, Crown-Zellerbach Headquarters
Building, San Francisco (project
completed by Charles Bassett, 1959)

Returns to SOM's Chicago office

Plans, Inland Steel Building, Chicago
(completed by Bruce Graham, 1957)

U.S. Naval Postgraduate School,
Monterey, California

Directs design team, U.S. Air
Force Academy, Colorado Springs,
Colorado (completed 1958)

U.S. Air Force Academy Cadet
Chapel, Colorado Springs,
Colorado (completed 1963)

1955

Becomes member of the American Institute of Architects (AIA)

The Academy Master Plan exhibition at the Colorado Springs Fine Arts Center (May 13–15) unveils designs for the U.S. Air Force Academy

Made partner at SOM

1957

Buildings for Business and Government exhibition at the Museum of Modern Art, New York (February 25–April 28) includes designs for the U.S. Air Force Academy

1959

Harris Trust and Savings Bank (first expansion), Chicago

Burling Library, Grinnell College, Grinnell, Iowa

Two Buildings San Francisco 1959 exhibition at the San Francisco Museum of Art (August 21–September 20) includes drawings and models for the Crown-Zellerbach Headquarters Building; travels to Portland, Oregon (October 6–November 1)

1960

Skokie Public Library, Skokie, Illinois

1961

Fine Arts Building, Grinnell College, Grinnell, Iowa

University of Illinois Circle Campus, Chicago (completed 1965): includes the Art and Architecture Building, University Hall, the Science and Engineering South Building, University Library, among other buildings *(Note: In 1982 it became the University of Illinois at Chicago.)*

1962

Paul V. Galvin Library, Illinois Institute of Technology, Chicago

Grover M. Hermann Hall, Illinois Institute of Technology, Chicago

Plan, Northwestern University Lakefill expansion, Evanston, Illinois

1963

Marries Dawn Clark

1964

R. S. Reynolds Memorial Award for U.S. Air Force Academy Cadet Chapel

Master plan, Lake Forest Academy, Lake Forest, Illinois

Northwestern University Library, Evanston, Illinois (completed 1970)

1965

The Forum, Grinnell College, Grinnell, Iowa

Center for Materials Science and Engineering (Building 13, also called the Vannevar Bush Center for Material Sciences), Massachusetts Institute of Technology, Cambridge, Massachusetts

Silver Medal for Design and Craftsmanship from the New York Chapter of the AIA for colored-glass windows in the U.S. Air Force Academy Cadet Chapel

1966

Lindheimer Astronomical Research Center, Northwestern University, Evanston, Illinois (razed 1995)

Total Design Award from the National Society of Interior Designers for the University of Illinois Circle Campus

1967

Elected to AIA College of Fellows

Illinois State Bar Association Office Building (now Illinois Bar Center), Springfield, Illinois

John J. Madden Clinic (now John J. Madden Mental Health Center), Maywood, Illinois

1968

Honorary doctor of fine arts degree from Lawrence University, Appleton, Wisconsin

Louis Jefferson Long Library, Wells College, Aurora, New York

Rebecca Crown Center, Northwestern University, Evanston, Illinois

1969

St. Matthew United Methodist Church, Chicago

1970

Joseph Regenstein Library, University of Chicago

Behavioral Sciences Building, University of Illinois Circle Campus

Science and Engineering South Building, University of Illinois Circle Campus

Superior Craftsmanship Award from the Concrete Contractors Association of Greater Chicago for Northwestern University Library

Master plan, "New Town-in-Town," Newark, New Jersey

1971

O. T. Hogan Biological Sciences Building, Northwestern University, Evanston, Illinois

Sunburst Youth Home (also known as the Winnebago Children's Home), Neillsville, Wisconsin

Core urban renewal plans, Pruitt-Igoe housing project, St. Louis, Missouri

Conceptual plans and urban design, Paired New Towns, Detroit

Living with Art: Selected Loans from the Collection of Mr. and Mrs. Walter A. Netsch exhibition at the University of Iowa Museum of Art, Iowa City (September 15–October 21)

Master plan, Montgomery College, Takoma Park, Maryland (completed 1980)

1972

James Madison Barker Library of Engineering (remodeling), Massachusetts Institute of Technology, Cambridge, Massachusetts

Sherman Fairchild Electrical Engineering and Electronics Complex of the Research Laboratory of Electronics, Massachusetts Institute of Technology, Cambridge, Massachusetts

Lindquist Center, University of Iowa, Iowa City

Basic Sciences Building (now Bowen Sciences Building), University of Iowa, Iowa City

Frances Searle Building, Northwestern University, Evanston, Illinois

Urban design and transportation study, Indianapolis

1973

Health Sciences Library (now Hardin Library for Health Sciences), University of Iowa, Iowa City

Industrial modular housing system, Indianapolis (for Operation Breakthrough, U.S. Department of Housing and Urban Development)

Master plan, New Town, Poinciana, Florida

Master plan, Research and Development Center and site development, Westinghouse Electric Corporation, Churchill Borough, Pennsylvania

Addition, Skokie Public Library, Skokie, Illinois

1974

Walter Netsch home and studio, Chicago

Barler Hall of Music, Wells College, Aurora, New York

Henrietta Campbell Art Studio (now Campbell Art Building), Wells College, Aurora, New York

John Wesley Powell Federal Building, U.S. Geological Survey National Center, Reston, Virginia

Feasibility study and remodeling programs, Organization of American States, Washington, D.C.

Honor Award from *Wisconsin Architect* magazine for the Sunburst Youth Home (also known as the Winnebago Children's Home), Neillsville, Wisconsin

1975

Master plan for wild animal reservation and recreation center, Dirab Park, Riyadh, Saudi Arabia

Harris Trust and Savings Bank (second expansion), Chicago (completed 1977)

1976

Art Institute of Chicago, East Wing (now Columbus Drive Building)

Chicago Architects exhibition at Cooper Union, New York (February 27– March 22) includes works by Netsch; travels to Harvard University, Cambridge, Massachusetts (March 26– April 23), the Time-Life Building, Chicago (May 1–June 20), various Illinois Arts Centers (July and August), the Illinois Institute of Technology (September), and the University of California, Berkeley (October)

1977

Regenstein Hall of Music, Northwestern University, Evanston, Illinois

Seeley G. Mudd Library for Science and Engineering, Northwestern University, Evanston, Illinois

1978

William G. and Marie Selby Public Library, Sarasota, Florida

Miami University Art Museum, Oxford, Ohio

Baldwin Building, Community Pediatric and Adolescent Medicine, Mayo Clinic, Rochester, Minnesota

Regenstein Eye Center, Rush-Presbyterian-St. Luke's Medical Center, Chicago

Honor Award and Bartlett Award from the AIA

Library Building Award, AIA/American Library Association

1979

Original concept drawings, Central Library, Sophia University, Tokyo

Department of Music, University of Chicago

Honorary doctor of humanities degree from Miami University, Oxford, Ohio

Transformations in American Architecture exhibition at Museum of Modern Art, New York (February 23–April 24) includes works by Netsch

Gives address on creativity at the Jungian Conference, Miami University, Oxford, Ohio

Certificate of Architectural Merit from the Association of School Business Officials

Mary Couts Burnett Library (expansion and renovation), Texas Christian University, Fort Worth, Texas (completed 1983)

Retires from SOM

1980

"Case Study: The University of Blida in Algeria," presentation at "The Search for Form: Places of Public Gathering in Islam," fifth seminar in the series "Architectural Transformations in the Islamic World," Aga Khan Award for Architecture, May 4–7, Amman, Jordan

Late Entries to the Chicago Tribune Tower Competition exhibition at the Museum of Contemporary Art, Chicago (May 30– July 17) includes an entry by Netsch; travels to the La Jolla Museum of Contemporary Art (September 12– October 12), the Walker Art Center, Minneapolis (April 12–May 31, 1981), Yale University Art Gallery (September 8–

October 20, 1981), Forth Worth Art Center (November 7–December 13, 1981), and San Francisco Museum of Modern Art (January 7–March 7, 1982)

Honorary doctor of fine arts degree from Northwestern University, Evanston, Illinois

Fort Wayne Museum of Art, Fort Wayne, Indiana (completed 1984)

Serves on the U.S. Commission of Fine Arts (term completed 1984)

1981

Watercolors and sculpture exhibited at Zolla/Lieberman Gallery, Chicago (April 2–May 5)

1983

Living with Art, Two: The Collection of Walter and Dawn Clark Netsch exhibition at the Miami University Art Museum, Oxford, Ohio (September 10–December 16); travels to the Snite Museum of Art, University of Notre Dame, South Bend, Indiana (January 22–March 25, 1984)

Chicago, 150 ans d'architecture exhibition, organized by Paris Art Center, Musée-Galerie de la SEITA, and L'Institut français d'architecture, includes works by Netsch; at various institutions (October 5, 1983–January 14, 1984)

Designs for the Peak Residential Club competition (not won), Hong Kong

1984

Three student housing communities, University of Annaba, Algeria

University of Blida, Algeria (completed 1986)

1985

Interviewed for Chicago Architects Oral History Project

150 Years of Chicago Architecture, 1833–1983 exhibition at the Museum of Science and Industry, Chicago (October 1, 1985–January 15, 1986) includes works by Netsch

1986

University of Tizi-Ouzou, Algeria

Appointed to the Board of Commissioners, Chicago Park District: president (1986–87), commissioner (1986–89)

1990

Establishes private consulting practice, Chicago

1991

Living with Art, Three: The Collection of Walter and Dawn Clark Netsch exhibition at the Miami University Art Museum, Oxford, Ohio (March 26–August 4)

Honorary doctor of landscape architecture degree from Purdue University, West Lafayette, Indiana

1995

Interviewed for Chicago Architects Oral History Project

1996

U.S. Air Force Academy Cadet Chapel receives AIA Twenty-Five Year Award

2001

Excellence in Architecture Award from the Illinois Institute of Technology

2002

Daniel H. Burnham History Maker Award for Distinction in Architecture and Design from the Chicago Historical Society (now Chicago History Museum)

2004

U.S. Air Force Academy Cadet Area added to the U.S. National Register of Historic Places; commemorative U.S. postage stamp issued to honor 50th anniversary of the Academy

Life Member of Northwestern University Library Board of Governors

2006

Walter Netsch and the Northwestern University Library exhibition at Northwestern University Library (February 7–March 31)

2007

AIA Lifetime Achievement Award

2008

Honorary doctor of architecture degree
from the University of Illinois at Chicago

Deering Family Award, Deering Society
and Library Board of Governors,
Northwestern University Library

Essays

ROBERT BRUEGMANN

It isn't easy to forget a first meeting with Walter Netsch.

I met Walter about 1980, just after my arrival in Chicago. John Zukowsky, also newly arrived in the city to oversee the architectural collections at the Art Institute of Chicago, asked if I would be willing to serve as guest curator for an exhibition he wanted to do on the work of three Chicago "maverick" architects — Harry Weese, Bertrand Goldberg, and Walter Netsch.

I was thrilled to get this opportunity. All three were still active in 1980, and they were already legendary figures. It seemed to me, a young historian just starting a career, that meeting them would be a chance to catch a glimpse of an era that already seemed to belong to some distant past. Each of them had played a key role in architecture in the decades after World War II, in which the torch had been passed from an earlier generation of modernist architectural pioneers — men like Ludwig Mies van der Rohe, Le Corbusier, Walter Gropius and Frank Lloyd Wright — to a younger generation.

By 1980 Weese, Goldberg, and Netsch had created a considerable body of work in which the principles of modernism were extended, enriched, and adapted for use in America. However, all were considered mavericks because they had highly individual approaches to design that didn't fit easily into the aesthetic of minimal geometric forms that was introduced to Chicago by Mies and considered the gold standard by many architects in the city.

In the case of Walter Netsch, I knew that he had recently retired from Skidmore, Owings & Merrill, an enormously successful firm that, during the postwar decades while Walter had worked there, had quickly expanded to become Chicago's largest. I knew that his extremely prolific career had included such major works as the master plan and buildings at the United States Air Force Academy, the Joseph Regenstein Library at the University of Chicago, a master plan and numerous buildings at Northwestern University, and the master plan and most of the buildings at the University of Illinois at Chicago Circle (soon to become University of Illinois at Chicago), where I was teaching. From the minimal modernism and glassy walls of the earlier buildings, Walter's work — like that of a great many architects of his generation — had moved toward a heavier, more complex approach, often involving intricate rotated geometries in a system that he called, with a half-ironic nod to Albert Einstein, "Field Theory."

By 1980 I also knew that there had been a strong reaction to modernist architecture and to the work of people like Walter. This was the high-water mark of the "postmodern" response to architectural modernism. According to many postmodernists, modernism had led architecture into a cul-de-sac. The minimal glass boxes of Mies, so admired just a few years previously, were called boring, energy inefficient, and insensitive to local context. Walter's later buildings were routinely described as too massive, gray, and brutal. Many people also considered the rotated geometries too complicated and disorienting.

And so it was one morning that I arrived at the door of the Netsch house on Hudson Street in Old Town. It was a building I had seen from the outside many times before. At first glance it was relatively unassuming. Although it clearly looked different from the neighboring houses, its massing, materials, and landscaping made it seem to fit in. The largely blank walls gave little sense of what might be inside, and I was very curious.

I rang the bell. Walter opened the door. From the front door I could look diagonally upward and see that the majority of the house was a great volume of space brilliantly lit from a few windows. Visible on the walls were several large pieces of art, most notably a huge Lichtenstein painting. From invisible speakers came the sound of some insistent modern music. Walter took me upstairs and showed me drawings of his latest project. The large dining table was strewn with dozens of sheets of yellow tracing paper, each one covered with geometric patterns, the "fields" of rotated squares that formed intricate matrices, out of which Walter would designate and trace buildings or rooms or pieces of furniture. Then I turned on the tape recorder and he started talking about his career.

As it turned out, the exhibition at the Art Institute never happened. But I was hooked. That first visit began a process that continued for many years, where I would visit Walter at home, hear about his latest projects, and then sit down to record what he could remember about his career. What he could remember always astonished me. Although the names sometimes didn't come easily, he could almost always answer any question I had about why he had chosen a particular material or designed a specific detail, even for projects that he had completed decades earlier. He conveyed vividly the sense of architecture as a mission: the creation of buildings that would make their occupants more comfortable, productive, and happy.

One thing that never changed was Walter's oversize personality. There is something about Walter that commands attention. It isn't his booming voice, although that is certainly memorable. His presence is deeply felt even when he isn't speaking. It isn't his physical size. He is a tall man but not overwhelming in stature. Even in recent years, when Walter has been confined to a wheelchair and suffering from many infirmities, his presence is huge. He seems to fill whatever room he is in.

It seems that what commands attention is, instead, an attitude, the way everything he says or does — even the way he simply sits in a chair — seems to express an absolute conviction that he is part of something larger than himself. That something isn't religion or politics. It is modern architecture. Walter was raised in the true modernist faith, and he has never

fig. 1 Walter Netsch with Robert Bruegmann, 2006

wavered in his belief. Design — good modern design — can solve human problems. To be an architect designing good modern buildings is one of the highest callings in the world.

This belief sustained him through all kinds of adversity, and it comes across almost instantly to anyone at all attuned to this way of looking at the world. For many years, particularly in the 1970s and 1980s, his unyielding faith in the power of rational modernist problem solving and his impatience with the ironic, detached play of imagery that marked the postmodern reaction to modernism made him seem like something of an anachronism, a vestige of a long-vanished world. But even in those years his presence was impressive.

Today, as modernism is again resurgent in schools of architecture and his buildings start to reach the age when they are ready for designation as historic landmarks, Walter Netsch provides a connection back to the heady years of the last century, when modernism and America emerged from World War II ready to take on the world.

Walter Netsch: A Biography

RUSSELL CLEMENT

"Netsch's work was the soul and the spirit of the people."
— Nathaniel Owings

Walter Andrew Netsch Jr. was born at home — 6807 Paxton Avenue, a block south of Jackson Park on Chicago's South Side — on February 23, 1920. His father, Walter Sr., was from Manchester, New Hampshire, the son of German immigrants, and had attended Dartmouth College on scholarship. There he met Anna Calista Smith, a devout Christian Scientist who descended from an established New England family. Anna's mother, Lizzie Smith, was the second wife of a wealthy meatpacker and maintained homes in Nashua, New Hampshire, and Jacksonville, Florida. In 1917 Walter Sr. and Anna married.

Anna's father offered Walter Sr. a large share of the family business, which he declined. The offer may have established Walter Sr.'s goal of joining the meatpacking industry, however, for in 1919 the Netsches moved to Chicago, where Walter Sr. worked for Armour & Co., rising to the position of vice president. At the time of Walter Jr.'s birth they lived in the South Shore community, a few blocks from Lake Michigan and several miles from the Union Stock Yards. A girl, Nan, was born 18 months after Walter.

As a baby, Walter returned with his parents to Nashua from Chicago in 1920–21, when his grandfather was ill. Henry, an elderly freed slave, rocked him in a bedroom above the dining room.

From an early age, Walter was fascinated by patterns and geometries found in nature. His mother's family

fig. 1   Walter Netsch with his mother, Anna, c. 1921

owned a summer home on Lake Winnepesakee in New Hampshire, where Walter recalls collecting leaves and rocks, watching shadows, and wanting to be an artist. His parents indulged his proclivities by enrolling him in drawing classes at the Art Institute of Chicago. He also built play structures out of containers brought home from work by his father. He was bright, thin, and small. He recalls roller skating, playing baseball (he became an ardent White Sox fan), and riding horses.

Horses were something of a constant in Walter's childhood and youth. His father rode on horseback in the immense Union Stock Yards — a way to supervise his staff while remaining above the effluent — and Walter recalls being taken for a horseback ride to see the carnage after a fire in the stockyards. His father purchased a hunter that was shown in stock shows and then a prized four-gaited horse named Tommie Boy. Walter recalls riding the city's wide bridle paths on the hunter while his father rode Tommie Boy. Walter himself rode Tommie Boy with the National Guard stationed at the armory in Washington Park, where he could show off to classmates from Hyde Park High School.

While his mother exposed Walter to art and music, his father expected him to excel in school, attend Dartmouth, and become a businessman. At that time South Shore was a new part of town, served by public transportation and schools that appealed to upwardly mobile families such as the Netsches. Walter attended O'Keefe Elementary School and Hyde Park High School. At Hyde Park he concentrated on college-entry-level courses in

figs. 2, 3 Walter Netsch at ages 2 and 12

math, science, Latin, and English. His extracurricular activities included the Psychology Club, the Chicago Tour Club, the Bit and Spur Club, and the Election Committee. An avid reader, he frequented the public library at 73rd Street and Exchange and, later, the Blackstone Library in Hyde Park.

Architecture was already a strong interest of Walter's, and he hoped to study architecture at Princeton University. As a junior he wrote a paper titled "What Is Modern Architecture?" that discussed works by Le Corbusier, Alvar Aalto, and Frank Lloyd Wright and made his own surveyor's transit and plotted every square foot of Wooded Island — which featured a Japanese temple built for the 1893 World's Columbian Exposition — in Jackson Park for a trigonometry project. Neighborhood architecture impressed Walter. Barry Byrne's modern geometric apartments were located nearby, between Paxton and Crandon on 69th Street. While attending Hyde Park High School, Walter discovered and visited Wright's Robie House and Blossom House. In addition to these unadorned geometric designs, he was drawn to Louis Sullivan's Carson Pirie Scott & Co. Building and to Sullivan and Dankmar Adler's Auditorium Building.

Walter recalls biking to the 1933–34 Century of Progress International Exposition. At the exposition Plymouth Motors sponsored a competition on air flow that Walter entered (his entry featured a drawing of the knee action and a car spring in the background, over which he typed his competition report). He also saw the Travel and Transport Building (whose tensioned roof could be raised and lowered) and Fred Keck's Crystal House, touted as America's first glass house. (Interestingly, facilities for the Armour & Co. pavilion at the exposition — including a hot dog booth — were designed by Nathaniel Owings and Louis Skidmore before they incorporated as an architecture firm in 1936.)

As his graduation approached in 1937, Walter was set on becoming an architect, while his father insisted on business school at Dartmouth. As a compromise, Walter completed a postgraduate year of high school at Leelanau for Boys, a college prep school in Glen Arbor, Michigan, where he took one class and taught geometry. Upon his return, Walter's father relented on Dartmouth, and Walter Netsch enrolled in the architecture program at the Massachusetts Institute of Technology.

According to Netsch, MIT's architectural program in 1939 was in transition from a traditional Beaux-Arts orientation to a more modern approach. Netsch felt that he was better prepared than his classmates and vividly recalls asking a fellow freshman, "What do you think about Le Corbusier?" and receiving the reply, "Who?" Because of the impending world war, the freshman class was small — only nine students. He names Lawrence B. Anderson, Herbert Beckwith, and John Lyon Reid as MIT's most progressive architecture professors.

During Netsch's time there, MIT was primarily a design school that relied heavily on the case study method. As part of MIT tradition, first-year architecture students together designed and built a colonial house that was sold to provide funds for the next year's project. Netsch's admittedly rebellious and modern proposed design, which burrowed into a hillside, was severely criticized.

MIT freshmen and architecture students from Harvard were assigned weekend sketch problems that were critiqued by architects and professors from both institutions. Netsch recalls a conversation after one such review with two architects over lunch in which discussion turned to the war. Netsch made spirited statements against fascism only to discover that his audience was Philip Johnson and Walter Gropius.

The coming war was felt in other ways, too. Finnish architect Alvar Aalto found a wartime home at MIT, and Netsch relates that having a resident genius like Aalto on campus was terrific (and recalls the odd detail of Aalto's jacket pockets being stuffed with paper money). MIT research was vital to the war effort, and students were exposed to prefabrication and large-scale programming that stressed functionalism based on modern design aesthetics. Netsch recalls, "As families were fleeing the Russians, we were designing houses. For his thesis, I. M. Pei designed a beautiful, movable structure. Gordon Bunshaft (before my class) was doing beautiful Beaux-Arts renderings, and Bill Hartmann, brick/cube MIT modernism."

At MIT Netsch took advantage of Boston and the surrounding region, both culturally and socially. One year he had a 1937 Ford that enabled him to visit family in New Hampshire as well as the region's modern architecture. Along with contemporary architecture and design, he particularly enjoyed contemporary music and art. Every August he received a $25 gift from his parents that paid for his season tickets to the Boston Symphony. Before Friday night concerts he often visited the Museum of Fine Arts.

Netsch was a member of Beta Theta Pi. Gaunt throughout adulthood, Netsch grew to six feet two inches and 128 pounds. In 1941–42 he experienced severe arthritis and returned to Chicago (and traveled to the Mayo Clinic) to convalesce for nine weeks, but he managed to keep up with course work.

Netsch also returned to Chicago during summers. One summer he secured an unpaid internship at the firm of Fisher and Patton, which had designed Collegiate Gothic buildings at Carleton College and elsewhere. Netsch recalls working alone in a spacious drafting room that could hold 40 or 50 people but was vacant because of the war. His project was a church, and he was supervised by an architect named Faulkner:

> Mr. Faulkner was building Christian Science churches (that's how I got my "experience"). He designed our church [Netsch's mother was a very active Christian Scientist — ed.] — modern Near Eastern, domed, at 73rd and Coles — but his specialties were classic frontal-façaded or three-dimensional colonials. Our effort [that summer] would never have [been] accepted by the firm. It really was an argument, a box, that if it had a reference would be to a Viennese glass block. I did learn the habit of going to work every day.[1]

Netsch's fourth-year thesis at MIT was titled "Renewal of Public Housing in South Boston," a work that reflected his lifelong social conscience. His fifth-year thesis, "Characteristics of the House as Determined by Space-Use, and its Applications to Storage," dealt with growth and change in residences in relation to family size and storage needs. His theory was that, as families grew, different types of storage units evolved and changed enclosed and open spaces, thus reshaping the volume of the typical domestic family home.

After Pearl Harbor male students throughout the country knew that they would likely serve in the military. Netsch recalls examining aerial photographs of Pearl Harbor that MIT faculty studied to determine the extent of damage to key buildings. His class was pushed ahead and attended classes all summer during their fifth year so that they could graduate in January 1943. They all entered military service by March or April of that year.

Netsch was inducted into the U.S. Army on March 1, 1943, at Fort Sheridan, Illinois. He scored high on mechanical aptitude tests and was selected to become an engineer. Basic

fig. 4 Walter Netsch with his parents, Walter Sr. and Anna, at the dedication of the U.S. Air Force Academy, 1955

training was at Fort Belvoir, Virginia, where he was chosen for Officer Candidate School but failed the physical examination. At that point he could have left the service but chose to stay on at Belvoir as a noncommissioned officer (a corporal) in cadre so he could train others. From Virginia he traveled to California and Canada en route to Alaska, where he was supposed to be a Caterpillar tractor operator. Netsch explained to the colonel that he was a "city rat" who couldn't drive a tractor and would endanger lives if he tried. He was promptly sent "down the chain" of Aleutian Islands to Atka Island, which was populated by 30 soldiers. The troops had built an emergency landing strip and a prefabricated hospital in preparation for a Japanese attack that never happened. Netsch's first commissioned work was a movable five-hole privy that was mounted on a sled. He proudly designed it in a New England modern style with vertical siding.

Besides air-strip maintenance and running Armed Forces Radio programs, Netsch taught other soldiers how to read and provided key evidence for the court martial of a deranged and tyrannical captain. When the war ended, he was transferred to Fairbanks (where he designed a house for an enlisted man from Connecticut) and ultimately to Great Falls, Montana. He was discharged on March 29, 1946.

When he returned to civilian life, Netsch was emotionally and physically spent. Always thin, he was an undernourished 138 pounds when he arrived in Chicago. He drew a building in three-point perspective to use in job interviews[2] and found work in the small Kenilworth, Illinois, office of L. Morgan Yost (1908–92), a Frank Lloyd Wright aficionado. Yost's office — which consisted of Yost, Netsch, and a third employee — specialized in North Shore homes. Netsch designed plans, Yost prepared elevations, and all three completed the working drawings. The firm's income was supplemented by supplying plumbing and heating drawings for building magazines. Yost also exposed Netsch to the work of Arts and Crafts architects from the West Coast such as Greene & Greene. Netsch was paid $40 per week.

Netsch's year with Yost got him back into architecture and taught him how a small firm worked. He also gained important building supervision and superintendent experience. While the relationship was cordial and professional, Netsch never regarded Yost as a mentor. When the opportunity came, he was ready to move to larger projects at a major firm. Years later, Yost remembered Netsch fondly:

> *Walter was quite a talented guy, as we know now. He impressed me because he was willing to come to my office in Kenilworth from the South Side. He lived down near the University of Chicago. He'd come by a couple of railroads and so on and get off at the Kenilworth station, which was right across from our office…. I was impressed that he would think enough of coming to work for me to go through the hardship and time involved in traveling that distance. He was a very talented man. Of course, soon he was able to take some of the design load…. He had a great natural ability and formal ability, too…. He later went on to do many great things with Skidmore, Owings and Merrill. I tried to get Walter to stay with me but he wanted to go with a big firm. He had that in mind….*
>
> *We certainly had some good discussions. I remember once I gave a talk down at the Museum of Science and Industry on a Sunday and he came to hear me and he laughed at all the right places.*[3]

Acting upon the suggestion and encouragement of Robert Allen Ward, an architect who had also worked for Yost, Netsch interviewed in November 1947 for a design job with Skidmore, Owings & Merrill (SOM) with John Merrill at his Chicago office at 100 West Monroe Street. Netsch was offered $60 per week and told to be in Oak Ridge, Tennessee, on a certain day. Netsch recalls that it was after Thanksgiving, as he had to wait for the results of his AIA registration licensing exam, taken November 19–22.

Oak Ridge, located west of Knoxville, had been selected in 1942 as a site for developing atomic materials for the Manhattan Project. The town was a closely guarded secret during World War II (it was unnamed and left off maps until 1949), and its population swelled from 3,000 in 1941 to 75,000 in 1945. SOM was contracted to provide a layout for the town and designs for its first permanent houses, schools, community services, roads, and shopping facilities.

Netsch drove to Tennessee in his Raymond Loewy–designed yellow Studebaker convertible, to which he had attached a propeller on the front as a joke. According to his contract with SOM (dated December 2, 1947, and approved by the U.S. Atomic Energy Commission), Netsch was hired as a "Designer, Arch." at the newly negotiated sum of $75 per week, and his estimated period of employment was "indefinite."

At Oak Ridge, Netsch designed prefabricated homes, apartments, and dormitories built of "cemesto" (bonded cement and asbestos panels) that could be erected quickly. He headed up a team that designed 500 houses and worked on the shopping center and high school. He learned on-site grading — putting each house on the lot and grading it out to the roadway so that water would not run into the house. Netsch liked landscaping, and the chore was good practical training but also boring.

It was at Oak Ridge that Netsch met Nat Owings, who became his mentor and protector at SOM. The Oak Ridge team was an informal group large enough for socializing and good picnics — Netsch's trademark "grey ice cream" was notorious, especially among women colleagues, as a design failure realized by mixing multiple colors — and the source of long-term relationships. For years the team held annual Oak Ridge reunions at Christmas.

Netsch was frequently dispatched from Oak Ridge to the Chicago office of SOM, where he observed the large working-drawings operation and was introduced to the design floor, presided over by William Hartmann. In 1949 he was transferred to the Chicago office, where he completed working drawings for the Oak Ridge High School, assisted with the Lake Meadows Shopping Center in Chicago, and, with engineer Jack Train, helped design the first automated baggage retrieval system at Midway Airport. Owings later called Netsch one of the "young men who had come our way — gold nuggets of pure design talent discovered at Oak Ridge."[4]

In 1951 Netsch was assigned to SOM's San Francisco office to work on the U.S. Naval Postgraduate School in Monterey, California — a project Netsch describes as his big career break. The school was located on the site of Hotel Del Monte, which the Navy had purchased along with 627 surrounding acres. When Netsch convinced Louis Skidmore that SOM couldn't possibly build the Navy's barrack-like plan — which would have uprooted the site's handsome gardens and trees — it was dropped. In its place Netsch reviewed the Navy's course catalog and converted it into his building program. Netsch's elegant presentation charts were later published in *Architectural Record*.[5] He also created

fig. 5 Netsch (third from right) at an SOM partners meeting at Nat Owings's house, Monterey, California, c. 1950s

schematics and a large plywood-and-cardboard model that was a nuisance to transport. The more humanized concept was approved by the Navy, and Netsch was given a month to design the full scheme. Netsch and John Hoops, a San Francisco–based SOM engineer, worked feverishly in an attic space in the Naval Academy in Annapolis, Maryland, and their designs were reviewed each evening by Rear Admiral Ernest Edward Herrmann, the first head of the U.S. Naval Postgraduate School.

The U.S. Naval Postgraduate School — one of the earliest examples of campus programming in North America — was a success for Netsch, who credited MIT's focus on large-project programming with providing him with the requisite skills to accomplish the plan. The project also positioned SOM for the U.S. Air Force Academy commission. Netsch recalled:

> The Naval Postgraduate School moved Skidmore into a new field, and it gave me my entry into noncommercial work with clients as users, not financiers. I no longer competed with other designers in Skidmore to get an office building or to get this or to get that. I had, in a sense, made a niche for myself. No joke — "Niche Netsch."
>
> Sadly, [the project] proved a real tragedy for the Admiral, whose support was essential…. Passed over for promotion after all his efforts, Admiral Herrmann committed suicide in his office….[6]

While working for SOM in San Francisco, Netsch designed Trinity Lutheran Church in Oakland and collaborated with John Merrill Jr. on the Murray Matthew house in Monterey, the only home he designed at SOM that was built. He also ran the design team that worked on the Greyhound service garage (notable for its enormous trusses and large open span) that later became the home of the California College of the Arts. The building has outlasted three earthquakes, has been upgraded to stricter earthquake codes, and still makes a fine design school.

In 1953 Netsch and a team of SOM architects designed air bases in Okinawa, Japan. In Tokyo Netsch's team lived at the Dai-Ichi Hotel, which had been built for the 1940 Olympics that were cancelled because of the war. SOM partners stayed at the Frank Lloyd Wright–designed Imperial Hotel, which they all got to know well. Besides Netsch, the team included Carl Russell, John Weese, and Tallie Maule. They produced master plans and building designs for military bases at Sukiram, Kadena, and Naha, among other locations. Ralph Youngren joined the group on Okinawa, and Bruce Graham came in the "third wave of young SOM designers," after Netsch had returned to the United States.

Netsch worried about how he would respond to the World War II enemy and to the damage the United States had done, but he found Japanese culture and aesthetics strong and beautiful. His travels in Japan included memorable visits to Kyoto, where Kiyomizu was Netsch's favorite shrine, along with local Buddhist temples. Netsch fondly remembers Japan and acknowledged Asian influences in his work from then on. For Netsch, the tatami mat is an elegant module and a predecessor of his Field Theory. (For more on Field Theory, see Felsen and Dunn, pages 73–78.)

Upon his return to San Francisco, Netsch designed a military hospital in Anchorage, Alaska, and the high-rise Crown-Zellerbach Headquarters Building in San Francisco; the latter was finished by Charles Bassett in 1959. When Owings left Chicago in 1954 for the West Coast, Netsch returned to Chicago to take over the design team there as part of what became known at SOM as the "Netsch-and-cash-for-Owings trade." One of his first projects was the Inland Steel Building in Chicago.[7] This beloved and much-admired landmark building was Chicago's first fully air-conditioned building, the first with double-glazing, the first to provide indoor below-grade parking, and the first to use steel pilings (driven 85 feet through mud and clay into bedrock) to support a high-rise structure. It also pioneered the use of stainless steel as cladding material. Its unobstructed foundation (177 x 58 feet) accommodates the building's unprecedented interior open span. Core services are placed in an adjacent tower to the east. According to Owings:

> [Leigh] Block of Inland Steel had spoken to me in 1949 of a new building, but it was five years before he authorized the Inland Steel building which would be the first new office building to go up in Chicago in twenty-two years, squeezed in among the smoke-stained, weather-worn monuments to another era. This was one of Walter Netsch's endless ideas which forever tumbled in profusion, evidencing a spirit and a talent which almost consumed him. As a solution for just such a building, and in order to compete with the cheaper conditions in the suburbs, he would eliminate inside columns, thus providing a stack of rectangular and more flexible loft spaces like hot cakes one on top of the other. To do this, all services — elevators, power, sewer, water, toilets — were consolidated in an attached outside vertical shaft, services freed of entanglement with the twenty or thirty or forty floors of the useful building space.[8]

Netsch's avant-garde, high-tech design for Inland Steel predated Richard Rogers's buildings with exposed mechanical elements by 20 years.

Before the Inland Steel Building was finalized, SOM was awarded the commission for the U.S. Air Force Academy in Colorado Springs, Colorado. Netsch was designated to lead the design team, and Bruce Graham modified the design of the Inland Steel Building, which was completed in 1958. Netsch said, "Bruce Graham eliminated the double-glazing, but otherwise finished the building beautifully." Leigh Block, the client on the Inland Steel Building, and his wife, Mary, shared Netsch's talent for collecting modern art and later endowed Northwestern University's art museum.

Designing the U.S. Air Force Academy was unquestionably the high point of Walter Netsch's career.[9] He participated in the creation of the design competition brochure and at competition presentations. On July 23, 1954, SOM won this coveted commission over 300 other firms, including Kittyhawk Associates, a prominent group supported by Frank Lloyd Wright, and many other distinguished architectural offices. Netsch directed a young and enthusiastic design team that included Ralph Youngren (whom Netsch describes as his best friend and cohort), John Hoops, and Gertrude Peterhans. The SOM team worked closely with the Air Force Academy Construction Agency and top Air Force personnel.

The U.S. Air Force Academy site comprised 17,500 acres on a mesa that fronted 2,000-foot cliffs at the base of the Rampart Mountain range. Netsch's team designed the Academy from the barren sage-brushed ground up. As he later recalled, "Every morning for a month, the Air Force gave me a helicopter, and I flew up and down every mesa, every valley. They spread out like fingers. Then I would drive over the land in a Jeep. And as the master plan developed, I walked every road."[10]

For Netsch the most wrenching moment of the design process came at the first high-level meeting on May 13, 1955, when objections arose over his chapel design:

> *At the end of that presentation, everything had been going along so well, and all of a sudden the senator from South Carolina said, "Everything looks fine, except that chapel. I don't hear the rustle of angels' wings." And some senator from North Dakota said, "It looks like a bunch of tepees to me." All of a sudden the earth fell in on that poor little chapel design. I thought I had lost everything. I was in tears in the back of the room, and Nat [Owings] came back and said, "What's wrong with you? Everything is approved but the chapel, and you can always do another one"* — *that was Nat's way of thinking.*[11]

Owings suggested that Netsch redesign the chapel after visiting Gothic cathedrals in Europe. Netsch's three-week European trip started at Stonehenge in England. He was impressed by Wells Cathedral but not really moved by European church architecture until he saw Notre-Dame, Saint-Denis Basilica, and Sainte-Chapelle in France. The Basilica of San Francesco d'Assisi in Italy was another highlight — a chapel on two levels like

fig. 6   Walter Netsch (right), c. 1960s

Sainte-Chapelle. Driving to Chartres and seeing the cathedral arise over the wheat fields of La Beauce reminded him of the isolation and possibilities of the Air Force Academy site. He vividly recalls Chartres:

> It was sense of place — you know, [like] the Air Force Academy out in the middle of nowhere…. [I]t had all the guts and strength that I didn't see in Notre-Dame. It was tremendous. I walked inside and there was an organ playing…. It vibrated. There was a little wedding of a townsman and a townswoman, just a few people in a side chapel, getting married, and I was just breathless. I was under one of the towers. I had just hardly gotten in the building. I just couldn't believe it. I retreated, because I felt like I was intruding on a special moment, and walked around the building…. I found a restaurant that faced the church so I could look at the building and eat….
>
> What was important to me was … that it had been built over time and still had order. There wasn't a momentous change in style or anything at Chartres. And it had the early windows and the later windows, and you could see the structural density that was required for the original rose window and the later open rose window which was much glassier. You could see the evolution of structure in details like that. Then you realized that all of these people were putting this together out of what they knew, but with great skill — great skill. All of the skill that I had heard about in the lectures at MIT was nothing compared to what I was looking at. I just thought, how can I do this in Colorado? How? But the Gothic form, this soaring form, the complex geometry, was something that was inspiring. How could that be the final result?[12]

Inspired by the grandeur and luminosity of Chartres, Sainte-Chapelle, and Assisi, he designed a nondenominational Cadet Chapel based on walls of inverted tetrahedrons. Netsch credits Ken Nasland, an SOM engineer assigned to his team, with helping to refine his tetrahedron design:

> I had gotten this idea here in Chicago, working with my engineer, of the tetrahedrons and compiling the tetrahedrons together — you know, piling them up so they inverted. You get two tetrahedrons, one on top of the other, … and you get the inverse. That is an inverse tetrahedron, so inside you get the reverse. That just sent me. That was really terrific. So it really came very quickly…. Then the idea of running the glass between everything and then having the window. I thought it would be absolutely tremendous if these tetrahedrons were all made of onyx … so they would be translucent, white tetrahedrons.[13]

Predictably, Netsch's daring chapel design was controversial, even within SOM. The design was negatively reviewed in the popular press and politicized. Notable architects — including Belluschi, Saarinen, and others on the Air Force Academy Construction Agency advisory board — actively defended the design through letters of support and in other ways. On August 6, 1957, by a vote of 102 to 53, the U.S. House of Representatives voted to delay construction of the Academy Chapel. The debate and subsequent restoration of funding, as recorded in the *Congressional Record*, is captivating. Nat Owings shared this remembrance about Netsch's campaign to promote the chapel's design:

> *In the final approved chapel roof system there are five miles of one-and-a-half-inch-thick stained glass strips between the tetrahedrons. I know this because the design was laid out entirely by hand on brown paper, rolled up foot by foot as Walter Netsch drew and colored it on his living room floor. Showing it to anyone who would look, he carried a model of the chapel around with him everywhere in a little case, with Christmas tree lighting that could be hooked up to the nearest outlet, gaining from each of his partners approval to fight for that chapel's inclusion in the plan. With its seventeen tetrahedrons and five miles of glass besides, unchanged, the original design was finally finished two years after the rest of the academy was in operation. The framework was a lacy skeleton of tubular steel tetrahedrons stacked one on top of the other, reaching a hundred and fifty feet toward the sky — still the most striking example of this relatively new kind of structure in the United States.*[14]

After funding was restored the Air Force and SOM arranged an exhibition and forum in November 1957 at MIT to promote the chapel design and garner public support. Prominent architects, politicians, and clergy participated and expressed their satisfaction with and support for the project.

The design process dragged on, construction estimates increased, and delays continued. Construction began in August 1959, and the chapel was dedicated on September 22, 1963. Contrary to SOM's team tradition, the Cadet Chapel was the firm's first major building credited to an individual SOM architect. It established Netsch's reputation as a premier designer and as a maverick individualist within a large corporate firm. (For more on the U.S. Air Force Academy and Cadet Chapel, see Nauman, pages 42–72.)

During completion of the Air Force Academy commission, Netsch rose within SOM from an associate partner to "Partner of Design" in 1955. He later increased his standing in SOM's partner point distribution system by purchasing some of Nat Owings's points. As funds permitted, he indulged his passion for original modern art by purchasing paintings and sculpture by emerging American artists. In New York he visited galleries with Gordon Bunshaft and Ralph Youngren. He became a regular customer at contemporary art galleries such as the Green Gallery, the André Emmerich Gallery, and Leo Castelli Gallery, where he bought works by Roy Lichtenstein, Robert Motherwell, Hans Hofmann, Donald Judd, Robert Indiana, Ellsworth Kelly, and Jack Youngerman, among other artists. He became acquainted with the latter three artists and visited their studios in Coenties Slip, New York. Netsch's collection was publicly exhibited in 1971, 1983, and 1991, and pieces from it have been loaned to exhibitions around the world.

In 1960 Netsch met Dawn Clark when she called to ask if local Democrats could use his spectacular art-filled penthouse at 1360 Lake Shore Drive for a political rally. He agreed and now credits Dawn with enlarging his vision of political progress through service opportunities. In 1963 they married. Dawn, a Northwestern graduate (BA 1948, JD 1952), practiced law in Washington, D.C., and in Chicago, has been a member of the Northwestern School of Law faculty since 1965, and has been active in state and local government. She was elected to the Illinois State Senate (1972–90), was comptroller of Illinois (1991–95), and was the Democratic candidate for governor of Illinois in 1994. Since 1974 the Netsches have lived in Chicago's Old Town neighborhood in a spectacular multilevel home and adjacent studio that Walter designed with soaring ceilings and skylights. Essentially a 40-foot cube, the home has been showcased in several publications. The couple shares a love of art, music, travel, White Sox baseball, and Boston terriers.

fig. 7   Dawn Clark Netsch and Walter Netsch, c. 1980s

In 1956–57 Netsch established a separate and independent design studio of about 30 young architects at 22 West Monroe in Chicago. It was not always easy to say where an SOM project ended and where a Netsch studio project began — in fact the two were often intertangled — but the studio was responsible for attracting its own commissions and clientele, and it offered variety and alternatives to SOM's large-scale commercial projects. As Netsch later recalled, "Our studio became isolated from Skidmore simply because our clients were so different."[15] His design team embraced new technologies and was an industry leader in adapting computers to architectural designs. He encouraged architecture school deans to send him their brightest students, and he actively recruited and hired minority architects and started an architecture educational aid program for minority students. Several designers who started with Netsch moved into prominent roles at SOM and other firms or started their own firms.

Netsch's studio devoted most of the 1960s and early 1970s to academic projects, including university and college libraries, academic buildings, and art museums. He was the lead designer for the new Circle Campus of the University of Illinois in Chicago. Intended to be his fullest expression of Field Theory aesthetics, the project became a bittersweet experience for Netsch. Building designs were often either changed during construction or not built, and the campus underwent radical modifications and renovations, culminating in 1994 with the removal of the dual-level raised walkways and central core. Once again, architectural journals supported the designs, while the local and popular press mostly attacked them.

Library projects included the Paul V. Galvin Library at the Illinois Institute of Technology, Chicago (1962), Louis Jefferson Long Library at Wells College, Aurora,

New York (1968), Northwestern University Library (1970), the Joseph Regenstein Library at the University of Chicago (1970), the James Madison Barker Library of Engineering at MIT (1972, remodeling), the Hardin Library for Health Sciences at the University of Iowa (1973), the Seeley G. Mudd Library for Science and Engineering at Northwestern (1977), the Selby Public Library in Sarasota, Florida (1978), Tokyo's Sophia University Central Library (1979), and Texas Christian University Library (1983, expansion). (For more information on Netsch's library projects, see "Chronology," pages 15–20.)

In 2001 Netsch remarked that Wells College's Long Library was one of his best buildings, and a first in Field Theory:

> *I wanted to work with the environment, so I made it fit the site. In fact, the first design fit the site so well that I had to do the roof over again. I went to a meeting of trustees and was so excited when I explained that students could ski down the roof of this building. Afterward, the president said, "Walter, you better change the roof. The trustees were scared to death that the students will actually do that." So I changed the geometry, but it's still a very good building. It also fit the concept of what a library should be — a place where you study, put the book on the floor, and read on the floor or on pillows. It's not regimented. It has volume, it has space and perception. It has small rooms that you can go to, especially on the bridge. And it has native materials. It has brick and wood. So I felt it did all those things, plus. It's the first time we took three rotated squares and made them work together as a triad. The design of the library is based on that triad, a major geometric form.*[16]

Perhaps the most of important of these projects was the Northwestern University Library. Netsch developed the program and designs over six years in collaboration with the University's Library Planning Committee.[17] He recalls, "The design and programming of Northwestern University Library was one of the most satisfying experiences of my professional life." (For more on this project, see Goodman, pages 79–96.)

Other major projects by Netsch for Northwestern include plans for the Lakefill expansion project (1962–68), the Lindheimer Astrophysical Research Center (1966, razed 1995 — one of his favorite buildings), Rebecca Crown Center (1969), O. T. Hogan Biological Sciences Building (1971), Frances Searle Building (1972), and Regenstein Hall of Music (1977). At the University of Chicago he drew designs for combining the Stevenson Building and the Oriental Institute, helped save the Robie House, and designed the base of Henry Moore's famous *Nuclear Energy* sculpture, which occupies the exact location on Stagg Field where Enrico Fermi created the first atomic reaction.

In addition to the Paul V. Galvin Library, Netsch designed IIT's student union building, Grover M. Hermann Hall (1962), and assisted with other IIT buildings after SOM inherited the campus architecture commission from Mies van der Rohe. Netsch also fondly remembers buildings at Grinnell College, the University of Iowa, Miami University, and Wells College (Aurora, New York).

Netsch said that designing the University of Illinois's Chicago campus "got me on the lecture circuit," and it also resulted in a number of honors. From the 1960s through the

2000s he received honorary doctorates from Lawrence University (1968), Miami University (1979), Northwestern University (1980), Purdue University (1991), and the University of Illinois at Chicago (2008). Over the years he taught courses and seminars at the University of Michigan, the Rhode Island School of Design, MIT, Lawrence Institute of Technology, Miami University, the University of Illinois (as the Hill Visiting Professor), and the University of Minnesota.

Netsch's professional work combined with his keen sense of social responsibility in the 1960s and 1970s when he designed St. Matthew United Methodist Church in Chicago's Cabrini-Green housing development (1969). A few years later his SOM team drew plans for core urban renewal of Pruitt-Igoe, St. Louis's notorious public housing project, which was demolished in 1972. He designed Sunburst Youth Home (sometimes referred to as the Winnebago Children's Home) in Wisconsin for troubled children, completed a study for a high-speed urban transit system in Pittsburgh for Westinghouse, and designed Detroit's Paired New Towns (which were not built).

For his alma mater he designed the Center for Materials Science and Engineering (Building 13, also called the Vannevar Bush Center for Material Sciences, 1965) and the Sherman Fairchild Electrical Engineering and Electronics Complex of the Research Laboratory of Electronics (1972):

> Probably the building I consider best at MIT is the Material Science Building, which fits just behind the dome.... It's just best looking, it's the most high tech, it had the clearest program, and it had a great position in the façade. Then, of course, there was the restoration of the dome, which is, again, a beautiful project.... The rest of the [MIT] buildings I did were linear buildings, that have a façade that relates back to the existing building, but they're not anywhere near as handsome as the Material Science Building. The Electrical Engineering Building is also a good building.... It has a great knuckle where one building joins another, and a marvelous staircase — just pretty and bright yellow. But the rest of the buildings were pragmatic buildings.[18]

Netsch was responsible for the Art Institute of Chicago's East Wing (1976), which included McKinlock Court, studios and classrooms for the School of the Art Institute, remodeling of the Prints and Drawings Gallery, and preservation of the Chicago Stock Exchange Trading Room, which had been designed by Louis Sullivan and Dankmar Adler. He also designed the museum's Terrace Gardens. Another important museum commission in the late 1970s was the Miami University Art Museum (1978), his last major Field Theory design, which he has called "my Louvre." The Netsches exhibited some of their art collection there and donated important works to the permanent collection. Concerned about art for his buildings, he often donated or commissioned works upon their completion.

Hospitals and clinics formed another component of Netsch's niche at SOM. Among others, he designed or remodeled the Eye Clinic at Chicago's Rush-Presbyterian-St. Luke's Medical Center and the Baldwin Building at the Mayo Clinic in Rochester, Minnesota (where Netsch was a patient in 1941–42).

Outside the United States, Netsch designed student housing and other campus buildings for the University of Blida, Algeria (1984–86), an elaborate theme park and zoo in Saudi Arabia (never built), the extension of the Far Eastern Institute for the Shah of Iran, government buildings in Brisbane, Australia, and an entry to the competition for the Peak Building in Hong Kong (not won). Foreign travel and cultures shaped major parts of his life and work. He once acknowledged, "My life has been a cultural parade, in a sense, of meeting all these different cultures — Japan, Algeria, Saudi, Iran. They were all different."[19]

Netsch retired from SOM in 1979. Health issues, including open-heart surgeries, were a major factor in the decision. Regarding his career at SOM, he said:

fig. 8   Walter Netsch, c. 2000s

I had the chance to explore a new field. I had a chance to explore my own aesthetic sensibilities because Nat [Owings] had established this freedom for me…. [I]f I was successful, … SOM allowed me to be. It didn't always help me, but they allowed me to be. And then, of course, I had all of those resources — the engineering — that were very important to the success of a building and how you finally get it made and built. I think what really happened was that systems — I'm talking about managerial systems — began to take over the pattern of the firm as the kind of work was dominated more and more by office buildings.[20]

In retirement Netsch has remained extremely active as an architect, designer, and professor, as well as an energetic public servant and spokesman for high-quality design and sustainable architecture. He has consulted on many projects, including the Fort Wayne Art Museum, Montgomery College in Takoma Park, Maryland, and Chicago waterfront and park designs. He has also designed furniture, including the Vasarely chair and exquisite gingko chairs based on leaf patterns, and he patented a Field Theory game.

In 1980 he submitted an innovative computer-assisted 3D design for *Late Entries to the Chicago Tribune Tower Competition*, an exhibition held at the Museum of Contemporary Art; his elegant high-tech concept and computer-generated design garnered considerable attention and press coverage. In 1980 he was appointed to the Commission on Fine Arts in Washington, D.C., by President Jimmy Carter; the only other SOM architect to share this honor is Gordon Bunshaft. Netsch's term, which lasted until 1984, saw the final approval of the Vietnam Veterans Memorial designed by Maya Lin. His watercolors and sculpture were exhibited at Chicago's Zolla/Lieberman Gallery in 1981.

Netsch is a lifelong social activist. In the late 1960s he joined an ad hoc committee to defeat a proposal for a road through Jackson Park. Work had already commenced when Netsch helped to mark trees that would be destroyed (see fig. 9). The group's actions prompted Mayor Richard J. Daley to appoint a review committee, headed by Netsch. The committee's lengthy report recommended that the city cease further destructive acts in the city's parks. Netsch recalled:

> *Word got out that we had a "tough report," and the papers were anxious to get a copy. Dawn and I were celebrating someone's birthday at Adlai and Nancy Stevenson's house. I received a phone call from a transportation engineer who was a committee member. The engineer said that a group from the mayor's office planned to arrive at his home in the morning to pressure him to deny the report and challenge its accuracy. I remember coming down the stairs and hollering at Dawn, "You and your damned Democratic Party!" I then called the other committee members and asked them to be at the engineer's house with coffee and donuts at 8 a.m. to meet the visitors. They were shocked to see us there en masse. I politely explained that only the mayor would receive the report.*
>
> *Subsequently, I received a request to see the mayor. I gathered the committee again, and we waited in the visitor's room outside the mayor's office until I was called in. I had never seen the mayor close up. I saw a man red, white, and blue — so patriotic: his face was red, his shirt was white, and his suit was blue — who cordially invited me to sit down....*
>
> *He came quickly to the point and offered a suggestion. If the report was not revealed, he would agree to appoint an outside planning architect and landscape group to review the parks and Lake Shore Drive. That sounded good to me, but I explained that I had to have the committee's approval and that they were outside in the visitor's area. We decided that this was a good bargain, but we had to agree not to reveal anything in our report. I returned to the mayor's office and told him our part of the agreement. A short time later, the mayor announced that Johnson, Johnson & Roy, a national urban planning and landscape firm, had been chosen to review the parks and Lake Shore Drive. They were to make their report a number of months later.*
>
> *The planning groups and general public were relieved. The Chicago press editorialized that the report must have been as tough as the Emancipation*

fig. 9   Walter Netsch in Jackson Park, late 1960s

Proclamation. Johnson, Johnson & Roy made the most of their opportunity
and provided solid programs for good park practice and maintenance. The
57th Street intersection was designed to go around the Museum of Science
and Industry and several destructive and poorly designed alignments
were corrected. They also suggested a series of landscaped pedestrian
bridges from the west side of Lake Shore Drive to the lake that were never
completed. I can't recall what I did with my copy of the report.[21]

In 1986 Netsch was appointed president of the Board of Commissioners of the Chicago
Park District by Mayor Harold Washington. Netsch served as president until 1987 and
remained on the board until 1989. During his tenure, which was fraught with political
battles and maneuverings, Netsch and Ed Uhlir (former Chicago Park District planning
director and later director of design for Millennium Park) discovered Daniel H. Burnham's
original drawings and documents for his famous 1909 *Plan of Chicago*[22], and the Park
District oversaw restoration of the historic South Pond Refectory (now known as Café
Brauer) in Lincoln Park. Netsch insisted on historically correct roof tiles at Lincoln Park
Zoo and improvements to parks throughout the city.

At 88 years of age, Netsch continues to conceptualize, consult, and design on his
home computer. He is presently developing models for futuristic living in sustainable
environments. Netsch once summarized his core design principles as follows:

Sometimes someone asks, "What do you think are the important buildings
you've done?" You think of why. One, this broke the rule; two, it has
good social purpose; three, it works; and four, you see them in place in the
environment and they don't look strange. In fact, they look so natural
sitting there that you think the rest of the world looks just like that.[23]

fig. 10   Netsch with library staff at the exhibition *Walter Netsch and the Northwestern University Library,* 2006

Notes

In 1985 and, more extensively, in 1995 Netsch was interviewed by Betty Blum for the Art Institute's Chicago Architects Oral History Project. A rich and remarkable combination of history and memoirs, the entire 474-page transcript is available at www.artic.edu/aic /libraries/caohp/netsch.html.

The majority of Netsch's papers, drawings, and archives are housed at the Chicago History Museum. The Art Institute of Chicago's Department of Architecture and Design holds several models, including the original concept model for the Inland Steel Building. SOM archives are another rich source of primary material.

1. Walter Netsch, interview with author, February 2007.

2. A copy of the rendering is held by the Chicago History Museum.

3. L. Morgan Yost, "Oral History of L. Morgan Yost," interview by Betty J. Blum, May 13–15, 1985, transcript, Art Institute of Chicago, 112–13.

4. Nathaniel Alexander Owings, *The Spaces In Between: An Architect's Journey* (Boston: Houghton Mifflin, 1973), 178.

5. "The Navy's Graduate Engineering School at the U.S. Naval Postgraduate School, Monterey, California," *Architectural Record* 117, no. 4 (April 1955): 159–71.

6. Netsch, interview with author.

7. Netsch's innovative conceptual model resides in the Art Institute of Chicago's Department of Architecture and Design.

8. Owings, 121.

9. Several outstanding histories present the fascinating story of its design and construction and document Netsch's major contributions. See, in particular, Robert Allen Nauman, *On the Wings of Modernism: the United States Air Force Academy* (Urbana: University of Illinois Press, 2004) and Robert Bruegmann, ed., *Modernism at Mid-Century: The Architecture of the United States Air Force Academy* (Chicago and London: University of Chicago Press, 1994). Stunning photographs of the site, buildings, and the Cadet Chapel appear in Elizabeth Gill Lui, *Spirit and Flight: A Photographic Salute to the United States Air Force Academy* (Colorado: U.S. Air Force Academy, 1996).

10. Robert Cross, "A Man Who Dreams of Classic Parks: But Architect Walter Netsch Suddenly Finds Himself Recast as a Pivotal Political Player," Tempo, *Chicago Tribune,* July 6, 1986, A1, 4.

11. Walter Netsch, "Oral History of Walter Netsch," interview by Betty J. Blum, May 10, 1985, and June 5–28, 1995, transcript, Art Institute of Chicago, 117 (hereafter cited as Blum), and Netsch, interview with author.

12. Blum, 137–38.

13. Ibid., 140–41.

14. Owings, 159.

15. Blum, 160.

16. Walter Netsch, "Walter Netsch Interviewed by Detlef Mertins," *SOM Journal* 1 (2007): 149.

17. The original members of the planning committee were Clarence L. Ver Steeg, chairman, professor of history; Richard D. Ellman, professor of English; David Jolly, assistant librarian; Jens Nyholm, University librarian; Moody E. Prior, dean of the Graduate School; John C. Sanderson Jr., director of plant properties; and Robert H. Strotz, professor of economics (and later president of the University).

18. Blum, 344–45.

19. Ibid., 322.

20. Ibid., 420.

21. Netsch, interview with author.

22. The *Plan of Chicago* documents discovered by Netsch and Uhlir are preserved in the Chicago History Museum.

23. Blum, 256.

A Timely Design:
Walter Netsch and the United States Air Force Academy

ROBERT ALLEN NAUMAN

On April 1, 2004, a ceremony took place at the United States Air Force Academy that celebrated the Academy's importance to the history of American architecture. It included the designation of the Academy's Cadet Area as a National Historic Landmark District and the unveiling of a United States commemorative stamp picturing the Cadet Chapel — the focal point of the Cadet Area (fig. 1). The date marked the 50th anniversary of President Dwight D. Eisenhower's passage of Public Law 325, providing for the establishment of the United States Air Force Academy. Constructed during the Cold War, the Air Force Academy was one of the largest architectural projects of that period. It was a government commission and, even though it was an educational institution, the expectation was that

fig. 1   U.S. Air Force Academy Cadet Area

it would function as a national monument, symbolically representing both the United States' emergence as a global power (if not *the* global power) following World War II and the Air Force's role in establishing and maintaining that position. Subsequent arguments and discussions in Congress and the public realm over the appropriateness of the Academy's modernist vocabulary polarized its supporters and critics, both summarizing and precipitating many of the architectural debates of the mid-century era.

As Air Force jets passed overhead during that 50th-anniversary celebration, few in the crowd remembered the debates and controversies that swirled around the Academy design. Nor did most Americans who would purchase the commemorative stamp — honoring a work of architecture that has become an American icon (and is the most popular man-made tourist attraction in the state of Colorado) — realize that the chapel itself was a lightning rod for much of that controversy. In fact, the vast majority of Americans, and perhaps even some of those in attendance at the anniversary celebration, would be hard pressed to name the architect who designed the chapel. Some would perhaps link the design to the corporate architectural firm of Skidmore, Owings & Merrill (SOM), the firm that had overseen the Academy construction, but that is only partially true. The chapel design can actually be attributed to a single SOM architect: Walter A. Netsch Jr.

Netsch was, in fact, SOM's designer in charge of the entire Academy project — remarkable considering he was only 34 years of age at the time. While accounts of the Academy construction have been written from various points of view, this one will look at the project from the standpoint of Netsch's involvement and the impact that he had on the design.[1] The story is both heroic and tragic: Heroic, in that Netsch persisted with many of his design ideas in the face of overwhelming adversity from the public, Congress, the military establishment, and even members of his own firm. Tragic, in that many of those ideas were compromised by bureaucratic and budgetary constraints. Netsch's involvement with the Academy project can be traced to its very beginnings, with the architect selection process. A brief summary of Netsch's education and early career with SOM reveals his experience to be a contributing factor to the firm's success in attaining the Academy commission.

I

Netsch received his bachelor of architecture degree in 1943 from the Massachusetts Institute of Technology, where he studied with Lawrence B. Anderson, Herbert Beckwith, and Alvar Aalto.[2] Netsch recalls that his other "heroes" while he studied at MIT included Walter Gropius and Le Corbusier, in large part due to their experiments in providing low-cost housing following World War I.[3] This was a social concern that Netsch himself was given an opportunity to address immediately after joining SOM in 1947, when he worked on additions to the Manhattan Project town of Oak Ridge, Tennessee, as it evolved from a closed, secretive wartime city to an open, "real" postwar city. Netsch was involved in master planning for the community, overseeing designs for 500 garden apartments, a shopping center, and a high school.[4]

In 1949 Netsch was sent to SOM's San Francisco office as chief of design. Initially dispatched to develop a shopping center for Del Monte properties in Monterey, Netsch was quickly placed in charge of SOM's Okinawa project in Japan. In that capacity he oversaw the designs for warehouses, town centers, chapels, schools, and other buildings for Army and Air Force units stationed at Okinawa.[5] During that same period (1949–54) Netsch was placed in charge of the design for the U.S. Naval Postgraduate School in Monterey. Splitting his time between the Naval Academy in Annapolis and SOM's San Francisco office, Netsch developed the master plan and designs for a complex of buildings to accommodate the needs of approximately 800 students. Those buildings included laboratories, classrooms, an auditorium, and a library — all designed employing a modernist vocabulary that some observers have termed "Miesian."[6]

The questionable impact of Ludwig Mies van der Rohe's modernist style on Netsch has relevance to the Air Force Academy design, so Netsch's thoughts on the issue are worth examining at this point. Netsch discounts the impact of Mies, stating that Mies's Chicago work was actually a refinement of the accomplishments of Chicago School architects such as William Le Baron Jenney. Of Jenney's impact on his own work, and the impact of the Chicago School in general, Netsch said:

> To me, he's one of my heroes and mentors, you might say, as a designer. So if you take a look at the Naval Postgraduate School, you will find a grid…. You will find, however, the auditorium sitting down, being depressed — so that as you look out, you look out at the trees. You will find that the concrete structure is exposed, the trusses are exposed, but they aren't in the manner of Mies's methodology. Mine comes from, I would say, MIT's pragmatism and the Chicago School's historicism…. I agree they're gridded. I won't argue they aren't gridded, but they aren't Miesian.[7]

Netsch's comments reveal an awareness of a very American architectural context that developed in Chicago through the work not only of Jenney but also of Sullivan and Wright. For Netsch the Naval Postgraduate School design was informed by both a sensibility of place, as defined by the dialogue between nature and the manmade (in terms of the auditorium siting), and by the practical and structural demands resulting from the development of tall-building types in Chicago.[8] Equally important is that, although he situates himself within this American context, Netsch never denies the impact of European modernism. He has mentioned, for example, that Sigfried Giedion's *Space, Time, and Architecture* was "the bible" at MIT.[9] Giedion's promotion of Gropius's architecture and of the Bauhaus and their attempt to heal the breach between industry and society led Gropius to invite Giedion to deliver the Norton Lectures at Harvard in 1938 that were the basis of *Space, Time, and Architecture*. Giedion's philosophy, which stressed addressing social concerns through city planning, would also reverberate throughout the U.S. Air Force Academy plan.

II

With his involvement in these postwar projects, it is obvious that Netsch was very experienced in community planning and campus design by the time the Academy competition was announced in April 1954. The task — to design an academy to educate and train future Air Force officers — would include administration, academic, laboratory, training, and office buildings; cadet and airmen barracks and mess halls; a library, a museum, a hospital, and chapels; family and officer housing; a gymnasium, a field house, a swimming pool, and other athletic and recreational facilities; and shops, warehouses, power and heating plants, utilities, roads, an airfield, and other operational support facilities.[10]

In sifting through SOM's archives, it is apparent that the firm used Netsch's connections and experience from the outset in garnering the Academy commission. Realizing that Colonel Leo J. Erler, who had supervised SOM's work in the Far East, would be a key figure in determining the Academy architect, SOM contacted him several days after the competition questionnaire was mailed to interested architectural firms and informed him that Netsch would be one of its main people involved with the project.[11] Several weeks later SOM wrote Erler to advise him that Netsch would be visiting his office to show him material the firm would be presenting for its application.[12] Netsch was also listed in the application as resident architect of the project, responsible for architectural coordination.[13] In fact, Netsch's experience informed also SOM's Academy presentation. At their final interview for the Academy contract, SOM partners presented their master plan and design schemes on a 15-foot long, 6-foot high screen — a format Netsch had developed when working on the U.S. Naval Postgraduate School and Okinawa projects.[14]

Not surprisingly, given its experience with military contracts, SOM was awarded the Academy project on July 23, 1954. A preliminary contract signed on August 4 stipulated that the following work be initiated: analysis and development of the project's academic, architectural, and engineering requirements; preparation of a master plan; development of sketch designs and preliminary drawings with design analysis and material lists; preparation of scale models as requested; preparation of cost estimates; and site investigation, including topographic and engineering surveys.[15] Earlier in 1954 an estimate for the construction of the entire facility had been quoted at $125 million in Congressional testimony from Secretary of the Air Force Harold Talbott. This was despite the fact that in 1951 the firm of Holabird, Root and Burgee had estimated the facility would cost approximately $182 million; further, prior to the 1954 Congressional hearing, an estimate by the firm of Gugler, Kimball, and Husted (in association with Harbeson, Hough, Livingston and Larson) — a firm that Talbott hired specifically to do a cost analysis of the project — had projected costs at more than $145 million. Netsch was promoted to full partner at SOM in 1955 and placed in charge of one of the largest American architectural projects of the decade, in the process assuming Talbott's budgetary restraints.[16]

Netsch later recalled that one of his earliest tasks was to determine the project's physical boundaries.[17] The mountains and the Pike National Forest established the western border. The north and south borders were determined by hills that would obscure future and possibly conflicting land use on adjacent property, while the east boundary was established east of an existing highway and railroad, so that no future development along the highway would impinge on the Academy sightlines. The far-reaching effect of that planning can be seen today. Colorado Springs has expanded to the boundaries of the Academy, but due to Netsch's original vision, the Academy grounds still serve as something of a regional park. The splendid sightlines afforded by 18,000 acres of Academy land encourage a dialogue between the Academy buildings and the natural environment — something that Netsch envisioned from the outset.

After determining the boundaries of the site, Netsch identified the four major components of the Academy: the school itself, the living community and the staff amenities, the airfield, and the service and supply area. He then positioned those components in the vast Academy terrain. The flatter eastern terrain was an obvious choice for the airfield and, since it would have to be reached by railroads, the service and supply area. Locating the other components presented less obvious solutions. Netsch later related that at least five different areas were considered for the Cadet Area, which would include the cadet quarters, the academic building (including classrooms, lecture halls, and the library), a dining hall, a social hall, an administration building, and a chapel. Options ranged from placing the Cadet Area in a valley to placing it on a more prominent area on the site — atop Lehman Mesa. Eventually, the Lehman Mesa site was selected, giving the Cadet Area a prominent position that allowed both an expansive view over the plain and a very visible presence — befitting a national monument— from the highway below. As Netsch would later relate:

> We got as close to the mountains as we could. Everyone will feel, I think, that he is on a foothill of the mountains, looking toward their heights or out on the plains. Situated close to the mountains, you can feel their grandeur.... [L]ooking out over the expanse of the plain, you can feel its grandeur, too, and this is better than sitting out on the plain, looking at the mountains too far away and the plain too omnipresent, and thus missing the grandeur of both.[18]

Of course, the prominent placement of the Cadet Area also allowed for Greek Acropolis analogies, appropriate for an architectural ensemble that had an abstracted classical pedigree, both in terms of its formal components and modernist rhetoric.[19] Evoking the precinct of Athena, goddess of war and wisdom, was also a powerful metaphor in establishing a tradition for this newest branch of the service academies.

As for the residential communities, they were situated in valleys (Pine Valley and Douglas Valley), with the community center that serviced them both situated on a ridge between the two. Netsch's concept in placing these developments in the valleys was that the residents would be forced to interact with the natural environment during their daily activities, driving in and out of the valleys to go to other areas on the Academy site. Given Netsch's respect for Sigfried Giedion, it seems appropriate to draw parallels to Giedion's discussion of the role of parkways in urban planning. In *Space, Time, and Architecture,* Giedion notes that a parkway is not laid out "for the sake of the most direct and rapid transit. Instead it humanizes the highway by carefully following and utilizing the terrain, rising and falling with the contours of the earth, merging completely into the landscape."[20]

The original concept for the housing in these residential communities also seems to pay heed to Giedion's suggestion that "schools, playgrounds, and athletic fields will be so related to the rows of houses that greenery will penetrate the body of the town to the greatest extent."[21] Netsch's solution, however, was again inspired not just by European dogma but also by an awareness of American architectural developments and how those radical applications might be adopted to a Western landscape. In a design that Netsch said was indebted to Buckminster Fuller (specifically, the Dymaxion House), each house was suspended or cantilevered from concrete supports, resulting in a design that would have minimal impact on the landscape. Netsch explained that he and fellow SOM architect Carl Kohler initially designed a house that was "a cube, in a sense."[22] The one-story housing units, which measured either 28 or 35 feet per side, were supported on a 10-foot-square concrete base that contained a large storage area and staircase. The cantilevered design allowed the home's occupants to drive into a courtyard and park beneath the overhang. The individual units were arranged in staggered square patterns.

Netsch and Kohler proposed a simple modernist design with flat roofs and windows that extended to the living room floors.[23] The Air Force hierarchy, however, rejected that plan. Eventually, the housing was administered as a Title VIII (Capehart) Housing Project. Under the conditions of that federally funded program, SOM was forced to affiliate with a firm that had Title VIII experience. Netsch feels the result was mediocre housing design at the Academy.[24]

III

The radical and somewhat utopian context of Netsch's vision, and the belief that the military hierarchy would embrace that vision, may seem naïve, but it is in fact indicative of Netsch's training and a result of his experience with military projects. Embracing technological solutions to design problems would have been part of Netsch's architectural training at MIT. And with his design for the U.S. Naval Postgraduate School, Netsch had waged and won a battle with the government over environmental concerns (meaning, in this case, a respect for and dialogue with the existing landscape). The Navy's original plan for that project was to destroy the historic landscaping on the site, the grounds of the former Del Monte Hotel. Netsch's plan, which was eventually realized, situated buildings within the existing landscaping.[25]

The integration of buildings and landscape was to become one of Netsch's guiding principles in designing the Academy buildings themselves, and it is worth addressing, since it is a complex issue. The Academy's site, situated beneath the Rampart Range and Pikes Peak, is spectacular and cannot be ignored. But what, precisely, was to be the relationship of men, materials, and design to this region and environment? In Netsch's concept the Academy buildings would provide a series of carefully orchestrated views that responded to the site while at the same time creating a hierarchy of spaces that addressed concerns both functional and metaphorical. But how did that concept determine form and dictate

fig. 2 Vandenberg Hall — Cadet Quarters

materials? Netsch himself provided many of these answers in subsequent interviews and discussions.

Functional concerns determined the master plan of the Cadet Area, both in terms of the buildings' individual designs and their relationship to one another. The Cadet Quarters building (fig. 2) was situated against the north side of the mesa, with Netsch providing an ingenious solution to its functional demands. He called it his "two up and two down" solution. From the pedestrian level, the building appears to be a three-story design, although it is actually a six-story building. The pedestrian level reveals itself as an open loggia, as does the first level on the north-facing side (originally both these stories were to be open arcades). The loggia, Netsch noted, provided shade from the sun or cover from rain or snow. At the same time the design solution serves another practical function: The cadets are only two floors away from the pedestrian level and the main academic area. From below the pedestrian level, on the other hand, the six-story profile creates a monumental presence.

The Cadet Quarters, designed to hold 2,640 cadets, is organized on the principle of the squadron. Four squadrons form a cadet group, and each group is located around a quadrangle. Those courtyards were originally designed with free-flowing biomorphic gardens to contrast with the geometric forms of the architecture. Each cadet's room featured two large windows — one facing out and framing the larger natural landscape, and one facing the courtyards and framing the smaller manmade landscape. Netsch provided the rationale for the large windows in each cadet room: "I can't imagine living in a cadet room without wanting to have a full eyeful of the country instead of peering through a porthole or a Pullman window."[26]

The Academic Building was sited perpendicular to the Cadet Quarters, forming, in effect, the short leg of an "L" design. This building contains classrooms and the library, and its location adjacent to the Cadet Quarters was determined by the cadets' need to move regularly and quickly between the buildings. The library is on the north end of the building, midway between the Cadet Quarters and the classrooms. Although both the Cadet Quarters and the Academic Building have interior courtyards, Netsch was disappointed to learn that classrooms were required, by the military hierarchy, to be interior rooms without windows. To alleviate that sense of containment, the corridors were designed with external views.[27] As in the work of other modernist architects, such as Le Corbusier's Villa Savoye or Mies van der Rohe's Tugendhat House, these windows abstracted nature into a series of views. These views are notable in that they appear within the context of both the natural environment of the western United States and a military academy. They acknowledge both the mythic force of the region and the cadet's place within that cosmos. Netsch's concern in the design was the human element. He considered how the cadets would interact with the Colorado terrain as a complement to their military activities. Netsch's interest in social activism informs the Academy. His design decisions are based on a dialogue with the natural environment that promotes reflection and self-awareness — qualities he values and respects as an important aspect of leadership.

The Dining Hall was situated next to the Academic Building, opposite the Cadet Quarters, and was also intended to promote a dialogue with nature. It was conveniently close to the former buildings yet allowed enough spatial separation for the mandatory formation of the cadets prior to meals. Netsch originally envisioned a glass-enclosed dining hall that offered panoramic views of the spectacular surroundings, with kitchen services on the floor below servicing the dining area via elevators. Unfortunately, the military hierarchy vetoed the plan, fearing an electrical outage could cripple the elevator system. As constructed, glass walls enclose three sides of the Dining Hall, while a masonry wall defines the north side. The fact that the building could not be realized as planned was another disappointment to Netsch.[28]

Eventually, some of the stark stone planes that comprised the Cadet Area buildings were enlivened with mosaic tiles. In keeping with his attempt to integrate the building ensemble with the landscape, Netsch had proposed that the mosaic walls be green and blue, but Gordon Bunshaft convinced SOM to use "Bauhaus colors" — the primary colors of red, yellow, and blue — for the tile mosaics.[29]

The entire Cadet Area was organized on a seven-foot grid. The module determined not only the structural bays of the buildings but also fenestration and façade detailing, room width, and even bed length. The grid was clearly demarcated in the marble strips that delineate the terrazzo pavement, reminding the cadets at every step of the rational underpinning to both the Cadet Area design and their own education. Netsch has noted that the grid was in part determined by his experience in Japan: "Falling back on my Japanese experience of the tatami-oriented world, the module of 7' x 7' was selected, and multiples or divisions of this proportion were used. This meant that within any structure system, the solids and voids would relate." It would, Netsch said, reinforce a geometry that "would contrast with nature's more complex character."[30]

While Netsch related the grid proportions to Japanese aesthetics, they also fell within the context of modernism, standardization, and proportional systems. In his 1923 *Vers une architecture (Towards a New Architecture)*, Le Corbusier, for example, wrote of the "regulating lines" that bring order to nature: "For, all around him, the forest is in disorder with its creepers, its briars, and the tree-trunks which impede him and paralyze his efforts. He has imposed order by means of measurement."[31] In discussing the Academy design, landscape architect Jory Johnson made a similar observation: "At the Cadet Area, nature is experienced as measures of control on a continuum."[32] Comparisons to Mies van der Rohe's 1929 Barcelona Pavilion might be appropriate as well, in that Mies's design also was based on a dialogue between the implied infinite bounds of nature and a rational, classical, proportional grid — although the decidedly spiritual foundation that informed Mies's conceptual framework was perhaps not as strong here.

A comparison to religious models, however, isn't too far-fetched. The model of St. Gall Monastery, for example, comes to mind: a medieval monastic community in which a module determined every element of the design, from buildings to gardens, paths, room size, and bed length.[33] Le Corbusier's Convent of La Tourette, constructed between 1953 and 1957, also offers an interesting comparison to the Cadet Quarters. Like the Cadet Quarters, Le Corbusier's plan presented a monumental five-story façade from a distance, while receding to three levels in the rear, with each room having a view over the surrounding landscape. It too was designed on a modular principle. At La Tourette, monastic frugality readily lent itself to standardization in terms of interior furnishings. The rooms were ideal for contemplation, although their interiors were adaptable to each individual's taste. Interestingly, at the time of the Academy construction, Netsch hinted that the cadet's life was likewise monastic: "The cadets, unlike ordinary college students, are isolated. They cannot go into town every night for movies or girls or beer. The cadet is so limited that his room is not only a place to sleep and a place to study; it is really his living space for four years."[34]

The Cadet Area ascends hierarchically from the parade grounds and physical education buildings to the academic area (comprising the Cadet Quarters, Dining Hall, and Academic Building) and finally to the most public area, the Court of Honor (containing the social hall, the administration building, and the chapel). Physical, mental, social, and spiritual domains were thus metaphorically defined as a series of levels representing the development of the individual and his responsibilities to self and community. In the original plan the south side of the Cadet Area was to remain open, allowing nature to penetrate — and providing both harmony with and contrast to the natural environment. The buildings would, as Netsch said, "confine yet open out … contain and release and relax within an exhilarated space which is an earthbound version of the sky."[35] Architectural historian Kristin Schaffer has commented on this effect:

The seven-foot grid of the module organized the buildings and the space, but never constricted or confined them, as the buildings were shifted away from the corners, which were open and implied.... [E]ven though a considerable visual momentum was created when one looked down their length, they never seemed to collide with one another, nor was there any sense of collision with the foothills behind.... This is a Modernist treatment of space, to be sure.... Yet here the great length of the buildings and the elevation of the entire terrace over the surrounding terrain created a sense of soaring, not just of expansion.[36]

It is interesting to note that Netsch made no attempt to either define or integrate the buildings with any notion of "Colorado architecture" or to use indigenous materials. In a 1958 interview with MIT architectural historian John Burchard, Netsch addressed the issue of the Academy within the context of Colorado architecture:

Don't you remember the night you ridiculed the idea that there was a Colorado architecture? You asked whether it was Mesa Verde? The dismal shacks of the silver towns? The Victorian opera houses...? The fire station in Georgetown, Colorado? The quaint wooden houses in Leadville...? You asked whether it was the imported Swiss chalets of the motels of Aspen, or the imported modern architecture of Herbert Bayer in the same town, or the brick of [Charles Z.] Klauder's university at Golden, or [John Gaw] Meem's museum at Colorado Springs, or the Broadmoor Hotel, or [I. M.] Pei's Mile High Center in Denver? I agree with you when you insist that there is no such thing as Colorado architecture in the sense that there is New England architecture, or even Prairie architecture, à la Frank Lloyd Wright. No, in the narrow sense, there is no

fig. 3 Dining Hall under construction

Colorado material, no Colorado architecture. The mountains are the architecture
of Colorado…. What is Coloradan is the land and the sky and the flora.[37]

In the same interview Netsch defended SOM's choice of materials:

Colorado is the site, but the Academy is national, and it will bring students not
only from every state, but from many other nations, too. I see no reason in this
day why the solution should be parochial. The idea never dawned on us that
this was reasonable…. No, the materials really evolved from the program.[38]

While the first quotation reinforces the strong connection that Netsch felt to the
Western landscape, the second quotation reveals his perception of the architecture's
responsibility to a national mission within the context of the Cold War. Although he
noted that the materials were determined by the Academy's program, they — along with
the construction techniques — also reflected technological advances developed during
World War II. They metaphorically referenced an academy that represented a new age of
aerial technology. At the same time, Netsch was expanding upon technological solutions
that had been explored by European and American modernist architects, such as Fuller
and the architects involved in the postwar Case Study House program.[39] Large areas of
glass (Netsch commented that glass was perhaps more generally acceptable than stone
for contemporary architecture), precast concrete, and extruded aluminum were used in
structures that, with the help of computer technology, employed innovative construction
techniques. As Netsch later said:

In the post WWII years, the building industry … was hungry for new ideas
and products, [focused] on extending the available and unused technology, and
we as designers were only too willing to participate. We saw this component
as the American addition to the modern movement born in Europe.[40]

One example of the application of new technological methods was the Dining Hall
roof, which was composed of a prefabricated truss roof system 308 by 308 feet, assembled
on the ground and lifted into place by hydraulic jacks in just six hours (fig. 3). Another
would be the Cadet Chapel.

IV

The Cadet Chapel was the centerpiece of the Cadet Area architectural ensemble. It was
a building that Netsch would later call his first "iconic" building.[41] That a chapel should
have been assumed from the beginning to be the focal point of the Academy design may
seem curious. This was, after all, not only a service academy but was also one of the largest
government commissions of the time and was intended to serve as a national monument,
symbolically representing the United States and the Air Force. However, an examination
of postwar American culture elucidates the issue.

In his 1955 publication *Protestant — Catholic — Jew,* author Will Herberg observed that
during the 1950s religion had become "religiousness without religion," a way of simply
"belonging," and that "being a Protestant, a Catholic, or a Jew is understood as the

specific way, and increasingly perhaps the only way, of being an American and locating oneself in American society."[42] In fact, Supreme Court and Congressional mandates had underscored this fact. The 1952 Supreme Court ruling *Zorach v. Clauson* allowed release time from regular classes in public schools for the purpose of religious instruction. The military academies West Point and Annapolis, where cadets attended compulsory chapel, were cited in that court case.[43] At both academies chapels were focal points: The chapel at the Naval Academy, designed by Ernest Flagg in 1905, was modeled after Jules Hardouin-Mansart's church of Les Invalides in Paris (c. 1680); and Cram, Goodhue and Ferguson located their picturesque Gothic chapel at West Point, designed in 1910, on a promontory overlooking that academy. During the early 1940s *Life* magazine depicted worship services at both West Point and Annapolis. Several years after *Zorach v. Clauson*, Sen. Homer Ferguson (R-Michigan) introduced a motion to insert the words "under God" into the Pledge of Allegiance. Congress passed the motion, and President Eisenhower signed it into law on Flag Day, June 14, 1954 — several months after he had signed the bill establishing the Air Force Academy. The fact that the phrase "In God We Trust" would be adopted as the national motto in 1956 was simply a continuation of these Cold War sentiments — a reaction to "godless Communism."

The chapel program seems to have been first discussed at an Academy design meeting in February 1955. It was decided that a single chapel design would best serve the three religious groups into which most of the cadets fell. Netsch was at that meeting, as were Air Force representatives and Major General Charles Carpenter, chief of chaplains for the Air Force. The original design was divided into three areas: the Protestant section would accommodate 1,600 men, plus 150 more in the choir loft; the Catholic section held 600 men, plus 50 more in that choir loft; and the Jewish section served 100 men. The numbers were determined by demographic studies that were recorded in the meeting minutes: "Experience factors in the percentage of cadets in each faith were discussed. It was agreed that the following factors would be the most reasonable to apply to the Cadet Wing: 25% Catholic; 72% Protestant; and 3% Jewish."[44]

Netsch was given full responsibility for the Cadet Chapel. His original design was a concrete building with a freestanding carillon. He described it as "a folded-plate chapel containing two chapels on the grade level, one for the Catholic services, one for the Protestant services, and a Jewish chapel on the mezzanine."[45] The form itself evoked Gothic churches, albeit in a very abstract fashion. The folded-plate concrete technique was structurally innovative.[46] Both form and materials visually separated the chapel from the Cadet Area buildings (figs. 4, 5). As with Le Corbusier's Chapel of Notre-Dame-du-Haut at Ronchamps (constructed between 1950 and 1954), Netsch's solution to a religious structure was both sculptural and expressive. While Le Corbusier's building referred back to the Parthenon and the ceremonial processions with which it was associated, Netsch mentioned Mont-Saint-Michel as an inspiration. While Le Corbusier's chapel was situated on a hilltop, Netsch's was situated on a podium overlooking the main Academy area and the Court of Honor. Ultimately, Netsch's design more specifically represented a synthesis

figs. 4, 5 Renderings by George Rudolph from *The Academy Master Plan* exhibition, May 13–15, 1955, Colorado Springs Fine Arts Center

between the two great architectural traditions — Gothic and classical — and both the building's form and siting underscored that synthesis.

On May 13–15, 1955, at the Colorado Springs Fine Arts Center, SOM first presented the Academy design, including Netsch's chapel, to the public and members of the press and Congress. The art and architectural press, sympathetic to International Style Modernism, was enthusiastic about the design. A writer for *Progressive Architecture* stated that the design was "above all, beautiful, lastingly beautiful."[47] *ARTNews* reported:

> *What the architects and these others have produced is a wonderful series of*
> *man-made geometric forms amid the pines and peaks of the Rockies — open*
> *glass and steel boxes and pyramids that belong to the landscape, and at the same*
> *time just as much to the workers who inhabit them, as did the great wide-flung,*
> *low-arched Romanesque monasteries of the pilgrimage roads of the Pyrenees.*[48]

Some of the Congressional response to the overall design, and particularly to the original folded-plate chapel design, however, was unfavorable to the point of insult, and Netsch later recalled being in tears at the back of the room. Nat Owings comforted Netsch, assuring him that the overall design was fine and suggesting he travel to Europe to study church architecture and then design another chapel.[49]

Subsequently, Netsch took off for Europe (a trip he had to finance himself) to study church design. He began in England, where he was impressed with Wells Cathedral (although he didn't like the "fussiness" of English Gothic). In France it was Sainte-Chapelle, flooded with colored light, that impressed Netsch. The fact that Sainte-Chapelle had a chapel on two floors also caught his attention. Visiting Chartres, Netsch was overwhelmed by both the structural detailing of the edifice and the quality of its light. In Italy the Basilica of San Francesco d'Assisi also caught his attention, again due in part to its two-level design.[50] Netsch later recalled the impact these buildings had on him: "I came home with this tremendous feeling of, How can I, in this modern age of technology, create something that will be as inspiring and aspiring as Chartres ... with the light of Sainte-Chapelle?"[51]

Returning from Europe, Netsch began to redesign the Cadet Chapel and reconsider its placement within the Cadet Area. The chapel, as both the signature building and the religious focus of the Cadet Area, carried the burden of defining the Academy in the Cold War era as a national monument. Modernist classroom or dormitory designs were one thing, but a church, many felt, had to have certain traditional features. To deflect public and Congressional concerns, a "generic" chapel model replaced the earlier folded-plate design. While SOM released a statement saying that the new model "may not in the least resemble the final concept," the July 3, 1955, issue of the *Colorado Springs Gazette-Telegraph* noted: "The new model conforms more to conventional American ideals of a place to worship and is complete with steeple and stained glass windows."[52]

As mentioned, Netsch had originally planned to romantically situate the chapel on a podium overlooking the Academy area and the Court of Honor. Eero Saarinen, one of the consultants on the Academy project (and the consultant whom Netsch most respected), suggested at an October 1955 meeting that the chapel be moved down to the Court of Honor.[53] Saarinen also suggested it be reoriented (turning it 90 degrees) to make it parallel with the mountains. Both of these suggestions were implemented in February 1956 and would continue to define the chapel's location and axis throughout the design process. As Netsch would later admit:

> *In the beginning we took a sort of medieval approach to its location in the*
> *community, and I think we were wrong. The Mont-Saint-Michel aspect would*

have been wrong. Cadets are not monks, and there was no reason why they should be made to climb 125 feet to go to church. So I am glad the first proposal was rejected.[54]

Disappointingly, when the revised chapel plan was submitted in February 1956, Secretary of the Air Force Donald Quarles rejected it and suggested SOM develop four or five additional models for the chapel.[55]

Quarles's rejection of the revised plan belied a more serious problem: the fact that the specifics for the chapel program and its budget had never actually been approved. A design directive dated June 1, 1955, called for two cadet chapels — one to serve Protestants and Jews, and one to serve Catholics. On October 18, 1955, another directive called for a single interdenominational chapel, and on June 9, 1956, a five-page memorandum from the commandant of the cadets stated that three possibilities existed for the chapel design: a single nondenominational chapel; three separate facilities; or one structure housing three chapels.[56] On December 27, 1956, a directive was finally issued for three separate chapels to be located in one building: a Protestant chapel for 900, a Catholic chapel for 500, and a Jewish chapel for 100. Unfortunately, no sooner had the program been set than the budget began to fluctuate. In the December 27 directive, the budget was set at $4 million, but on February 1, 1957, was cut to $2.55 million.

By March 1957 Netsch had settled on a two-level design, inspired by Sainte-Chapelle and the Basilica of San Francesco d'Assisi. It was also at that time that he and an engineer devised the chapel's distinctive structural system, using tetrahedrons. This structural system determined the chapel's form, in the same fashion, said Netsch, that stone determined Gothic form:

> *Returning from my trip to Europe I was seeking an appropriate form that would have a three-dimensional character like a Gothic cathedral. The stone was the structure, the stone was the decoration, the stone was the pattern, the stone was the form…. [T]he tetrahedrons were the three-dimensional form I was seeking — structure, shape, decoration.*[57]

Originally Netsch envisioned tetrahedrons made of translucent white onyx. (Yale's Beinecke Library, designed in 1963 by SOM's Gordon Bunshaft, gives a sense of how light would have been diffused through this material.) But Netsch was persuaded by SOM's Robertson Ward, an architect who had been hired to set up a separate technical and materials research group for the Academy project, that, because the pieces of onyx would have been very small, thousands of joints would have been required, and leakage would have been unavoidable.[58] The tetrahedron concept, however, remained. Between each of those forms, spaced two feet apart, Netsch inserted a one-inch thick panel of stained glass. As Netsch later recalled, "By literally placing the tetrahedrons on top of one another, I made an enclosure that embodies the concept of light and space — and that is the dominant part of church architecture."[59]

In order to present his design to the SOM hierarchy, Netsch made a model of the chapel in section that was approximately 2½ feet high. Unbeknownst to Netsch, it precipitated an internal crisis at SOM, with some of the firm's partners calling the design "crazy" or saying it wasn't in keeping with SOM's philosophy.[60] As for Netsch, he later recalled his enthusiasm over the design:

> My team, of course, was terribly excited. We had something this time. We had Bucky Fuller, we had our geometry, our tetrahedrons; we had technology with Robertson Ward and all these pipe columns. This was a very contemporary thing, and in a sense it was Gothic in its form. We couldn't fail. It was everything that we wanted, and it was beautiful to boot.[61]

The model, along with color renderings, was presented to the Academy consultants, the Secretary of the Air Force, and other Air Force and Academy staff members at a Pentagon meeting on May 15, 1957, and the response was enthusiastic.[62] Netsch's solution synthesized the Gothic European tradition with technological applications specific to the mid-20th century while acknowledging the influence of American architects such as Fuller. This was a building that drew on tradition yet reflected its own modern and national context.

By the next month Netsch had designed a chapel with an upper level for Protestants that would seat 1,200 and separate Catholic and Jewish chapels on the lower level for 550 and 100 persons, respectively. Netsch immediately began to design the windows, a process he later recalled:

> I had in the meantime sat at home on my own and done some windows. I picked four points: I did the Creation out of Genesis; I did Saul to Paul, the famous event on his horse when he is converted; and the Apocalypse, which is Revelation.... I'm sure I did four, but those are the three I remember. The first one, Genesis, [depicted] the waters under the sea and the waters above the sea. So I remember doing the window for Genesis, ... there were ... different kind of blues, striped blues ... gradually turning into red for the sun.[63]

Netsch described the design as "Matisse-like." Unfortunately, the Academy chaplains found the designs unacceptable, and Netsch and Ward were forced to come up with an alternate design for the glass. They designed new frames that would be a foot wide and about three feet long, divided into panes. The stained glass pieces would be chipped off at the edges so the light would filter in across the faceted edges. Again, Netsch recalled working on the new design of both the stained glass and the chapel in general:

> So we had the system of how to do it, and I wanted the windows to, in a sense, start from Genesis, being dark colors, and go to gold over the altar.... Since I had a mile of this glass to do, I then had a pallet of blues and purples and reds and greens and then yellows. I would sit in my living room of my little penthouse at the top of 1360 Lake Shore Drive with little chips of colored pencil and a drawing of a facade of the building. I would make that blue and that red and that purple and so forth and so on, and as the window went up towards the apex it would get lighter so you would see this transition of color horizontally and vertically. Since the tetrahedrons crossed, they would meet and come back again....

[T]he Jewish chapel and Catholic chapel were on a 21-foot module. The Protestant chapel was on a 14-foot module. I was layering and crisscrossing. I was making very complex geometries. Not only was it tetrahedrons and triangles, but also the regular, straightforward, horizontal geometries were being changed. And the Jewish chapel was a circle, to represent the tent. There I used purple glass, very differently glazed. I did panels in the Catholic chapel, and they had their own artist do the stations of the cross. [64]

It was also during this time that Netsch contacted Walter Holtkamp to design organs for the Protestant and Catholic chapels. (Holtkamp had been the organ designer for MIT's chapel and Kresge Auditorium, both Eero Saarinen projects.)[65]

V

Congress had its own issues with the chapel. It continued to question the modern design and argued that the $3 million revised budget that had been submitted was too expensive. On August 6, 1957, the House of Representatives voted 102 to 53 to delay the chapel construction. Opposing the design on the basis of its inappropriateness to a Rocky Mountain setting and its materials, Rep. Errett Scrivner (R-Kansas), noted, "Three million dollars should build a cathedral … one spire is good, but why should there be a polished aluminum cathedral with 19 spires? This design and material is completely incompatible with the greatest beauty of all … the natural grandeur of the Rocky Mountains."[66] He called the design a "19-spire polished aluminum monstrosity … that will look like a row of polished teepees upon the side of the mountains."[67]

Rep. Daniel Flood (D-Pennsylvania), defended the design as appropriate to its natural setting:

I can assure you that when the 19 spires that were spoken of so lightly rise to the heavens of the Rockies … and when you see the teeth of the white-capped Rockies match the spires of this beautiful chapel … every requirement of your esthetic senses will be met to the fullest, and I believe these lines of pure Gothic majesty — not cubism — will meet the requirements. [68]

Rep. Alfred D. Sieminski (D-New Jersey) further supported the use of materials: "As for aluminum, the boys fight and die in aluminum planes…. They can worship in aluminum if they can die in it, can they not?"[69]

The following day, August 7, 1957, the Congressional debate over the chapel resumed. Rep. Edwin Dooley (D-New York) endorsed the design on the basis of a technological metaphor: "Is it not a fact that the chapel is supposed to represent flight in architecture…. The flying buttresses of a cathedral are replaced by the ailerons of the planes wings and the bow of the plane pointing skyward are the spires. I like it."[70] On August 8 Congress reversed its previous decision and voted 147 to 83 to restore the $3 million funding for the chapel. The debate over the cost, however, had ramifications for the design. Ultimately, the budget was cut. In November 1957 Netsch was forced to reduce the number of spires from 19 to 17, resulting in an overall reduction of the interior space. He also simplified the chapel's structural system and eliminated an elevator and air conditioning in order to lower the estimated cost of the building.

Ironically, that same month an exhibition and symposium focusing on the chapel design was held at MIT, and prominent church leaders from around the country defended and praised the design. Rabbi Aryeh Lev, chairman of the National Jewish Welfare Board, was "completely satisfied" with it, especially the fact that it included all three faiths in one chapel. Reverend Edward Fry, executive director for church architecture of the National Council of Churches, declared, "It is as daring as the early development of Gothic in the churches. I could worship here." The Very Reverend Joseph Marbach, Cardinal Spellman's assistant in the Military Ordinate appointed by the president, praised it for its "farsightedness." And Walter Taylor, chairman of the commission on architecture for the National Council of Churches, added, "No man has a right to decide whether God approves or disapproves a house of worship. I feel it is in the best religious tradition that this new style of church architecture be developed."[71]

At approximately the same time, Academy consultant Eero Saarinen issued a press release praising the chapel design:

> I think the chapel is very beautiful. It is well located in relation to the other buildings and can be seen from all sides. The form is strong and simple, as it had to be with the mountains behind. The basic shape is a pointed roof like hands held upward in prayer. There are pinnacles at the top, which give it a relation to Gothic spires. The main thing is to capture that indefinable spirit that makes a chapel a religious building and different from any other. This is achieved by the shape of the building and the way the light is used.[72]

Congress finally approved Netsch's $2.85 million budget for the chapel in December 1957, but the debate over the chapel funding continued through the next year. In fact, SOM later noted 33 separate design directives and reviews in 1958. As if that wasn't enough, there were still disagreements about the design from within SOM. Nat Owings expressed concern regarding the window designs. In a letter dated May 12, 1958, Netsch (working in the Chicago office) complained to Gordon Bunshaft (working in the New York office) about Owings's suggestions:

> Much to my surprise and chagrin, I feel the big north and south windows on which we have been laboring did not appeal to him design-wise…. Nat's feeling on the window was that the unit looked too vertical, which, unfortunately, was just what I was trying to establish…. Nat has suggested a precast concrete grille. This I cannot agree with as we have kept all the concrete for the terrace level in trying to maintain the light structure relating to the tetrahedrons and the vertical space.[73]

These letters and comments reflect the vehement battle that Netsch had to continually wage to get his chapel design accepted and completed. Unbelievably, the battle continued into 1959.

As the design process dragged on, costs rose. When construction costs were quoted at $3.3 million in August 1959, Congressmen suggested the glass between the tetrahedrons be eliminated. In response, Netsch wrote a letter to Secretary of the Air Force James Douglas:

> *Mr. Ferry [Special Assistant for Installations at the Academy] has asked what savings could be made if the glass between the tetrahedrons is removed and the structure re-analyzed and simplified. This change would be of substantial nature because of the three-dimensional characteristics of the tetrahedrons and would involve a complete structural analysis, architectural analysis, and would be a major change to the drawings involving architectural costs that would negate some of the economical advantages gained…. This cost would never compensate for the loss in character and the change in concept or additional design costs.*[74]

Finally, on August 28, 1959, the Santa Fe firm of Robert E. McKee Inc. was awarded the contract for the chapel, and construction began. The tetrahedrons, made of welded tubular steel, were prefabricated in Missouri and transported to the Colorado Springs site via railroad. Rising over 150 feet from their granite abutments, each of the tetrahedrons was 75 feet long and weighed over five tons (figs. 6, 7, 8). Embossed aluminum panels covered the exterior, while plaster panels with aluminum surrounds were used on the interior.[75]

Photographs of the chapel's skeletal structure appeared in numerous national publications, while the texts metaphorically linked the design to aerospace technology. The May 1961

fig. 6 Cadet Chapel, exterior

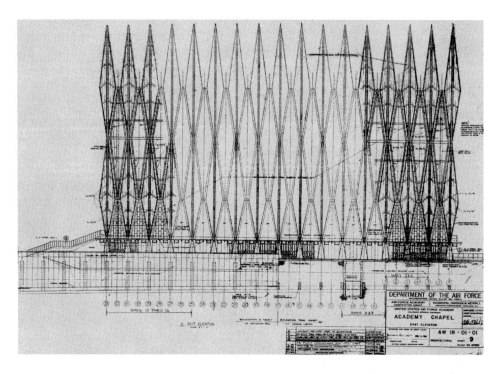

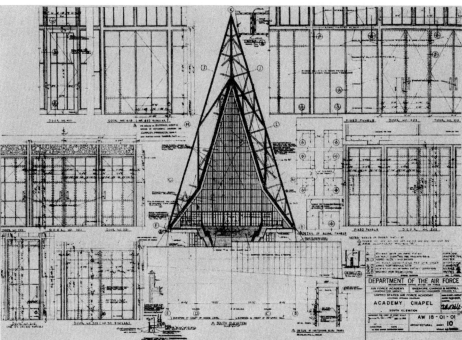

figs. 7, 8 Cadet Chapel, east and south elevation plans

issue of *Architectural Forum*, for example included several photographs of the skeletal system with the following remark:

> Interestingly, the Air Force several years ago thought seriously of building tubular metal hangars, but dropped the idea. Now it has a tubular steel chapel as big as a hangar, the result of independent thinking by its architects — a truly modern frame enclosing a space of impressive scale and promising beauty.[76]

A year later *Time* magazine concluded an article on the chapel by poetically linking its form to its natural setting:

> Most important of all, the building's metallic majesty, visible across the countryside like the church spires of rural Europe, is in perfect harmony with the spirit of the Academy. Its materials and basic forms are largely those of an airplane, and its spires do not merely point — they soar.[77]

The chapel was eventually completed in the summer of 1963 and dedicated on September 22, 1963.

Protestants worship upstairs at the Cadet Chapel, while the Roman Catholic and Jewish chapels are located on the lower level. The Catholic chapel is approached by two sets of steps from the south, while the Jewish chapel has separate entrances from either the east or west sides. Netsch's concept for the various chapels was explained in a 1962 *Time* magazine article:

> Each religion would have a chapel of its own. The Protestants, being in the majority, got the largest, and since the Academy is fairly formal, the chapel was endowed with lofty grandeur.... The Catholic Chapel, with its gentle arches and stonework, suggests the architecture and masonry of the Romanesque cathedral.... The Jewish chapel is housed within a round wooden screen from which all structural elements have been eliminated. This ... goes back to the ancient tents of the wandering Tribes of Israel, for each tent created ... a nonstructural space.[78]

The Protestant chapel soars to 150 feet and is the Academy's showcase for visitors. One-foot-wide strips of glass illuminate the interior by day and glow on the exterior at night. Netsch described the effect: "The colors change from darker blues to reds to gold as the altar is approached and at the junctions of the tetrahedrons starbursts occur."[79] The Catholic chapel is essentially rectangular. Its exterior walls are constructed of precast concrete panels with stained glass inserts providing illumination. Soft light filters through the amber-stained glass panels that define the area. In contrast, a circular wooden screen with inserts of white opalescent glass spatially defines the Jewish chapel. Originally the interior of the Jewish chapel was to be lit with a continuous neon light strip that defined the diameter of the room; florescent lights now fulfill that function. The violet, green, and blue glass panels on the east and west walls of the foyer heighten the soft glowing effect of the Jewish chapel.

Other artists and architects also contributed to the chapels' interiors. Harold E. Wagoner designed the liturgical furnishings for the Protestant chapel, while Luman Martin Winter executed the glass mosaic reredos in both the Protestant and Catholic chapels. Frank Greenhaus was the supervising architect of the Jewish chapel. Interestingly, that chapel's foyer floor was paved with Jerusalem brownstone, donated by the Israeli Defense Forces.[80]

In addition to the Catholic and Jewish chapels on the lower level, Netsch included an All-Faiths Room, devoid of specific religious symbolism. Practitioners of other religions, such as Buddhists and Muslims, have used it over the years. Netsch's inclusion of this room in the design is particularly revealing. It indicates that ultimately the chapel design was informed as much by spiritual considerations, both denominational and nondenominational, as by subtle and evocative transitions of light and enclosures of space.

Any metaphorical associations between the chapel spires and missiles or fighter planes are not in keeping with comments Netsch has made regarding the design. For example, he vigorously objected to the references to propellers and jet technology on the pew ends and to the aggressive, dagger-like design of the cross in the Protestant Chapel, but he was overruled by the National Council of Churches, which provided funding for the furnishings.[81] The technological metaphors that he embraced in the Academy design, it is clear, were meant to present technology in the service of mankind, not as a machine for war.

VI

Recognition and praise for both the Academy generally and the Cadet Chapel specifically has come slowly from the architectural community, perhaps due to the backlash against modernist design that began in the 1960s. In 1996 the Air Force Academy Cadet Chapel received the American Institute of Architects Twenty-Five Year Award. The AIA citation read:

> An outstanding collaboration of design and technology. This icon of cleanly
> articulated structure connects earth to heaven — its spectacular rocky mountain
> surroundings to it ecclesiastical purpose. Within the chapel, too, the eye is
> drawn upward, naturally, reverently. Artistically ahead of its time, the
> Cadet Chapel continues and will continue to inspire worship and awe.[82]

In endorsing Netsch's nomination for the award, Denver's Modern Architecture Preservation League noted:

> Netsch's design for the Air Force Academy campus is the finest example of
> 20th-century architectural design in Colorado and is one of the premier
> examples post-World War II site planning in the world. The Chapel, which
> constitutes the centerpiece of the plan, is exceptional for the dramatic sculptural
> quality of its design and its use of advanced materials and technology.[83]

Just prior to the designation of the Cadet Area as a National Historic Landmark District in 2004, SOM was approached to begin restoration work on the Cadet Chapel — to "restore the chapel to its original form and detailed profiles."[84] In discussing the restoration project in a recent publication, a representative of the firm said of the chapel:

> *Originally the Cadet Chapel took seven years to design and construct amid much public debate. When finally completed in 1963, it became the first SOM project credited to a single designer: Walter Netsch.... Inspired by ecclesiastical icons of the Middle Ages, the Cadet Chapel has itself become an icon of the Modern Age. The chapel was designed to be provocative and iconic, and symbolic to the mission of the newly created Air Force. Its design forged ahead in form and materials from the typical building conventions of the time.*[85]

Architectural historians have discussed the Air Force Academy — and the controversy it engendered — as a pivotal moment in American architecture.[86] Built in the late 1950s and early 1960s, the Academy was precariously balanced on the edge of a transitional period that would profoundly affect American society and culture — and the face of architecture. Netsch himself has noted that the chapel marked a transition in his approach to design. The geometric solution that the tetrahedrons provided for the chapel design would reemerge with his design for the University of Illinois's Chicago campus, based on the geometry of the rotated square. Defining the tetrahedron as a "three-dimensional enclosure object," Netsch noted that the next logical step was to move to the rotated square as a basis for the architectural plan.[87]

In summarizing the U.S. Air Force Academy design, it seems fitting to allow Walter Netsch to have the final words. Recently, PBS did a television special on the Academy titled *Jewel of the Rockies*. During interviews for the special, Netsch was asked about his design: "Nathaniel Owings said in a 1958 article in *Fortune* that the architecture of the Academy was 'timeless.' Others have identified the architecture with modernism of the 1950s. What do you think? Would the design differ significantly if you were to do it today?"

Netsch replied succinctly: "Design in our time is only timely if it is a good example."[88]

Notes

Frequently cited sources are identified by the following abbreviations:

Blum   Walter Netsch, "Oral History of Walter Netsch," interview by Betty J. Blum, May 10, 1985, and June 5–28, 1995, transcript, Art Institute of Chicago. The entire 456-page interview may be viewed online at www.artic.edu/aic/libraries/caohp/netsch.pdf.

RAFACA   Records of the Air Force Academy Construction Agency, record group 461, National Archives, Federal Records Center, Denver; followed by box number and folder title.

SOMA   Skidmore, Owings & Merrill archives, Chicago; followed by drawer or box number and (if relevant) file number. (Distinctions have been made between interdepartmental memos and outgoing letters.)

1. Historic accounts of the Academy include the following: M. Hamlin Cannon and Henry S. Fellerman, *Quest for an Academy* (Colorado Springs: United States Air Force Academy, 1947); George V. Fagan, *The Air Force Academy: An Illustrated History* (Boulder: Johnson Books, 1988); Robert Bruegmann, ed., *Modernism at Mid-Century: The Architecture of the United States Air Force Academy* (Chicago and London: University of Chicago Press, 1994; hereafter cited as *Modernism at Mid-Century*); and Robert Allen Nauman, *On the Wings of Modernism: The United States Air Force Academy* (Urbana: University of Illinois Press, 2004; hereafter cited as *On the Wings of Modernism*). Air Force Academy records are also located in the Special Collections Branch of the Air Force Academy Library in Colorado Springs.

2. Walter Netsch, interview with author, May 20, 1993. In 1937 Anderson and Beckwith formed the firm of that name.

3. Netsch noted that Mies van der Rohe was not included in this list because he was discredited in Boston due to his Nazi associations. Netsch recounted these events in Blum, 22.

4. In the 1993 interview (see n. 2), Netsch noted that the Oak Ridge apartments were similar in design to the 1927 Weissenhofsiedlung apartments at Stuttgart.

5. For Netsch's background and work for SOM before the Academy project, see his testimony before the Air Force Academy Contract Appeals Panel on January 13, 1960: SOMA, drawer 46, (no file no.), 31–41.

6. The library was never built. Netsch later published an article that provided an analysis of the design factors for the Naval Postgraduate School. See "Programming the U.S. Naval Postgraduate School of Engineering," *Architectural Record* 115, no. 6 (June 1954), 150–57.

7. Blum, 83–84.

8. Of course, the concept of the "Chicago School" is itself complex. For more on issues of the Chicago School, see Robert Bruegmann, *The Architects and the City* (Chicago: University of Chicago Press, 1997). Joan Draper and Robert Nauman also addressed this issue in their entry "Chicago, Illinois" in R. Stephen Sennott, ed., *Encyclopedia of 20th-Century Architecture* (New York: Fitzroy Dearborn, 2004), 241–43.

9. Blum, 18. Giedion shared Netsch's enthusiasm for Jenney's architecture and the Chicago School. See Sigfried Giedion, *Space, Time, and Architecture: The Growth of a New Tradition, 3rd ed.* (Cambridge, MA: Harvard University Press, 1954), 366–75.

10. For specifics of the Academy competition, see *On the Wings of Modernism*, 9–35.

11. Nathaniel Owings to Colonel Leo J. Erler, letter, 13 April 1954, SOMA, drawer 51, file 01. The letter announcing the competition was sent out to firms by the Department of the Air Force on April 6, 1954. Erler was deputy director of installations for the Air Force under Maj. General Lee B. Washbourne. He was appointed director of the Academy architect selection board the following month (May 1954).

12. Owings to Erler, letter, 23 April 1954, SOMA, drawer 51, file 01.

13. SOM proposal for the Academy commission, SOMA, drawer 51, file 01.

14. Kristen Schaeffer, "Creating a National Monument," in *Modernism at Mid-Century*, 62.

15. Contract No. AF 33 (600)-28303, 4 August 1954; Contract No. AF 33 (600)-26116, 12 August 1954, SOMA, drawer 50, file 11.

16. For the budgetary projections and Talbott's testimony, see *On the Wings of Modernism*, 11–18. Netsch, meanwhile, had been transferred to Chicago in 1954 to begin design on the Inland Steel Building. Due to his increased responsibilities with the Academy, he was relieved of that project.

17. See "A Conversation about the U.S. Air Force Academy between Walter Netsch and John Burchard," in *Modernism at Mid-Century*, 175–76.

18. Ibid., 183–84.

19. An obvious example would be Le Corbusier's 1923 treatise, *Vers une architecture*, in which he compared the "spirit that built the Parthenon" to contemporary design solutions.

20. Giedion, 728.

21. Ibid., 714.

22. Blum, 130–31.

23. Ibid., 132.

24. Schaeffer, 64. Although this discussion of the Academy focuses on the Cadet Area, much could be done with an examination of other areas of the Academy, including the original housing designs and community center plans.

25. Blum, 75, 79–81.

26. "Walter Netsch and John Burchard," in *Modernism at Mid-Century*, 183.

27. Ibid., 181.

28. Ibid., 182.

29. *On the Wings of Modernism*, 95.

30. Elizabeth Gill Lui, *Spirit and Flight: A Photographic Salute to the United States Air Force Academy* (Colorado Springs, CO: U.S. Air Force Academy, 1996), 89. Interspersed with Lui's photographs of the Academy are "Memories" written by Netsch.

31. Le Corbusier, *Towards a New Architecture*, (New York: Dover, 1956), 71.

32. Jory Johnson, "Man as Nature," in *Modernism at Mid-Century*, 110.

33. The classic text on St. Gall is Walter Horn and Ernest Born, *The Plan of St. Gall* (Berkeley: University of California Press, 1979), although subsequent authors, such as Lawrence Nees, have contributed to the discussion of this famous plan.

34. "Walter Netsch and John Burchard," in *Modernism at Mid-Century*, 178–79. It is important to remember that in the 1950s the Academy was miles from Colorado Springs, and most of the cadets did not have cars.

35. Ibid., 185.

36. Schaeffer, "Creating a National Monument," in *Modernism at Mid-Century*, 53–54.

37. "Walter Netsch and John Burchard," in *Modernism at Mid-Century*, 184. Klauder's university, to which Netsch refers, is the University of Colorado in Boulder. Meem's museum is the Colorado Springs Fine Arts Center.

38. Ibid., 180.

39. The Case Study House program has been discussed by Esther McCoy in her book *Case Study Houses* (Hennessey and Ingalls, 1977) and in *Blueprints for Modern Living*, the catalogue of an exhibition organized by Elizabeth A. T. Smith (Los Angeles: Museum of Contemporary Art; Cambridge, Massachusetts: MIT Press, 1989).

40. As quoted in Lui, xxiv.

41. Blum, 67.

42. For a summary of religion in America in the 1950s, see Douglas T. Miller and Marion Nowak, "Ain't Nobody Here but Us Protestants, Catholics, and Jews," in *The Fifties: The Way We Really Were* (Garden City, New York: Doubleday, 1977), 84–105; and Paul A. Carter, "Under God, By Act of Congress," in *Another Part of the Fifties* (New York: Columbia University Press, 1983), 114–40. The Herberg quote is from Miller and Nowak, 102.

43. Carter, 121.

44. Minutes, 28 February 1955, RAFACA, box 701, General Correspondence, Academy Chapel.

45. SOMA, box 46, Vol. I and II, Chapel, ASBCA No. 5593, 12. Netsch meticulously recalled the entire history of the chapel project from June 1955 through October 1959 in two grueling days of testimony before the Air Force Contract Appeals Panel. His testimony is contained in Vol. I and II, Chapel, ASBCA No. 5593, 1–208, dated 13–14 January 1960.

46. Marcel Breuer had also used the folded-plate construction in his 1954 design for a Benedictine monastery in Collegeville, Minnesota.

47. George A. Sanderson, "Air Academy: U.S. Air Force Exhibits Plans at Colorado Springs," *Progressive Architecture* 36, no. 6 (June 1955): 90.

48. "Grown Up At Last," *ARTNews* 54, no. 4 (Summer 1955): 23.

49. Lui, 29.

50. Blum, 136–38.

51. Ibid., 140.

52. The new design appeared in a front-page photograph in the July 3, 1955, edition of the *Colorado Springs Gazette Telegraph* and in the July 10 edition of the *Colorado Springs Free Press*.

53. SOMA, drawer 55, file 61.2, SOM — Consultants Meetings.

54. "Walter Netsch and John Burchard," in *Modernism at Mid-Century*, 185.

55. Quarles's rejection of the redesigned chapel was the subject of a memorandum, titled "Subject: Design of the Academy Chapel" and dated March 9, 1956, from Colonel Albert Stoltz, director of the Air Force Academy Construction Agency, to General Lee B. Washbourne: RAFACA, box 59, INS 3-3C, Chapel — Correspondence — 1955–57.

56. Much of this information dealing with the Chapel design is recounted in *On the Wings of Modernism*, 108–31.

57. Lui, 109.

58. Blum, 141.

59. "Spires That Soar," *Time*, July 27, 1962, 39.

60. Netsch stated that it was Bruce Graham who led this dissension to the point of trying to convince SOM partner and designer Gordon Bunshaft that the design should be scrapped. See Blum, 142.

61. Ibid. Netsch also recalled Fuller's Dymaxion House and the effect of Fuller's work on him in the 1930s: "He was one of the idols of the new world. I mean, he was representative of what was going to happen." See Blum, 32.

62. Minutes, Consultants Meeting, 15 May 1957, Washington, D.C., SOMA, drawer 35, file 62, SOM — Consultants Meetings. Representatives for SOM at the meeting included Owings, John Merrill, Bunshaft, and Netsch.

63. Blum, 144.

64. Ibid., 145–46.

65. Netsch to Walter Holtkamp, Holtkamp Organ Company, Cleveland, memorandum, 5 June 1957, SOMA, drawer 72, file P-141-000, Academy Chapel 1955–August 1959.

66. *Congressional Record*, 85th Cong., 1st sess., vol. 103, pt. 10 (August 6, 1957): 13769–70.

67. Ibid., 13788.

68. Ibid.

69. Ibid., 13789. Scrivner's and Sieminski's remarks appeared in "Air Force Gothic," *Time*, August 19, 1957.

70. *Congressional Record*, 85th Cong., 1st sess., vol. 103, pt. 10, (August 7, 1957): 13926–28.

71. Press release by the Office of Information Services, Air Force Academy Construction Agency, 6 November 1957, RAFACA, box 59, INS 3-3C, Chapel — Correspondence — 1955–57. See also "Memorandum for Secretary of the Air Force," 23 October 1957, RAFACA, box 42, REL 2-2, Civil Liaison 1957.

72. "Academy Designed to Fit Site, Says Local Architect," *Colorado Springs Gazette Telegraph*, September 14, 1957.

73. Netsch to Gordon Bunshaft, memorandum, 12 May 1958, SOMA, drawer 72, file P-141-000, Academy Chapel 1955–August 1959.

74. Netsch to the Honorable James H. Douglas, memorandum, 10 August 1959, SOMA, drawer 72, file P-141-000, Academy Chapel 1955–August 1959.

75. See Sheri Olson, "Lauded and Maligned: The Cadet Chapel," in *Modernism at Mid-Century*, 156–67; James S. Russell, " Learning from Industry," in *Modernism at Mid-Century*, 152, 154–55; and "Air Academy Chapel Shapes Up," *Architectural Forum* 114, no. 5 (May 1961): 128–29.

76. "Air Academy Chapel Shapes Up," 128.

77. "Spires That Soar," 39.

78. Ibid.

79. Lui, 117.

80. For details of the Chapel furnishings, also see the U.S. Air Force Academy's publication *The United States Air Force Academy Cadet Chapel*, now in its 21st edition.

81. Olson, 167.

82. Lui, xxii.

83. Diane Wray, director, Modern Architecture Preservation League, and Michael Paglia, chair, Preservation Committee, to Fremmill Smith, American Institute of Architects, Washington, D.C., 27 September 1992.

84. When the chapel's aluminum exterior cladding was removed, large areas of flashing were discovered to be missing where the structural tetrahedrons join. Those areas would have been the most difficult to flash, and hence were subject to the unfortunate Congressional budgetary cuts when the chapel was under construction, but they were also the areas most susceptible to leakage. As Diane Ghirardo noted: "The commission to restore the structure's aesthetic and functional integrity allowed SOM to incorporate better performing materials … in effect regaining structural integrity while maintaining the building's distinctive profile." "Introduction," *SOM Journal 4* (Ostfildern-Ruit, Germany: Hatje Cantz, 2006), 9.

85. Ibid., 93. On restoration efforts at the Academy, also see Robert Allen Nauman, "Preserving a Monument: The United States Air Force Academy," in *Future Anterior* 1, no. 2 (Fall 2004): 32–41.

86. See, for example, Bruegmann's essay "Military Culture, Architectural Culture, Popular Culture" in *Modernism at Mid-Century* or Nauman's *On the Wings of Modernism*.

87. Blum, 155–56.

88. "Proposed Questions for Walter A. Netsch Jr., Skidmore, Owings & Merrill Director of Design for the Air Force Academy," April 25, 2002, 6.

Field Theory: Walter Netsch's Design Methodology

MARTIN FELSEN AND SARAH DUNN

Architects draw while considering the possibilities and outcomes of design problems, and they create drawings to represent ideas and issue instructions. Reyner Banham, the renowned writer on architecture and design, noted that methods of drawing have always had "such crucial value for architects that being unable to think without drawing became a true mark of one fully socialized into the profession of architecture."[1]

Walter Netsch is one such architect who recognized the potential of *drawing* as a critical design tool. He developed a systematic approach to conceiving buildings in which the act of drawing itself was fundamental to the design process and the primary device for architectural speculation and production. Netsch called this design methodology "Field Theory." "We were interested in a systems-based approach to design, not an *a priori* approach," Netsch said.[2] He thought Field Theory had the potential to transform the aesthetic and functional standards of modern buildings. "We keep trying to find new ways to see things," explained Netsch. "Our Field Theory is a process of looking at things differently, and of ordering too."[3]

In the mid-1950s, when Netsch began working at Skidmore, Owings & Merrill (SOM), Field Theory was a concept from the discipline of behavioral science employed to interpret interoperational relations between groups of people with an emphasis on human actions and events. Netsch borrowed these relational ideas, merged them with his own concepts of organizational and spatial hierarchy, and transformed them into a highly functional visualization and planning methodology. Field Theory became a systematic tool of inquiry for generating families of hierarchical, organizational, and spatial design options.

Field Theory is a geometrically based design methodology that mobilizes sets of functional requirements, programmatic relations, and environmental forces. It posits holistic relationships between buildings, and parts of buildings, within a continuous, mostly two-dimensional geometric field. Using Field Theory, Netsch investigated part-to-whole

fig. 1 Photograph of an Italian hill town by Robertson Ward, 1975. The photo (and others like it) inspired Netsch to develop a systematic drawing technique to represent the architectural qualities he saw in this photograph: an ordered, geometric, two-dimensional field of optical data.

relations across multiple compositional and associative scales; essentially, it was a formal process of planning a building's entire site while simultaneously organizing the practical and material complexities of a building.

As a disciplinary approach, Field Theory served Netsch in three primary ways. First, it provided aesthetic and psychological variety. Netsch referred to a particularly apt field as possessing "existence will," a term formulated by Louis Kahn.[4] Second, Field Theory was flexible and adaptable to nearly every design problem in that it was an open-ended design system: If a program or structure could not be rationalized within a particular geometric field, the field could be easily transformed via infinite mathematical variation. Third, because of its preestablished unifying objectives, Field Theory was a design system anyone could employ, which was vital in the large corporate office of SOM. "The interesting thing was, it was not an egoistic direction. Anybody could do it," Netsch said of his decision to adopt Field Theory as an operational directive.[5] Under Netsch's guidance, Field Theory became the fundamental technique and procedure of architectural production in Netsch's design studio at SOM at a time when he oversaw the erection of several buildings per year.

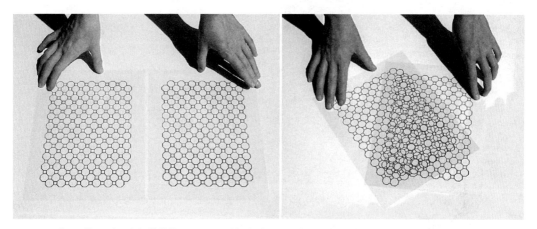

fig. 2 Illustration of the Field Theory process: A lattice is created by superimposing grids printed on transparent acetate sheets.

The Field Theory process began with a grid printed on a sheet of transparent acetate (fig. 2). Several sheets were then superimposed onto one another, creating a moiré or "lattice." Netsch said, "A lattice is when you rotate a sheet that has these forms and then you put another sheet over and you draw it all over again. In fact, you draw it a third time."[6] In this iterative search came discovery at multiple scales: Everything from building plans to furniture layouts were found by tracing the moirés. Netsch and his team made thousands of tracings by hand, revealing a great number of modular and nonmodular geometric patterns. Netsch would name the patterns that would appear, referring to them as "a pack of four or six, octagon ring-slipped fields, double fields, latticing, [and] the figure-ground of the field."[7] In an era before computer animation, Netsch and his team made films of three-dimensional geometric patterns in an effort to accelerate the process of uncovering novel formal solutions. Ostensibly, the Field Theory design process was begun without preconceived formal notions or ideal models: The objective was for the process itself to release the potential for each field to "will" its own emergence.

Writing about Field Theory during Netsch's prolific career, architecture critic Mildred F. Schmertz commented that

> *proportional systems have always been used in architecture, fundamentally as symbols. The triangle and hexagon, for example, have meaning for the religions of the East and West; the square and the octagon are also universal images. Until the Modern Movement declared that form must follow function, all architecture was geometrically ordered, and during the modern revolution and since, all good architecture continues to be.* [8]

Field Theory was inspired and motivated by historic rules of ordered proportion, patterning, and shape. Netsch gained confidence that his design approach was meaningful as he rediscovered past geometric systems and created new ones with Field Theory. He said, "We use an age-old aesthetic attitude that goes back to the Gothic Cathedral days. They took their programs, what the cathedral was to achieve, and used the geometric definition of form as the factor to establish the character and quality of space." [9]

fig. 3   Walter Netsch, c. 1980s

Netsch designed two buildings that incorporated elements of his emerging aesthetic prior to fully articulating and engaging the geometrical language of Field Theory: the U.S. Air Force Academy Cadet Chapel (1954–63) and the Northwestern University Library (1964–70). In Netsch's mind, the inherent complexities of these buildings not only galvanized the necessity of developing a systematic design approach but also germinated the core principles of Field Theory itself.

For the Northwestern University Library, Netsch devised a unique set of complex building requirements. He hierarchically reorganized the typical functional relationships favored by contemporary library planners in order to formalize more user-friendly design solutions. For example, a typical functional approach to library design might prohibit public access to book collections in order to maximize space for book storage or to assure maximum manageability and security of book collections. Alternatively, Netsch chose to create a "book complex" at Northwestern, where all members of the community had open and unhindered access to book collections and free access to a variety of spaces for intellectual collaboration or individual contemplation. "The idea for the library was to think about books, not big rooms," said Netsch.[10]

The Northwestern University Library Planning Committee asked Netsch to create a library as social center, and Netsch took its directive literally. He conceived three research towers, or minilibraries, that were designed around radial vectors emanating from social spaces in the exact *center* of each tower. These social centers allowed for informal reading and collaborative book searches. Netsch said, "We imagined people go[ing to] the middle of the square to orient themselves in their search for books."[11] He designed squares about the social centers, a maneuver geometricists refer to as "squaring-the-circle," and used them to order the main structural column grid. The peripheral areas contain private spaces, such as the seminar, study, and carrel alcoves. Radial collection stacks are arrayed between the center and the periphery, visually and acoustically buffering purposefully small-scale environments. Today, walking freely through the stacks, comfortably searching for books, one still becomes fully engaged in the physical act of tracing the orientating public/private paths originally conceived by Netsch.

Northwestern University Library literally formalized Netsch's innovative and "intimately centered" programmatic concepts. The geometries deployed in the library were invented specifically for the program and structure of the library itself; they were not randomly applied. Where later Field Theory projects would typically emanate from the superimposition of rotating 2D geometries, Netsch developed the vector/plane geometries of the library as a unique solution to an innovative set of programmatic constraints. During the design of the library, Netsch said the use of Field Theory methodology was "subliminal."[12] Looking back now, we can certainly see the ancestral mathematical relationships between the library and later Field Theory buildings. (For more on Northwestern University Library, see Goodman, pages 79–96.)

Buildings designed by Netsch immediately after the Northwestern University Library depended heavily on 45-degree-angled geometrical planes. About this reliance Netsch said, "The rotated square was the way we broke the box, by rotation."[13] The first box-buster to be designed was the Architecture and Art Laboratories building at the University of Illinois at Chicago Circle (1964). The organization of the building was developed from fields of rotated squares inscribed by geometries of circles. Mathematically related to the squaring-the-circle geometry of the Northwestern University Library, the Architecture and Art Laboratories building was created from a clustered and continuous set of "latticed fields."

The lattice was the big organizational breakthrough. The technique produced iconic yet rational programmatic hierarchies that were structurally sound, functionally efficient, and economically feasible. Because the design methodology was a systematic generative process, Netsch could fairly easily communicate its rigors to his team and corporate sponsors. Through the teaching and continual updating of Field Theory, Netsch could also make certain it did not devolve into capricious pattern making — and he could make certain the building designs did not lose their organizational and functional efficiency in favor of simplistic visual aptitude. The self-organizing robustness of Field Theory solutions, Netsch said, avoid "the willful, cute angularities that are sometimes designed in for sculptural variety."[14]

Notes

1. Reyner Banham, "A Black Box: The Secret Profession of Architecture," in *A Critic Writes* (Berkeley: University of California Press, 1996), 298.

2. Walter Netsch, interview by the authors, February 22, 2007.

3. C. Ray Smith, *Supermannerism: New Attitudes in Postmodern Architecture* (New York: Dutton, 1977), 28.

4. Mildred F. Schmertz, "New Museum by Walter Netsch of SOM Given Order by His Field Theory," *Architectural Record* 167, no. 1 (January 1980): 119.

5. Walter Netsch, "Oral History of Walter Netsch," interview by Betty J. Blum, May 10, 1985, June 5–28, 1995, transcript, Art Institute of Chicago, 209.

6. Ibid., 218.

7. Schmertz, "New Museum," 119.

8. Ibid., 111.

9. Nory Miller, "Two Libraries Miles Apart Yet Sharing a Family Origin," *Inland Architect* 15, no. 4 (November 1971): 8.

10. Walter Netsch, interview by the authors, February 22, 2007.

11. Ibid.

12. Miller, "Two Libraries," p. 11.

13. "Walter Netsch Interviewed by Detlef Mertins," *SOM Journal* 1 (2007): 144.

14. Smith, *Supermannerism*, 33

Walter Netsch: Five Imagined Histories

DAVID GOODMAN

Some of this really happened. Actually, it all did, just not in this way. The very idea that there could be a grand narrative — a story of the inexorable evolution of architecture, from Gothic to Renaissance to Le Corbusier and onward, without detour or contradiction — is so thoroughly discounted that one struggles even to explain why that is. How do you debate what seems a self-evident fact?

But what if things had worked out differently? What if architecture at the end of the 1960s had come to a moment of consensus, a sense that the discipline could only have evolved as it did, could only have arrived at that point? What if, instead of fracturing into apparently irreconcilable pieces, architecture had remained whole? New histories would have to be written; linear, inevitable histories would take shape, explaining this remarkable moment of agreement. And while the author is, for one, quite pleased that this consensus never emerged, it is at the very least useful to imagine how the disparate strands of work emerging at the end of the 1960s might be gathered together in order to create the illusion of a definitive movement.

Walter Netsch, while a vital if often overlooked part of the history of modern architecture, could scarcely be said to have been the central figure in that history. In fact, Netsch's work with Skidmore, Owings & Merrill (SOM) only recently seems to have been reincorporated into the history of architecture in tentative and halting steps. We are just now learning how to digest Netsch, where to file him away, into which of the many fractured narratives to insert his personal and occasionally disquieting investigations. Perhaps Netsch's work has been overlooked precisely because we simply don't know what to do with him. The iconic U.S. Air Force Academy Cadet Chapel (1954–63), the bewildering Field Theory geometry of the Behavioral Sciences Building at the University of Illinois Chicago Circle (1970), and the city of crenellated towers that forms the Northwestern University Library (1964–70) could easily be placed within any number of histories of architecture but do not ultimately seem to belong entirely to any of them.

It is this very indeterminacy that makes Netsch's work so provocative. We could quite possibly situate his work at the center of any number of fictional moments of consensus. Like Woody Allen's chameleon-man Leonard Zelig, Walter Netsch, too, seems to fit within any context while not truly belonging to any of them. And while the Northwestern University Library is not generally considered a crucial work in the history of modern architecture, it is nevertheless an extraordinary project, incorporating ideas and formal strategies that would appear in all of Netsch's subsequent work and that were, at the time, fundamental to the discussion about how architecture should proceed. Part megastructure, part sculpted object, part functionalist machine, part contextual response, part exploration of pure geometry, the Northwestern University Library *could* have been a seminal work for any number of reasons. It *could* have defined a movement. This essay will present five imagined histories in which that was the case.

Imagined History 1: The Triumph of the System

The crisis of direction in modern architecture came to a definitive end with the opening of Walter Netsch's Northwestern University Library in 1970. Hailed as an infinitely expandable network and prototype for the organization of large-scale programs, Netsch's embryonic megastructure pointed the way toward a renewed consensus in architecture, serving as a standard-bearer for the nascent movement that would dominate architectural discourse and production for years to come.

The Northwestern University Library is more system than building — a series of towers containing book stacks and informal reading areas is plugged into a plinth of support spaces and lounges (fig. 1). The roof of this horizontal plane forms a student plaza that links the library to the existing buildings on site and provides a space of assembly at the

fig. 1 Walter Netsch, Northwestern University Library, 1964–70

fig. 2 Le Corbusier, Venice Hospital project, 1963–65

heart of the campus. Although this system was not ultimately extended, it promised a way to accommodate changes in use and the inevitable increase in the library's holdings merely by continuing the pattern established with the first three towers.

With its modularity and subordination of the overall form of the building to the idea of the network, Netsch's building was a vertical reinterpretation of Le Corbusier's Venice Hospital project of 1964 (fig. 2) or of the "mat" buildings of Alison and Peter Smithson or Candilis, Josic, and Woods.[1] The early mat buildings were less figure than fabric: dense horizontal networks that ostensibly valued patterns of use over form. At Northwestern, Netsch added verticality to the mat and, in so doing, also added a more assertive and extroverted form to a building type that had until that time been primarily explored through horizontal expansion into the landscape.

Writing in 1974, Alison Smithson would summarize this way of making buildings as one that "can be said to epitomize the anonymous collective; where the functions come to enrich the fabric and the individual gains new freedoms of action through a new and shuffled order."[2] Netsch's strategy at Northwestern was in large part based on a similar emphasis on individual freedom within a network. Unlike the existing closed-stack Charles Deering Library, Netsch's building would open the shelving to students. At the time this represented an innovation, and it was fundamental to the development of the "system building." Once the book stacks had become integrated into the public space of the project, the design of the building could no longer be that of a grand reading room with an attached mute volume for the storage of books. Books and readers would be interwoven, and the entire building would become a system for simultaneous storage, display, and use of books by unsupervised students. "By developing an individual-centered use," Netsch remarked, "the concept reflects the direction toward self-study."[3]

Megastructure projects, such as Kenzo Tange's 1960 project for Tokyo Bay (fig. 3), attempted to resolve the functional requirements of an entire region through the design of a single highly modulated building or system. Tange's project, with its interconnected suspension bridges and housing slabs, extends a mat-and-tower chain across Tokyo Bay. Other megastructures, such as Archigram's Walking City (fig. 4) and Plug-In City, were attempts to harness the technology of oil rigs, mass production, and the space program and apply them to the design of a building that, in itself, would constitute a city.

Netsch's Northwestern project had a decidedly more humble mission — it is, after all, a library, not a city — yet it applies a similar mode of thinking. The flexible network of towers and plinth was designed to house a broad range of program activities, both planned and unforeseen, and to organize the central core of the campus with a single composite building. There is in all of these projects — the mat buildings, the megastructures, and perhaps in Netsch's library as well — an apparent contradiction: These all-encompassing

fig. 3 Kenzo Tange, *Plan for Tokyo,* 1960

fig. 4 Archigram, *Walking City*, 1964

systems were intended by their authors to provide maximum individual freedom, maximum flexibility. Yet the architect ultimately remained the author of the entire complex. While the architect promised ultimate freedom, it was ultimately he who would design every last freedom-providing inch. Nevertheless, one cannot ignore the very real way in which Netsch's library allows for unexpected encounters and a radically decentralized vision of what the library could be.

Despite the eventual exhaustion of the movement it came to represent, Netsch's Northwestern University Library remained for years both icon and example to architects such as Rem Koolhaas, whose Nexus World housing in Fukuoka, Japan, suppressed the verticality of Netsch's tower pavilions, concentrating instead on the development of the plinth; Koolhaas used a series of undulating bands to create a network of private houses and gardens that together form a housing system more than a mere housing project.

With the Northwestern University Library, Netsch illustrated how the varied activities and spaces of a city could be condensed into a single building, how the very notion of building could itself become elastic to include several identical buildings knitted together to form a system — a composite whole. Architects of the late 1960s rallied around this concept and around Netsch's example, ending the years of fractious debate that increasingly had come to divide the discipline. With the Northwestern University Library, Netsch emphatically declared the triumph of the system.

Imagined History 2: The Triumph of the Operation

The crisis of direction in modern architecture came to a definitive end with the opening of Walter Netsch's Northwestern University Library in 1970. Hailed as a case study in how the careful and systematic application of a series of geometric operations could yield an architecture of formal complexity and programmatic invention, Netsch's starbursts of rotated and cantilevered carrel bays presaged his later explorations in Field Theory and pointed the way toward a renewed consensus in architecture, serving as a standard-bearer for the nascent movement that would dominate architectural discourse and production for years to come.

To look at Netsch's Northwestern Library in either plan or perspective (figs. 5, 6) is to immediately grasp its origins in pure geometry. Like Frank Lloyd Wright's S. C. Johnson and Co. Administration Building (1939) or Palmer House (1950), Netsch's library is based on the manipulation and repetition of primary geometric forms — in this case, a subdivided circle superimposed on a rotated square. Wright often employed primary geometry as an underlying ordering device for plan organization or as a repeated graphic motif, a technique perhaps inherited from his mentor Louis Sullivan. For Netsch, however, manipulation of geometry itself would become the subject of investigation. Netsch's is an architecture of easily legible operations: stacking, folding, rotating, offsetting, shifting, arraying. These operations do not speak of the universality of primary geometry, of purity, or of an innate harmony presumed to reside in the circle, square, or triangle but rather of purposeful modifications to accommodate the particularities of program, site, or iconography.

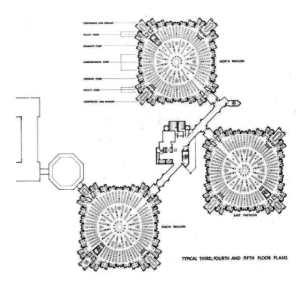

fig. 5 Walter Netsch, Northwestern University Library, plan, 1964–70

fig. 6 Walter Netsch, Northwestern University Library, perspective rendering, 1964–70

Fundamental to the idea of an operative architecture is that the operations be legible; the act of rotating or stacking is fundamentally rhetorical and ultimately would be useless were it invisible to the uninitiated. We know, of course, that the building itself has not truly been subjected to torsion or subdivision — Netsch's library was not, as a Gordon Matta-Clark piece might have been, built as a pure cube and then sliced, rotated, and pulled apart. An operative architecture, then, must make evident the traces of the operations used to arrive at the final form because those operations are ultimately the subject of the work.

Netsch's decision to use a radial geometry in Northwestern University Library was initially motivated by practical concerns. Clarence Ver Steeg, chairman of the Library Planning Committee, enthused during the unveiling of the project in 1964, "When a user walks to the center of the pavilion, he can see and reach 125,000 volumes that relate to his particular subject matter."[4] Netsch had spent months studying the organization of the book stacks, attempting to minimize the apparently inevitable back-and-forth walk through repetitive parallel bands of shelves. The radial scheme solved this problem while simultaneously freeing up the perimeter for group and individual study.[5] It was in the radial stacks that the geometric operations would begin.

Rather than directly expressing the circular perimeter of the stack layout at the building's edge, Netsch extended the radial field to create a jostled series of study carrels and seminar rooms. Like badly aligned books on a shelf, the wedges created by the radial stack arrangement are pushed and pulled, cantilevering beyond the square of the exterior column grid to form a serrated perimeter (fig. 7). Netsch's operations of radial division, sectioning, and jostling may have arisen as a functional solution to the problem of stack organization, but the decision to continue the geometric operations to the facade — where they were no longer necessary for purely functional reasons — is one that makes the geometric operation itself evident in the building's exterior image.

It is possible to argue that Netsch extends and expresses the radial stack arrangement with the jagged facade in order to communicate the deep organization of the building — a sort of rhetorical functionalism akin to Mies van der Rohe's decision to affix decorative

fig. 7   Walter Netsch, Northwestern University Library, 1964–70

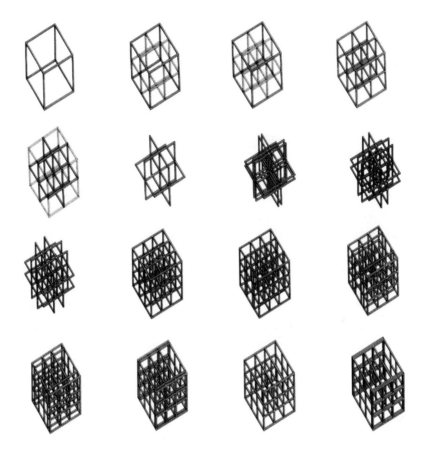

fig. 8 Peter Eisenman, House IV, 1971

wide-flange sections to the outside of the Seagram Building, where they indicate the concrete-encased steel columns within. There is, it seems, something of this ideal of functional transparency behind Netsch's facade strategy at Northwestern — an indexing on the facade of what goes on behind it. Ultimately, though, this project is more instructive as an example of Netsch's development of the geometric operation as a generative tool, whether or not it originated out of functionalist concerns.

Despite the eventual exhaustion of the movement it came to represent, Netsch's Northwestern University Library remained for years both icon and example to architects such as Peter Eisenman, whose work was, and in large part continues to be, based on operations applied to platonic fields, grids, and cubes (fig. 8). For Eisenman these formal operations are not, as they are for Netsch, related to functional requirements. On the contrary, they are intended to make architectural operations themselves the central focus of the discipline; in Eisenman's view, a truly "modernist" architecture — in the sense that Mondrian or James Joyce are "modern" — would not be related to function at all, but instead to operations intrinsic to the discipline of architecture.[6]

With the Northwestern University Library and much of his subsequent Field Theory work, Netsch illustrated how the sorts of operations Eisenman would later employ for "postfunctionalist" ends could be used to generate an architecture still based on underlying functionalist assumptions, but with a rhetorical emphasis on geometric operation as a key determinate of the building's overall form. Architects of the late 1960s rallied around this concept and around Netsch's example, ending the years of fractious debate that increasingly had come to divide the discipline. With the Northwestern University Library, Netsch emphatically declared the triumph of the operation.

Imagined History 3: The Triumph of the Machine

The crisis of direction in modern architecture came to a definitive end with the opening of Walter Netsch's Northwestern University Library in 1970. Hailed as a continuation of the heroic period of the early modern movement, Netsch's rationally planned and detailed machine for study pointed the way toward a renewed consensus in architecture, serving as a standard-bearer for the nascent movement that would dominate architectural discourse and production for years to come.

Netsch's Northwestern University Library takes a remarkably complex program — book storage, reading rooms, classrooms and study carrels, support spaces, assembly areas —

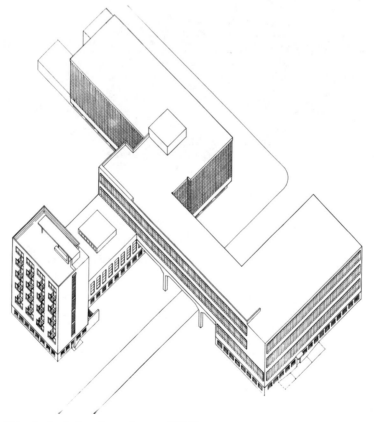

fig. 9 Walter Gropius, Bauhaus, Dessau, Germany, 1925–26

fig. 10 James Stirling and James Gowan, Engineering Building, Leicester University, Great Britain, 1959

and resolves it into discrete, efficient elements, each articulated as an independent piece of a complex machine. The three book stack–study carrel towers, with their segmented, vaguely gearlike facades, perch over a plinth that houses support programs. Elevator cores provide efficient access from the plinth to each of the individual towers, and an access corridor knits the towers together at all levels. Even the entrance is articulated as an independent element, separated from both towers and plinth. Netsch's machinelike approach to design is deeply rooted in his wartime training at the Massachusetts Institute of Technology, where problem solving was emphasized above all else, and more broadly in the early functionalist work of the 1920s.

Crucial to the ethos of the early modern movement was idea of the building as machine: Le Corbusier famously referred to the house as "a machine for living in," and early projects such as the Ozenfant House (1922), with its sawtooth skylight system, consciously adopted the image of the factory. Walter Gropius's Bauhaus at Dessau (1926; fig. 9) also borrowed from industrial architecture, with its proto-curtain wall along the workshop wing. More significantly, Gropius made a clear formal separation among programs: housing occupied a tower at one end of the building, workshops and classrooms were housed in their own separate volumes, and a bridge of public space and administration provided a link between programs. The articulation of individual program elements as separate volumes became a fundamental part of the modern canon — a basic principle of design. By the early 1960s the polemically functionalist ethos of the early moderns had so faded that James Stirling and James Gowan's Leicester University Engineering Building (fig. 10) would appear radical for its articulation of individual program elements and factorylike materiality.

Netsch, like Stirling and Gowan, had quite clearly been affected by these functionalist principles. His work with Bruce Graham on the preliminary planning phase for Chicago's Inland Steel Building led him to rethink how the typical office tower could be organized. In office tower design, various programs are typically combined into a single volume, without articulating the constituent parts. With the Inland Steel Building, however, Netsch and Graham separated the office wing from the elevators and toilets, articulating these support programs as a separate volume. Although this solution was rarely employed again in the design of tall office buildings, Netsch would continue to articulate differences in program by separating constituent elements — both in Northwestern University Library and in his later Field Theory projects.

Despite the eventual exhaustion of the movement it came to represent, Netsch's Northwestern University Library remained for years both icon and example to architects such as Norman Foster and Richard Rogers, whose buildings are often machinelike not only in their organization of program, but also in their explicit references to industrial prototypes and in their exposed structural and mechanical systems.

With the Northwestern University Library, Netsch illustrated that the functionalist ethos of the early modern movement was not yet a spent force. Architects of the late 1960s rallied around this concept and around Netsch's example, ending the years of fractious debate that increasingly had come to divide the discipline. With the Northwestern University Library, Netsch emphatically declared the triumph of the machine.

Imagined History 4: The Triumph of Context

The crisis of direction in modern architecture came to a definitive end with the opening of Walter Netsch's Northwestern University Library in 1970. Hailed as a sensitive and contextual intervention into an existing campus environment, Netsch's skillful reinterpretation of the collegiate Gothic pointed the way toward a renewed consensus in architecture, serving as a standard-bearer for the nascent movement that would dominate architectural discourse and production for years to come.

Immediately after the design for the Northwestern University Library was unveiled in 1964, Netsch discussed the project with the school newspaper, listing the primary design objectives in numerical order. While the first three objectives listed by Netsch dealt with the internal organization and usage of the library, the fourth dealt with the building in context. One of the primary goals, Netsch stated, was "to develop form and scale consistent with the existing campus structures."[7]

Netsch's remarks would scarcely be noticed today; the idea of acting without regard for the existing context on a campus like Northwestern's is one that few architects would entertain — or would be allowed to entertain — for very long. Yet in 1964, such concern for context was far from a given. Robert Venturi's *Complexity and Contradiction in Architecture* would not be published until 1966, and Jane Jacobs's *The Death and Life of Great American Cities*, which bemoaned the utter insensitivity of architects and planners to the richness of the existing city, had only been published three years earlier. Furthermore, little of

fig. 11 Walter Netsch, Northwestern University Library, 1964–70

fig. 12 James Gamble Rogers, Charles Deering Library, Northwestern University, 1933

SOM's work up to that point could truly be categorized as contextual, with the possible exception of the addition to the U.S. Naval Postgraduate School in Monterey, California, designed and programmed by Netsch in 1954. This project, a series of simple bar buildings, was carefully sited to avoid as many existing trees as possible; while there was little about the architecture that seemed to respond to context, the siting was executed with great sensitivity.

At Northwestern, however, Netsch produced a work that, in both its siting and vocabulary, is firmly embedded in its context. Given a site immediately adjacent to the existing Collegiate Gothic Charles Deering Library, designed by James Gamble Rogers (1933), Netsch establishes a new plaza at the rear of the existing building onto which the new library opens. On this plaza, directly adjacent to the Charles Deering Library, Netsch created a central entrance pavilion — a small building inserted between new and old, providing access to both. Instead of overwhelming the modestly scaled original library with a single volume more than four times larger, Netsch locates much of the program within the plinth that forms the plaza surface, breaking the library into three linked towers, none of them much larger than the original building.

fig. 13 Ernesto Rogers and Enrico Peressutti, Torre Velasca, Milan, 1956

Although one could only with great difficulty affix a "Gothic" label to Netsch's library, there is nevertheless an echo of the adjacent Charles Deering Library in the color and texture of the striated concrete and a similarity of rhythm between the arches on Deering's western face and the cantilevered carrel bays in Netsch's building (figs. 11, 12). Netsch separates the carrel bay volumes from the concrete columns ringing the building. These volumes are cantilevered several inches further with each additional floor level, making the columns appear to narrow as they ascend, as do the piers on the Charles Deering Library. The rhythm of carrel bays and columns in Netsch's building is, in effect, the negative image of the western facade of Charles Deering Library: while Deering's facade alternates diminishing piers and recessed glazed arches, Netsch establishes a rhythm of diminishing columns and projecting bays.

fig. 14 Louis Kahn, Indian Institute of Management Ahmedabad, India, 1962

Netsch was not alone in beginning to incorporate historical references in his work. Ernesto Rogers and Enrico Peressutti's 1956 Torre Velasca (fig. 13) in Milan plainly recalled an overscaled medieval tower; Robert Venturi's Vanna Venturi House of 1962 mixed surface decoration, a gabled silhouette, and tropes borrowed from early Le Corbusier; and Louis Kahn, as early as the late 1950s, had begun to experiment with brick arches that plainly recalled the Romanesque (fig. 14). Yet Netsch's Northwestern project achieved a subtle contextualism without literal imitation or quotation; his was a nuanced contextualism of modulation and scale.

Despite the eventual exhaustion of the movement it came to represent, Netsch's Northwestern University Library remained for years both icon and example to architects such as Alvaro Siza, whose Schilderswijk residential complex in the Hague and the Galician Center for Contemporary Art in Santiago de Compostela, Spain (fig. 15), respond to their immediate contexts in both materiality and massing without directly imitating them.

With the Northwestern University Library, Netsch illustrated how the massive building requirements of the postwar era could be made to harmonize in scale, material, and massing with the smaller scale interventions of an earlier time. Architects of the late

fig. 15 Alvaro Siza, Galician Center of Contemporary Arts, Santiago de Compostela, Spain, 1993

1960s rallied around this concept and around Netsch's example, ending the years of fractious debate that increasingly had come to divide the discipline. With the Northwestern University Library, Netsch emphatically declared the triumph of context.

Imagined History 5:
The Triumph of Expression

The crisis of direction in modern architecture came to a definitive end with the opening of Walter Netsch's Northwestern University Library in 1970. Hailed as a dynamic and formally expressive work, Netsch's series of abstract sculptural concrete volumes pointed the way toward a renewed consensus in architecture, serving as a standard-bearer for the nascent movement that would dominate architectural discourse and production for years to come.

Just after the opening of Netsch's Northwestern University Library, a

figs. 16, 17 Walter Netsch, Northwestern University Library, 1964–70

professional journal published by the American Library Association featured the project on its cover. One might have expected the journal, published primarily for librarians and those involved in the operation of libraries, to focus on the functional aspects of the new building — after all, Netsch's project had quite radically reshaped the programmatic organization of the traditional library. Reproduced on the cover, however, along with a series of dramatic exterior photographs, is the following assessment: "Your eye is pleased and delighted by the variety of forms, spatial relationships, thrusts, and indentations. It is a giant piece of sculpture that changes with the light of day and the angle of the seasonal sun."[8]

This poetic assessment of Netsch's work highlights what is, perhaps, its most salient characteristic: its expressive, sculptural form. The dramatically cantilevered carrel bays rotate slightly as they move around the tower, their "fish-scaled" skin of textured concrete highlighting the slight changes of angle (fig. 16). Some bays accommodate seminar rooms, and the cantilevers increase accordingly. Viewed from below and at close range, the building seems almost impossibly complex, impossibly varied. Viewed at a distance, however, these details tend to fade (fig. 17); the building appears flatter, more repetitive, and normative. Mute walls of concrete, occasionally pierced with gun-slit windows, punctuate the complex, a foil to the hyperarticulated towers.

The highly varied and ultimately personal expression of Netsch's Northwestern University Library can be traced to earlier expressionist architects such as Erich Mendelsohn, Bruno Taut, and Le Corbusier — especially his Chapel of Notre-Dame-du-Haut at Ronchamp (fig. 18) — and, perhaps most directly, to Paul Rudolph's 1962 Art and Architecture Building at Yale University. And while Netsch's work at Northwestern does not approach Le Corbusier's complete departure from Cartesian geometry at Ronchamp, it does significantly break out of the mold of orthogonal bar buildings that Netsch had previously designed for the U.S. Air Force Academy and elsewhere. But it seems to have been Netsch's work on the Cadet Chapel at the Air Force Academy that most prepared him for the highly varied and sculptural direction his work would ultimately take. In that project a series of folded tetrahedra create an enormous triangular nave. Having had his first chapel scheme rejected by a congressional committee for being insufficiently inspiring, Netsch was not likely to commit that error twice. Netsch's work at Northwestern does not reach the literal or metaphorical heights of the Cadet Chapel, but it is nevertheless a building of great sculptural complexity and sensitivity whose functional requirements are never compromised by concessions to willful form making.

Despite the eventual exhaustion of the movement it came to represent, Netsch's Northwestern University Library remained for years both icon and example to architects such as Enric Miralles and Frank Gehry, whose highly personal investigations of form produced buildings of a more varied and sculptural form than anything undertaken by Netsch himself.

With the Northwestern University Library, Netsch illustrated that the architect working within a corporate context could nevertheless produce work of great sculptural complexity and expressiveness. Architects of the late 1960s rallied around this concept and around

fig. 18 Le Corbusier, Chapel of Notre-Dame-du-Haut, Ronchamps, France, 1950–54

Netsch's example, ending the years of fractious debate that increasingly had come to divide the discipline. With the Northwestern University Library, Netsch emphatically declared the triumph of expression.

Perspective

None of the above histories tells the true story of Walter Netsch's Northwestern University Library. It is doubtful, of course, that there even exists a single true story at all. Netsch's work is complex enough, varied enough, and occasionally puzzling enough to convincingly fit into any number of narratives. Ultimately, it is possible to see in Netsch just what we want to see. His work is inconclusive and open, and it thus seems to leave room for our interpretation; our perspective is required in order to come to any sort of provisional conclusion. These are five histories of Walter Netsch's work. None of them can possibly be true, because the master narrative has yet to be written.

Notes

1. See Hashim Sarkis, ed., *Case: Le Corbusier's Venice Hospital and the Mat Building Revival* (Munich and New York: Prestel, 2001).

2. Alison Smithson, "How to Recognise and Read Mat-Building," in Sarkis, *Case: Le Corbusier's Venice Hospital*, 91.

3. "Bold Library Plan for Total User Experience" *American School & University* 37, no. 1 (September 1964): 48.

4. Ibid., 50.

5. Walter Netsch, interview by the author, February 23, 2007.

6. "Peter Eisenman, "Post-Functionalism," in *Architecture Theory since 1968*, K. Michael Hays, ed. (Cambridge, MA: MIT Press, 1998), 236–39.

7. "Concepts Behind New Library's Design Discussed by Architect," *Daily Northwestern*, June 4, 1964.

8. *American Libraries* 1, no. 5 (May 1970).

Statements by Walter Netsch

All statements are excerpted from published and unpublished writings and speeches by Walter Netsch.

Programming the U.S. Naval Postgraduate School of Engineering (1954)
Objectives in Design Problems (1958)
What Architecture Is and Is Not (1959)
On Political-Economic Horizons (1960)
University of Illinois at Chicago Circle — Revisited (1966)
The Philosophy (1966)
Living with Art (1971)
Postmodernism in Context (1978)
Creativity: A Personal View (1979)
Designing in the Third World (1980)
Late Entry to the Chicago Tribune Tower Competition (1980)
Lecture Notes, Stuttgart, Germany (1980)
Lecture Notes (1981)
Living with Art, Two (1983)
Notes for a Speech (c. 1984)
On Nathaniel Owings (1984)
Notes on a Field Theory Game (c. 1984)
Chicago Park District President's Report (1986)
Remarks (c. 1987)
Living with Art, Three (1991)
Lake Shore Park (1992)
The Cadet Chapel (1996)
Chicago and Architecture (2002)
2060 (2006)
Northwestern University Library (2006)

Programming the U.S. Naval Postgraduate School of Engineering (1954)

From "Programming the U.S. Naval Postgraduate School of Engineering, Monterey," Architectural Record *115, no. 6 (June 1954): 150–57.*

The programming procedure which must underlie any architectural venture is both a subjective and an objective undertaking; it requires thorough analysis of the particular needs of the client and of the potentials and limitations of the job, and a gift for transforming the dry statements of the program into the dynamics of structure, the special needs into line, volume and mass. Not only must this transformation fulfill the requirements of function but, if it is to qualify as architecture, it must also satisfy, visually and emotionally, the users of the structure — whether or not they are aware of this satisfaction. The program makes of architecture a purposeful art; without it, a project has about the same direction as a child's building of blocks....

Funds for the first new buildings at Monterey — to house the School of Engineering — were appropriated by Congress in 1951, and shortly afterward our firm was selected as architects for the project. Since no program as such existed, a team of architects from our staff — Lawrence Lackey, project architect, William Dunlap, John Hoops, Stanley Panski and myself — was sent to Annapolis to make an on-the-spot analysis of the requirements and from them to derive the actual program. There was barely one month in which to do this. The analytical procedure was so intensive and unremitting an effort to determine all the implications of the school's courses of instruction that the essential design, in the form of schematic space allocation studies, emerged simultaneously with the completed program.

Although a master plan was not originally included in this phase of the project, it became clear quite early in the analysis that this was not only a necessary but a natural accompaniment of the programming since another group of buildings — the School of the Line — was some day to be built on the site. The interim master plan which was prepared was a valuable aid in respecting, and taking advantage of, the natural assets of the site, a goal which we had set as an inherent part of the project.

The analysis which led to the program had two parts, one an investigation of the faculty's wants and needs in terms of space and function, as well as of interdepartmental relationships, which would make for sound functioning of the school; and the other an examination of the school's catalog of courses.

A close collaboration between the architects and the faculty was essential if a solution that was appropriate both to site and to academic requirements was to be achieved. This took the form of numerous discussions with the faculty members and of questions and answers (in questionnaire form) on the specific wants and needs of each department in space, equipment, utilities and room-to-room relationships. To make this basic information as helpful as possible, and as realistic, the faculty was encouraged to think in terms of the kind of quarters and facilities which would fully answer their teaching needs rather than of the cramped quarters to which they had had to adapt their teaching methods.... The information in the catalog describing the functions of the nine departments, the relationships existing among them, and the 16 "curricula" given by these departments, was converted by the architects into a graphic analysis of the School's whole program of instruction. The charts — one for each department — which resulted from this graphic analysis gave detailed information on the number of hours spent in laboratory and classroom by the student in each curriculum; number of students in each department and in each of its curricula; and the curriculum in which the student is primarily enrolled. These figures provided the information needed for arriving at the number of classrooms and laboratories required. The area requirements were included on the charts not as absolutes but relative to one another, and a diagrammatic arrangement of these areas, based on the preferences of the department's faculty, was shown on each chart.

Last, but of equal importance, the charts showed the specific utilities which each department needed and indicated whether or not direct access to ground or to roof for special experiments was desirable….

During the course of the programming, technical questions came up which demonstrated the impossibility of divorcing one part of the design process from another. Even at this presumably preliminary stage, certain technical decisions were made which proved valid throughout the execution of the project. These decisions, along with the program analysis, became the basis for the schematic solution which evolved simultaneously with the actual program.

The schematic solution follows closely the groupings by departments which the analysis had pointed out. For the laboratory sciences, whose requirements (laboratory, classroom, lecture-laboratory, research and office space) were so similar, a multi-story building became the appropriate solution…. In the actual design process these ideas were refined and expanded as necessary, but the basic decisions were not changed. The real determinant was the provision of optimum working and teaching conditions within the framework of the structure and mechanical services, not only in the laboratory sciences building but in the others as well….

An undercurrent in all our discussions of the project was the matter of the design character of the buildings. We felt that harmony between building design and the area's regional architectural character was as much a factor to be considered as full utilization of the potentials of the site. Instead of trying to achieve a harmonious relation by following local tradition, we decided to work toward it by relating the mass and volume of the buildings to the site on which they were to be placed, and in a way, the site itself was the key to this solution. The contours of the land and the three-dimensional qualities of the many kinds of trees (eucalyptus, pine, redwood, oak and others) on the site were a natural parallel to the same qualities in the buildings. The balanced and at the same time free relation of the natural forms to each other suggested a similar plasticity in the architectural forms. But too much plasticity would be inconsistent with the architectural, educational or economic disciplines which the School should express, so a definite, intentional order was injected into the design, in the form of a basic column spacing of 18' 8" and a standard unit of fenestration.

The program, therefore, became the basic instrument for the resolution of the design. No matter how well annotated or analyzed, however, the program is only one factor in the synthesis which becomes an architectural composition. The technical aspects of the structures themselves, the environment, the master planning of the group, the existing buildings on the site, and the detailed development of the individual technical problems were all factors in the eventual resolution of the design problems at Monterey. The ultimate value of a project, not only as something useful but as something which is creative of an environment, depends on the proper order and degree of all the facets of design.

Objectives in Design Problems (1958)

From "Objectives in Design Problems," Journal of Architectural Education *(Autumn 1958): 44–46.*

So much is currently being said of architectural style and the contrast in formal and plastic styles that the evolutionary and truly selective aspects of architecture are ignored. Any structure should reflect the use for which it is intended, not only in providing the technically organized physical requirements and the technological services to support those requirements, but also the spatial and conceptual qualities such requirements can achieve, as well as the external relationships with the surrounding environment — natural or man-made. The students' recognition that the opportunities of choice are, in the beginning, unlimited, gradually disappears with the evolution of the creative process, where decisions and determinations drastically reduce the choices available each succeeding step of the way. Correctly developed, the diminution of choice ceases to be limiting in character, but rather becomes the refined crystallization of the creative art. Much of this procedure is not statistically deducible: the broader the basic language, the better the methodology, the easier it is for the student — even the average student — to improve quality.

To provide the student with an opportunity to understand the advantages and limitations of his decisions is of greater academic advantage than providing a great variety of building types — especially complicated physical programs that would ordinarily require practitioners to consult with other professional groups....

Architects have evidently not accepted their responsibility for our physical environment; for if the quality of all professional work were high, natural leadership in our environment would be recognized. Education has the responsibility of determining this quality, and improvement therein can evolve a sound professional attitude in re-evaluating and determining what is required in an academic curriculum, when it is required, and to whom it should be taught. Architecture is not a business open to all, but a profession with the serious responsibility of creating the three-dimensional physical structures upon which our culture will be evaluated. Of greater importance, the opportunity exists for greater fulfillment of the society which must inhabit this environment today.

What Architecture Is and Is Not (1959)

From "What Architecture Is and Is Not," convocation address, Grinnell College, Grinnell, Iowa, October 17, 1959.

I think architecture in all civilizations has been the environmental structure arising out of human need and utilizing the materials and techniques of the particular era. Today, the multiplicity of human needs, materials, and techniques provides an infinite variety of spatial opportunities. The search for unity in this variety, the search for the nuances of need, and the search for visual order are the primary elements of today's total modern architecture.

One of the things that I wish to stress most clearly is that the architect is responsible as a creator of space. He is responsible for providing an environment. The quality of this environment is a function of the ability of the architect to understand and perceive the quality of the problem. It is the responsibility of the client, therefore, to develop and explain, to look for the nuances of the problem. It is with the combination that we improve our visual environment. And one of the things that today seems most important to us in the profession is that our environment keeps pace with the knowledge of science and the knowledge of our society that exists in the 20th century.

Architecture, especially today, is not archaeology. This is very difficult to explain. Many of you know of a special little problem that our office was involved in: Is an Air Force Academy chapel supposed to be Gothic, or is it supposed to be Georgian, or is it supposed to be contemporary? I think some of you have heard of that discussion. I think some of you have heard some of the things that the building was called. Well, it'll be built, and as it's built, it will be an opportunity for all of us to see that we are trying to carry forth the idea that all of the aspects of architecture must be brought forward.

Now, I think that in our times, more than in any others, we have a certain element: the clarity of structure. Our society, which has many technical advances, has an opportunity to develop — as we've seen again in the library — beautiful precast forms, and these precast forms are worthy of showing. They have clarity of structure and the kind of structure that can be expressed. There are times, of course, in which it is not expressed at all, but this is a deliberate order and a deliberate spatial environment that is being created. It is both in searching for clarity and in the recognition of both the materials and the methods that special character is created.

A drawing or a speech can be forgotten. It doesn't have to be inhabited. A building is inhabited, so all the ideas have to be put together well. The selection and use of materials is one of the important aspects of good architecture. It is important that the materials be related one to another, that they have a relationship of need and use, so they are friendly together. Unless you want to develop a jarring note in space, it is better to select materials that work together. So we are talking about the correlation of quality and consistency and integrity in craftsmanship, and once again, this is the joint responsibility in our society between the people who make the drawings, who put the building on paper before it's built, and the contractor who builds it as an actuality. And this is entirely different, for example, from earlier times, when we dealt with just one material, stone, when we could build one on top of the other without drawings. Today, with the great complexities of services like lighting and air conditioning, we must unite all these aspects, and we must build with a sensitive selection of materials.

All of these things, developing from a need in architecture, search for one thing alone, really — the quality of space. Without that, the real success and development of supplying a human need do not exist.

On Political-Economic Horizons (1960)

From "On Political-Economic Horizons," American Institute of Architects Journal *(June 1960): 82–84.*

Today what comprises the urban scene for us is first of all the home of an egalitarian society, a society of citizen-entrepreneur, with the responsibilities of both; it is a mobile society where one in five move; it is an expanding society where experts predict expansion of millions of persons in individual areas; it is a technical society where obsolescence and change is an accelerated constant; and as in all societies it is still a selfish society where so-called rights of the individual transcend the community.

And what are the human forces that must be accommodated for tomorrow? First of all not only more people, but a longer lifespan for persons, with continuing emphasis on the needs of the individual as baby, child, teenager, adolescent, young adult, adult, and aged — as a single person, as a family, as a group. Secondly, as a changing society where concepts of time, space, knowledge and education are accelerated. Thirdly, as a period where free time and recreation will increasingly be available. Where once work provided the absorber for our aggressive tendencies in the community, in the future free time must be the absorber.

...

[T]he changing horizon should provide new areas of opportunity for the changing patterns we already foresee in human needs. Here are mine:

1. As individuals, and as cities, we do not need any longer to be big — the community of urban areas should be defined — one of the principal foci is the edge of the sub-unit.
2. We should be less interested in status quo and more interested in the search for new urban patterns; the next piazza could be on the twentieth floor.
3. Research in new opportunities in urban scale. Where is our Institute for Advanced Studies?
4. Recognition of the greater demand for leisure time area.
5. Redefinition of active and passive responsibilities in democratic political process.
6. Greater use of evaluation of the principles of science rather than the artifacts of science.

Architecture, in all civilizations, has been the environmental structure arising out of human need and utilizing the materials and techniques of the particular era. Today the multiplicity of human needs, materials, and techniques provides an infinite variety of spatial opportunities. The search for unity in this variety, the search for the nuances of need, and the search for visual order comprise the primary elements of a total architecture.

As architects we should:

1. Intensify our own critical values for a personal philosophy.
2. Recognize through personal research the opportunities available through science and technology to give new solutions to human shelter.
3. Recognize that basic research in our field is a requirement now if we are to maintain a mature environment for future civilization.

University of Illinois at Chicago Circle — Revisited (1966)

From "University of Illinois at Chicago Circle — Revisited," in Architecture and the College: Proceedings of North American Conference to Consider the Critical Issues in Campus Planning and College Building Design, April 17–21, 1966 *(Urbana, IL: University of Illinois, Urbana, April 1966), 84–93.*

In planning an urban campus, one of the major problems is the arrival and departure of initially developed criteria of the campus. After checking almost 11,000 automobiles by the time we got to a 3-2-3 environment, this was even more than a shopping center will provide…. We also have had a series of problems in the relationship of the campus to the environment. I think it is safe to say that in spite of slums, it is involved in conservation and renewal, and it is located adjacent to one of the largest packets of low-rent housing in the Chicago area. It has problems in the social environment which exist on almost any campus in the Unites States…. One is utilization of teaching techniques, the evolution in which the top guards utilize the teaching techniques. The second one is a problem of flexibility. You can always correct and make something very small or something very large and change it in a disciplinary way within its relative scale or make modifications which are relative to the scale. The third one is the problem of living in an urban society — how can we make use of both high- and low-rise buildings?… We actually developed 27 different models. In all cases, we reviewed the criteria for 20,000 [students], and cut it back to 9[,000], 8[,000], 7[,000], 6[,000] in accordance with the then existing programs. This capacity of working from a number, although we recognized that 20 was not fixed, it gave us, at least, some method of evaluating the decisions we made as we went along…. This is a more traditional campus than we have here at the University of Illinois in Champaign-Urbana where you can see a green mall in the middle. We have essentially a rotational system which, of course, had problems because we could not expand easily…. That, of course, forced a re-evaluation of the site. As we look at the site and its specific problems, it had an agreed-upon position not to consider moving into the community. Immediately it had a fixed number of acres, 106, for an ultimate demand of 20,000 students…. Of course, the scheme is based primarily on the intensity of use…. [I]t is a simple intensity from the center out — from the very center is our major public space which is more than just a green swath. It is an active kind of young adult jungle gym, conference and meeting center which is above the lecture center, adjacent to classrooms, adjacent to the library, and adjacent to the student center.

With that intensity of use in the center, we fan out where the larger elements represent laboratories or special discipline centers — art and architecture — where the time spend in environment is longer and where they don't contribute to the intensity of housing environment….

This is a final model as it was developed, and you can see this instead of the Renaissance city hall. In the lower foreground, you can see the intensity of use of that central area of the campus. We have about 40 percent coverage within this area. We run, I think, a ratio of close to 2.4 people in 6, fully developed. We have the major urban space in the middle, and the garden space at both ends in the lower right and the far left. These were left open because of the utilities and their expanse and development. I think you can see from this drawing the intensity of use of the site. It is intended, in theory, as the one building scheme, although in essence it is not. It is a transitional road to a more continuous environment with walkways scaling the building forming a continuous network.

Here we can see the first phase of construction with the city in the background and you can see the wonderful play of the adjoining neighborhood which is Maxwell Street, the flea market. It is a wonderful contrast, and I think an exciting phenomenon, if we can inject the intensity of communication as it exists here into the social spaces of the final campus area. Here is the center of the campus, and you can see the development. It was initially benches located on the periphery, but it was decided it was more like putting sparrows on a telephone line.

It would be more socially responsive if we could devise ways in which students could form their own grouping. The amphitheater in the center is of a formal nature and also forms the staircase to the lower level and the left center beneath. You can see these walkways which come from the parking areas, come from mass transit and immediately develop a high-speed, quick means of access either at this upper good-weather level or at the lower bad-weather level and connect and unite all the buildings. They also tend to channel what small open space we have left to more passive student use and then to permit those areas to achieve their own characters. As you can see, it does function as an adult jungle gym….

The character of materials is very simple — granite, pre-cast concrete, brick. Here is the tall building. Most of you will notice that the spans change as they go up. It was a deliberate attempt to try to resolve these energy forces.

We decided very early in the project that it was a goal to use the same strength of concrete throughout the whole design, so that the problem, whether big or small, would not outweigh the intensity. We tried to use the forces of energy as directly as possible, so that there will be a means of communication in the cultural environment to students who may not have had this perceptual opportunity in the past; and for any student it makes, I think, a meaningful structure….

As we look back at the city from that same floor, we can see the proximity of the city to the environment. You can see the scale of the library which is actually 30 percent of size at this time. It doesn't reflect the needs for a graduate and research center in science and engineering, but as we enter into the central area we see the amphitheater in the middle, the lecture center, the library itself, and the large span with 2 simple cords — the evolution of flexible space....

We tried to pay attention to details, to changes in texture. We even designed the waste baskets as basketball hoops to try to encourage debris throwing. You will also notice great changes in scale between the small piazzas around the classrooms as compared to the larger scale of the major building....

You can see this as a projection of a matrix of a very complex society in which you can come and build any portion of this at any one time, and then you would add on to these knuckles.... You can look for patterns of expansion. You can develop different kinds of means of communication. You can change the field or pattern. You can begin to look at this as a topological environment in which these floors are not exactly at the same level and actually use the corridor as a means of moving space rather than down the desired corridor as one means of central communication to the other. In other words, if chemistry gets in its locale with instructional classrooms to be shared by others, how can this be located with better proximity to chemistry and still be allowed to be located as part of the general distribution of a classroom throughout the whole campus?...

One of the interesting comments we have gotten from the first phase of the U. of I. is that the professors say, "Do I have to have my office exactly like the next office?" How can we look and see for a variety of spaces, can we achieve different-sized offices in different areas? Most faculty members don't need or want the kind of office which is available for industry. They like to develop a sub-corner for a work center as well as an area to talk to the students. There are opportunities to use additional room to a specific advantage. So these are simply abstract studies to develop for ourselves a vocabulary which will tie this vocabulary back into the strict programmatic vocabulary, back into the total educational environment. Then we hope to come up with what we call a phase three for the Chicago Circle campus of the University of Illinois.

The Philosophy (1966)

From "The Philosophy," in "Comprehensive Building Systems: Threat or Promise?"
special issue, Building Research *3, no. 5 (September–October 1966): 8–11.*

In the future it is obvious that there are going to be several problems which will occur because there will be more concern about the control of the environment, both natural and man-made. It may be expressed by the national beautification program at this moment, or by problems in air pollution, but these are only symbols of what will be the need for expanding the sociological program preceding the physical structure. There will also be problems in urban density, in total environment, and their application to new systems construction.

There will probably be less attention paid to matters involving current transportation and current techniques. There will be more utilization of electronic techniques, and expandable, collapsible, build-it-yourself frameworks with a more enfolding, existing, open system environment.

The description of a possible new urban environment could be the description of a city by the contemporary painter [Victor Vasarely]. He is an artist who has an idea of what the city should be. What is the system for the city? The polychrome city — polychrome especially in the sense of the diversity of its inner and outer coating materials — appears to be a perfect synthesis: The fundamental principle is that the conjunction of the arts restores all the plastic disciplines in their complete function. The polychrome city proposes its most coherent application at this point of history in which we find ourselves after Piet Mondrian's and Kasimir Malevich's revolution. These two other artists of this century were involved in this search.

That the harmonic principle is eminently called for by the factor of historic evolution should be in itself a source of satisfaction to us. However, it must be added that the polychrome city achieves only an architectonic synthesis of a nature such as to associate to the plastic value of a physical space a real psychic dimension that implants this space-form-color in the universal consciousness. An image of such synthesis that proposed a space and its form of specific extension in a social structure was given, for example, in the Gothic period.

The "Gothic space" was first of all the cathedral and its plasticity, but it was, above all, the hold that mystical faith had on the faithful souls. During that time the cathedral, like a *perpetuum mobile*, manufactured the mysticism. Like the synthesis of remote times, the polychrome city, today's synthesis, is in fact the concrete construction capable of this essential extension.

This would be a world in which the emphasis would be on personal doing and interaction. The cost of this new urban form would manifest itself in responsive change. The first change would be in form. The past aesthetic judgment would be of little value. The sense of things as objects we know today — the grammar school, the factory, the shopping center — would disappear. The intuitive judgment of protest, the factor of ambivalence, all factors such as these would be strong, reflected in the use of an area which would change not only during the daily or seasonal cycle, but would be responsive to its neighbors.

It would be a psychic, perceptual area of change. It might be a preschool in the morning, a sun-play space in the afternoon, a meeting place for all in the evening. It could be a stage for a traveling play group or a concert group, or a space for a political rally, or a church service, or an electronic performance, or a wide-screen movie. It would be essentially an urban interspace; not a town center, not a cultural center, not the traditional city square. It would be all of these things. It would also be just one of the many interspaces existing among the networks of an urban environment. As a core for a new urban community, it would require new systems.

This is one suggested solution to the problem of systems and working with the change of scale in present-day society. There is a need, therefore, to consider the development of construction systems. Those factors that must be defined encompass scale, the project organization in all its esoteric values and in all its real values, as they are commonly called, the project size, the market size, and the systems application.

It is necessary to consider in the environment the project organization and its relative size, its market capability, and its application to new technologies. Then, systems will be an extension of the visual as well as the physical order.

It is probably true that, in the future, new organizations will be required. The traditional architect-engineer relationship and the traditional concept of industry; the traditional concepts of organization, economics, legal and fiscal policies will have to change.

Living with Art (1971)

"Statement," in University of Iowa Museum of Art, Living with Art: Selected Loans from the Collection of Mr. and Mrs. Walter A. Netsch *(Iowa City: University of Iowa Museum of Art, 1971), 4.*

These paintings and sculptures have, for us, been a great source of personal pleasure — more than aesthetic joy, more than intellectual confrontation. Most of the works were purchased near the date of the painting, often before a show and sometimes unstretched. For the commonality of the paintings expresses our enthusiasm of artistic effort and a confidence in the intellectual goals of the artists themselves: the consistent search in color field painting; the iconic symbols of number and word; the strong geometry in the figure-ground; the strong anger of the surreal.

This says something about the good fortune of being in the proper place at the proper time; for the time, we have no control, but the place is formed from contemporary patterns. Many see a relationship between the images in the art and my own work, and I, too, feel this. For ours is not a collection in the usual sense — one of each from a period — and it is restricted by funds available. The objects are really my visual library and, seen in our house packed closely together, make a visual noise, urban and dense in character. When a painter interested me, I would follow his/her work over time; thus you will find three Nolands, three Indianas, three Kauffmans, etc., [not] because we did not like their subsequent works, but because these were, for us, beyond our means.

Although I grew up wanting to be a painter, pasting MOMA reproductions on my wall (such as Picasso's red/green *Woman in the Mirror*), and painting like John Marin, there were no original paintings in the home, except for some "follow the numbers" of my grandmother. The opportunity to acquire "the proper place" came with my role on the Air Force Academy, which required trips to New York City, Washington, Boston and Los Angeles.

I must thank my partner, Gordon Bunshaft, who, sharing an equal devotion to art, but already owning a great collection of Joan Miró, Jean Dubuffet, and now Henry Moore, allowed me to share his then every-Saturday tour of the New York galleries. These tours introduced me to Mr. Sam Kootz and dissolved the mysteries of "the back room." With increased confidence that galleries were not about to ignore or embarrass, I started a tour of my own, discovering galleries that had artists closer to my aesthetic goals and my pocketbook.

For this I would save my money for a year and make a trip to New York, spend three or four days on a "visual binge," perhaps see 500 works, list the 10 I liked best, count my money saved, and buy from the 10 twice the sum in my pocket.

In the later fifties I also discovered the Green Gallery and Mr. Dick Bellamy. Dick was the central force for many young artists, and I was welcome, in his patience, to sit in his back room for hours or invited to visit a studio of an artist he was considering.

Living and working in the visual world makes these works speak to us more clearly than wall decoration, more beautifully than wallpaper, more heartily for their crowded environment, and more personally as the special province of the special effort and joy of man. For us art is best not in a museum, not for the sake of collecting, but as part of living.

Postmodernism in Context (1978)

"Postmodernism in Context," in "The Search for a Postmodern Architecture," special issue, CRIT, *no. 4 (Fall 1978): 17.*

These notes will try to compress, in a few words, a kaleidoscope of ideas and history. For many of us, my age, the revolution of the modern movement was real. Gropius and Aalto were alive and working and teaching in the U.S.A. Frank Lloyd Wright was berating all for not being revolutionary enough. Corbusier's book was being published, a sell-out, hot off the press. It was a time when architecture was synchronized with art, the new politics, and social change.

Up until the Second World War, much was still theory — revolutionary theory, with little body of accomplished radical contemporary work in the U.S.A. The official colonial house dominated the scene, the Tribune Tower competition was a rallying cry for the losers, and *The Fountainhead* remained a fantasy of the individual fulfilling the romantic revolution. Mies did not emerge until the technological skill of the Second World War was applied to the building industry, with 860–880 the password. For many, however, the search continued. Saarinen searched his way; Stone and Yamasaki sought beauty in their way; then there were the Brutalists — architecture as sculpture, etc. For myself, Field Theory.

A revolution has a soul and the leaders give the issues and the hopes. Today another event, the postmodernist, is projecting another order, and many are proclaiming leadership.

For some of us, there are other ways. The presence of movements, especially if the formats can be visual, intellectual and explainable in context with the stuff of architecture — materials and needs — then the impact will be greater and more useful. Yet, sometimes the technique chosen is dramatic....

So today, as before, there is a new right and a new wrong with a new search for final victory. Unfortunately, projects flaw theory. The Venturi & Rauch proposal for Pennsylvania

Avenue Plaza not only flaunts complexity but substitutes a comic opera totalitarian example of Mussolini Moderne. In the process, a sensitive artist, Richard Serra, is demolished. *C'est la guerre!*

Having moved from complexity and contradiction to metaphor and coding, the resultant mannerists' products now provide the student with another discipline and new images rather than a working philosophy.

I prefer a more personal way, or as Lou Kahn would say, "The existence-will." The reality of commitment for the architect or the artist must always be the lonely individual pursuit of idea; for each of us it should be different — both the pursuit and the idea.

Creativity: A Personal View (1979)

"Creativity: A Personal View," in Perspectives on Creativity and the Unconscious: Proceedings of the Jungian Conference, Miami University, Oxford, Ohio, *ed. Donald W. Fritz (Oxford, OH: Old Northwest Publication, 1979), 10–14, 34–37.*

Creativity is not really how you design, but how you get prepared to use the skills, the techniques, and the directed energy toward the design. Architects may, because theirs is a social art, have forces that channel creativity: the client, the commission — you might say the subject — their own personal attitude toward both the client and the commission as well as their trade, and of course their capability....

First, then, at issue many times for me is my work appeared [in] conflict: conflict with parents over goals, with teachers over aesthetics — in retrospect probably pure narcissism — with the military over principles, with partners over ethics, with clients over faith, and with staff over communication. These conflicts, however, honed training, not only in problem solving on the professional, educational level but in the ethics and decision-making of the craft. The assistance of conflict to force reassessment — that is, internal rather than external conflict — does much to challenge the issues of the design, or the site or the program, materials or needs, rightness or wrongness. Indeed that internal stress is more important than training alone. But without the internal conflict, nothing is honed, internalized, or learned. Without this impact of internal stress on training, creativity also suffers, for aesthetics as understanding ideas will then remain unclear and sloppy.

Second, let me mention the role of the ego in creativity. Ego is a tyrant and a crutch and a godsend — all not at once. As a tyrant ego impedes creativity. Lou Kahn, a very fine architect, used to say that a design has its own existence-will, as we call it, tramples creativity. The bravura faith cannot be called upon like a skill or training, but often exists as a hidden resource.

Third, we must remember that the times play an extremely important role in life for an architect or an artist, and in that the media, for one must substitute the media for the guild today in communicating. One must indeed be aware of the time. When I was in high school, only 125 million people inhabited the United States; only 25% of them were planning to attend college when I did, so I had the advantage of time and place. No matter how creative an architect may be, he must have an opportunity. Yet, with that opportunity must come utilization of the time and talents.

I personally have had to recognize the indifference — even antipathy — that appeared professionally regarding my so-called Field Theory style, my way of working. You must understand that for many, Skidmore, Owings & Merrill represents not only the Establishment, but a soulless, crass commercial organization. It is not expected that unique ideas can flourish in such an environment. Secondly, the Chicago School has for many years been interpreted as Mies van der Rohe, and any deviation from that School has been until recently Philistine. So, by location and practice, I automatically was isolated. And since my efforts were not developed in an academic environment, I did not have formal scholarly support. Yet it is most interesting that all my buildings were primarily for academic institutions; so that is where the freedom, for me, lay. And finally, since those of us who have been involved in the studio of the firm represent diverse groups, we not only had our isolation, but were multi-faceted.

In retrospect I see the forces that developed Field Theory coming out of practice in the concepts of aesthetics and technology. My generation, second-generation Modernists, felt the issues of the modern architectural revolution. For me as a student, Alvar Aalto lectured and taught at MIT while he was designing Baker House, and I was just a student. Walter Gropius and Marcel Breuer were at Harvard, Eero Saarinen in Detroit. Mies and Walter Peterhans, hardly even known in the United States, were starting out in Chicago. Laszlo Moholy-Nagy and others were establishing their design center at the Old Natural Museum in Chicago. America was being blessed by its freedom which was extended to those who fled from abroad. Frank Lloyd Wright was still alive and gave us all hell, students and faculty alike. It was still the time when colonial, domestic architecture and Royal Barry Wills were the enemy. Aesthetic changes came dramatically. Picasso, the Museum of Modern Art, the viability of strong social issues, Spain and the Lincoln Brigade, and above all the bursting giant — technology — were about to produce creations in abundance, making the Bauhaus seem infallible. Research and product development were very responsive. Products followed and flowed as if William Morris had realized his vision. Such was our world in the U.S.A. in 1940 with 125 million people by then, a righteous war for freedom, and an exploding society. This was the heritage and the working place for U.S. architects. Aesthetic questions came from Europe, Pier Luigi Nervi, Smithson, the Dutch; but the concepts were extensions of the original revolution from the Bauhaus.

For me, being a Chicagoan by birth, Sullivan, George Grant Elmslie, and Wright were visible patterns. Actually I chose to go to MIT because no god permanently resided there, and that of course I was told by Sullivan, Elmslie, and Wright. I wanted no local master's advice. My education and practice followed essentially the Bauhaus. My understanding and my faith in technology were complete. And, in fact, industry responded for me at the Air Force Academy. We developed our own research corps under Robertson Ward with brand new products — grey glass, mirrored glass, large extrusions of aluminum, the granite industry today, special sealants, floor tiles, etc., all appearing out of that marvelous four years — which now, of course, surfeit the industry.

However, all was not perfect. The box, to me, was not perfect. Programmatic needs needed programmatic design. My personal crisis then appeared with the Air Force Academy Chapel. The original folded-plate design was murdered in the press. One Southern senator said, "Ah don't hear tha touch of angel's wings." So there was a personal trip to Europe, my first, from Stonehenge and vertical Gothic to Michelangelo and the Baroque, via Chartres, Sainte-Chapelle, Notre Dame. It was for me my total immersion in and exposure to Sullivan's goals translated to the past: an alternative unresolved by technology, and a recognition that cognitive form came from program and geometry, not technology. And from this for me a new design process was created.

The Air Force Academy Chapel was controversial, both within my firm as well as outside — that's the second and final one. But few responded to early attempts at our aesthetics in latticing structure, articulating structural materials, metal and concrete. Personally the effort of designing the 5000 feet of windows convinced me that somewhere, I had to be able to articulate a more coherent way. Ralph Park Youngren, who was working with me in the studio, and I decided the Chapel experience as well as the Air Force Academy was a point of departure, not a beginning. Work on Chicago Circle was like the Chapel, embryonic, until another man working with me, Will Reuter, and I became totally immersed in geometry, in the rotated square, the triangle, the circle-square configuration, that had developed forms and aesthetics way in the past, and we sought to find means of relating them to today.

Issues explored by U.S. artists in their own context were going on at the same time. Robert Motherwell, Al Held, Kenneth Noland, Jack Youngerman, Gene Davis, Jules Olitski, Kauffman, Tony Delap, and others were doing their thing. Superreal, of course, was going on. There was Claes Oldenburg, George Segal, Roy Lichtenstein, Ed Ruscha, Bob Indiana, all of them searching and finding their particular answers. Contemporary artists had, for a long time, destroyed the picture plane, flattened, projected, reassembled, destroyed again, Mannerist and Renaissance form. The dissolution of the Renaissance form was for me not the primary issue, and it certainly was not the primary issue of Mies and Le Corbusier, but for them those were rather neoforms. Sullivan and Wright searched for the democratic aesthetic; and like Art Nouveau, sought the organic.

In architecture at this moment, all of these things are being taken into consideration. This building — the Miami University Art Museum [in Oxford, Ohio] — for example, is a very complex effort on my behalf. But originally the discovery of Field Theory freed us from the past; and once we'd established the programmatic priorities, we began our search for appropriate field or geometry, the potentials for that field, and all its ramifications and jargon — latticing, slipped fields, doubled fields. By following the progression of buildings year by year, we began to discover the potential of the geometry. Today, we have developed a vocabulary in the studio, which makes it easy for us to communicate with the language we have created.

But without conflict, opportunity, and threshold, again creativity starves. One doesn't go out to design a new system each day. One can't invent without disenchantment with the existing, without concern for personal achievement, or anger at existing situations, real or imagined. When young and full of hope and positive of one's future, one engages in dialogues of concern and criticism of existing concepts. Then aesthetics flow freely. At the completion of the Air Force Academy, for example, I was well known, probably categorized, but personally worried. After the Chapel design, which was a personal and emotional event over a long period of time, penetrated by political conflict and politics, I enlarged my search. The building, that building, when created, felt very good. By that I mean I was not concerned with the strangeness of the form or the proportion, or the impact of the unusual scale on the environment. It gave a sense of pleasure — a sense of personal pleasure. The act of building on the initial concept gave this and many more feelings. A feeling of rightness. It was an unconscious response to a series of conscious events. So the balance in creativity often has a kind of physical presence. It is not necessarily true that the design is at its very best at that point, but perhaps conceptually it is the most consistent. Then hard, more objective effort is necessary to combine it into a greater whole.

But at other times, things do not feel right. You get up in the morning nervous and unhappy, the drawings disappoint, even disgust you. When you feel out of touch, and "you can't go home again," life in creativity is a mess. The early design of Chicago Circle, for example, shows that kind of personal equivocation. The gradual assimilation of cross axes, the use of a primitive form, the historical alliteration of the Agora, the evolution of non-orthogonal issues all began, however, to rekindle in me an energy and a faith that there was intuitively some kind of form brewing. But these kinds of responses are available to you only if you've not already committed yourself. In fact Camus would call that non-commitment a commitment of its own. For now discovery begins.

So therefore, Field Theory grew as a visual language of discovery, not as an individual building like the Chapel. The body of a language in form and geometry already exists in some form previously. It is the discovery for yourself of the connectedness of the idea, the growth of the idea, the excitability of continuous creation that starts the different pattern of creativity. Then the theory outstrips the act, the building. Decisions in the name of theory may control logic, but then the design sometimes suffers as a totality.

...

In order for the field to work, it has to work both in relation to the program and to the site. The synthesis of these three culminates, of course, in the final design. The fourth factor I spoke about earlier, this feeling of rightness, plays a role at each step, and provides for that inner critical additive to the direct critical response of the act of designing. Architecture is a semi-solitary art; one can in a group share in the three procedural steps. The interaction with a like-minded confrere is positive and stimulating. The need to keep the beginning steps independent is simply learned from experience. Synthesizing too early robs the design of potential richness. It also keeps us all searching longer. The synthesis comes alone and along at the very special times, and the results can give different solutions that are obviously dependent upon the weight of each part in the synthesis. It is impossible to recreate totally the situation in which the design process actually occurs. In fact, it can never be entirely truthful, for time plays tricks.

At Wells College, for example, our selection as an architect for a library involved such soul-searching by the President and the Board of Trustees that I thought we were never going to be selected. They had to resolve the conflict between the desire for a unique building and a traditional campus and an architect 800 miles away. But when the resolution came each phase of the program took on a special dimension, particularly since that was a time when women were seeking an early kind of collective freedom. The sense of now and the future dominated the program: how can the program and design state and emphasize that change? How can the building share those goals, and be reflected, of course, in the President's goals for his students, their rights and freedoms, both intellectually and physically? The site was full of conflict and potential. Could we build without impacting on existing buildings? Could we use the ravine and the steep slope of the site? Once we solved some of those primary issues and rediscovered the diagonal paths of the students connecting the campus, we could continue. The intellectual work of the field related to the site and the scale and the simple problem of how book stacks could be assembled for both order and variety. There was no immediate synthesis. Two schemes were presented. The responses and interaction of the sensitive and probably very concerned clients assisted us. I remember actually the synthesis coming in a meeting, and all I could do was wait to try it out. I had to go with what we had done. I knew it was already the past, it was irrelevant, but I couldn't do anything else. It was one of those terrible times when the pencil sits there and you can't grab it, and you've got to wait. The result, of course, turned out to be a pretty marvelous building. This time it was much like the final result — it had an absolutely fantastic roof. It was geometrically wild and beautiful. They thought of all of Wells College skiing over it, in a massive slalom course — and it almost undid the client. So I had to accept reality and create a new roof. But the new roof gave really the existence-will of the way the windows and everything else fell together. The whole building began to fall into place — program, site, and field. It was of special satisfaction to us in the design, because the construction workers even enjoyed building the building.

Little things create images, and images create possibilities. The infiniteness of our fields for us provokes a richness. The problem is to be patient, have faith, and control your personal fears and ego. You will notice in the three designs for the Basic Science[s] Building at the University of Iowa the concepts of science (how you house science), the change in scale, and our effort in the Field Theory "Piranesian space." The Behavioral Science[s] Building at the University of Illinois, Chicago Circle — a long and very complex building — was an effort in complexity. We wanted to see if we could develop richness out of that complexity. It sometimes misleads people in corridors, but it has a major event and is probably the most complex aesthetic attempt we have made. And, of course, this museum had a very simple program with a very beautiful site. I had, fortunately, the past experience of designing my house and living in essentially triangular exhibition space. But here, it was just the opposite of the Behavioral Science Building. It was to create richness out of a unified setting: we developed everything, from the dimension of the windows to the height of the room to the size of the limestone, into a unified whole. However, we do not expect you to discover this; we expect that it makes the building quieter, more elegant; you feel a kind of personal satisfaction in being here. Then we, of course, have done our job.

Designing in the Third World (1980)

From "Designing in the Third World: Work in Algeria," George A. Miller Lecture, Center for Advanced Study, University of Illinois at Urbana-Champaign, Thursday, March 27, 1980.

If I have a guardian, it is Louis Sullivan, who gave the transcendental war cry for effort, faith, and conviction. Wright, the iconoclast, was every student's secret friend, for he espoused Sullivan, fought the system, and argued for a native architecture. In *Kindergarten Chats*, Sullivan argues for a language and a discipline....

The search in creativity is a personal, separate one; historians like Colin Rowe hypothesize and intellectualize about creativity. Rowe's description of La Tourette is architectural in form and character — formal and ordered. While it is compelling, tonight you are going to see another side of Le Corbusier, the side most architects know and understand — a more primordial order: How the cultural impact of history on us was the impact of primal vernacular forms on our goals and disciplines and our constant exposure to and faith in imagination, thought, and expression.

Tonight I am asking you, therefore, to relax, rely on your feeling and intuition, not forgetting your discipline or your intellect, but subduing those qualities, as Sullivan advises, for the first stages of creativity. As a young architect, Sullivan provided the hope that out of our new society would come a true, organic democratic architecture, and from Wright we were taught to be ourselves and distrust the establishment.

Growing up in two worlds — the secular, technological yet ideological world of MIT Class of 1943, and the indigenous efforts of the Chicago School — is my aesthetic base — dichotomy-diversity — and, I hope, my strength. This historical introduction is in a sense a confession that ideas do not spring full-grown, but are responses to your own responses to the aesthetic and professional life you lead.

Nationally, the first project of mine involved with national forces of pride, power, education, national uses of technology, curiously not a high budget, and the opportunity of interaction with consultants to the government (Eero Saarinen, Pietro Belluschi, Wallace Harrison, Welton Becket, etc.) was the United States Air Force Academy in Colorado Springs, Colorado.

Curiously, this project epitomizes the U.S. secular goals of technology, aspiration, and yet above the total ensemble, the building most responsive to the people, to the fusion of modern secular goals and religion, is the U.S. Air Force Academy Chapel. This building borne of joy and pain, conflict and support (from a few) not only is the pinnacle but my base for the future. After that I could not, as we say, go home again, but with this structure a new search started which is now called Field Theory architecture.

The following exposure to you will be intense, somewhat chaotic, as time compresses germination in ideas, the selection ends with the two new projects: my entry into

Late Entries to the Chicago Tribune Tower Competition, which is my alternative proposal to postmodernism as the current viable aesthetic, and a real project in the Central Library at Sophia University, Tokyo, Japan. Jesuit Father Armbruster, originally from Bavaria, is the client and librarian.

I shall, as the slides are shown primarily chronologically, emphasize the growth of the theory and its adaptation to projects, architectural philosophies beyond the discipline, and the impact of materials, technologies (or the lack of them) on the structures as architecture. Field Theory is a discipline in two-dimensional and three-dimensional order and proportion which, combined with human need, social goals, materials, and technology, forms the base for my design.

Late Entry to the Chicago Tribune Tower Competition (1980)

Statement concerning Netsch's entry in Late Entries to the Chicago Tribune Tower Competition *exhibition at Museum of Contemporary Art, Chicago. In Stanley Tigerman,* Late Entries to the Chicago Tribune Tower Competition *(New York: Rizzoli, 1980), 2: 54.*

TTTWO, a field theory butterfly tower in the chrysanthemum field: a soft/hard edged base developed from alternate series of equal and square root of 2 units, alternating, ascending with a 15° rotation latticed.

The facade contains 7 variations of transparency of silver reflective glass plus silver opaque.

The individual floors and roof are self-contained environmentally; including energy system trombe wall sections forming thermos type elevations on the south wall.

The classic problem of the high-rise extruded form here is developed into a field-topological environment.

Form, pattern, volume and site configuration are contained in variations of eight. The chrysanthemum field, the window progression, the structure and the tower declinations all follow this principle.

The drawing is programmed to the PDP 1170 using plotter xynetics 1101, 3073F transparent blue and 3073F transparent violet on silver mylar.

The design is dedicated to the Bartok piano sonata (1926).

Lecture Notes, Stuttgart, Germany (1980)

Introduction

Ladies and gentlemen, I wish to thank you for this invitation, especially recognizing the intensity of studies at this time of year. This, the last stop on a journey from Chicago, U.S.A., to Amman, Jordan, to the fifth Aga Khan conference on the search for form in Islamic society, with side trips to Petra and Jerasch, ancient ruins in Jordan, a visit to our

[SOM] projects in Algeria, contrasting with and reinforcing the ideas at the Aga Khan conference, and now Stuttgart, my first non-airport experience in Germany.

The United States of America is physically a large and variable climatic environment with a current population of 220 million. Yet, when I was in secondary school the population was 125 million. So, in my professional life I have been a participant in enormous and essentially affluent technological growth. For we realize that the primary growth spiral in the U.S.A. coincided with the Industrial Revolution and continued into the new electronic revolution. The citizens of the U.S.A., by good fortune in the environment and the time, coalesced their cultural and national diversities into a secular technological society, one without historic or cultural precedent, without an indigenous physical heritage, but developing a tradition of the new, encouraged by growth and change.

I personally was fortunate to be a student at the time that the leaders of the architectural revolution — Walter Gropius, Alvar Aalto, Le Corbusier, and Mies van der Rohe — were making their first statements in the U.S.A. Gropius had his houses at Lincoln, Massachusetts, and taught at Harvard; Aalto designed the Baker House dormitory at MIT (my alma mater); Le Corbusier founded his art center at Harvard, and Mies began a school of architecture at IIT in Chicago. To us, the aesthetic revolution in architecture was real, the opportunities enormous, and we assisted in routing the forces of eclecticism in the profession — the architect-designed Colonial house, etc.

If not terminated, careers were interrupted by World War II. Those returning found new materials, construction techniques, and growth to coalesce with the lessons learned from the secular leadership of the modern architectural revolution.

This represented another opportunity — the evolution of group practice at Skidmore, Owings, & Merrill, and direct participation in a wide assortment of projects big and small, located from many sections of the U.S.A. to the Far East — eventually beyond that. Today you will see many university buildings and the effort to join programs, technology, and architecture.

Tübingen

Yesterday I went to Tübingen. I saw an old city with old and new universities, a history of architecture, and ways of living. Tübingen is a busy, intense, beautiful city. The streets and squares are designed for people and activities. The architecture is busy, active, repetitive, and modest. The old city is an interactive way of life — made of many, many parts. The new university is about education, knowledge, and health and health service. The people and activities are specialized, and the architecture is specialized and technical. It was a special day.

Stuttgart

A large city, with a university, in which though the city has human scale, it is more impersonal, more anonymous, the architecture more specialized, more technical. Your city, Stuttgart, is more the world I come from, though the charm and intensity of Tübingen is fascinating.

Life: Programmatic Architecture and Field Theory

Life is the involvement of people in activities — people with people; also people with things. Programmatic architecture is about this.

Field Theory is a way of discovering proportion, order, and relationships in form and proportion. My architecture is about how people do things in handsome, well-proportioned university buildings — libraries, laboratories, student housing, hospitals, theaters, museums, art schools, and architecture schools.

It is also a voyage of discovery — program and architecture, form and architecture, materials and architecture, structure and architecture, and beauty and architecture. It is about the new university, but about architectural form as control, not specialization.

Lecture Notes (1981)

It is very difficult to display the concepts of 34 years' work. I shall use the high points to explain my Field Theory. I hope you can enjoy looking at the buildings as art. Of course, they must work — they had also to be on budget and mostly on time. However, those explanations would take too long. The same is true with campus planning.

So I hope the slides build the variety, the proportion, and the scale. The buildings are different for different locations. Pretend it is a dream trip without music, for the eyes, mind, and heart, and for the future. These buildings are a personal pilgrimage and hopefully build towards an imaginary landscape.

Every aesthetic has its order or combination of orders, from the Golden Section to the I Ching, from historicism to eclecticism, from the scale of the hand to the infinity of systems. None is right or wrong; all have been misused. The decision or choice finally becomes ethics or opportunity or both.

In many respects I fit the tradition of Chicago architects and architecture — a maverick architect involved in theory and practice. Trained in the Modernist mold with Lawrence Anderson, I had no one god, but felt an extension of the modern revolution — Walter Gropius, Alvar Aalto, but mostly Le Corbusier, with my Chicago base of Frank Lloyd Wright and Louis Sullivan. (Mies van der Rohe was not on the horizon in the United States in '39.)

If one is fortunate, one has a design crisis at the proper moment. Fortunately, for me, the crisis was the chapel for the Air Force Academy in 1954. The first design was turned down, demolished. Nat Owings always said that it was for the best — all the other designs were approved, I could always do another chapel. The new design changed my aesthetic career. I could not go back to the box. I could not do only chapels. What to do? This short lecture is about an aesthetic idea, the network-Field Theory, and how it happened, what it is, and what it does for me.

Before redesigning the chapel, I went to England, France, and Italy, to see the great Gothic, Romanesque, and Renaissance cathedrals — Wells Cathedral, Sainte-Chapelle, Chartres, but also Stonehenge, the Campidoglio, the Laurentian Library, Piazza Navona.

I rediscovered not stone, not style, but the unifying order of geometry, the unifying proportion no matter what style or what material.

The chapel at the Air Force Academy is not a Field Theory building but a break in approach — technical, geometric, aesthetic, a mixture of high tech and romance. I spent a winter designing the colored glass windows. The first Field Theory building is the Art and Architecture Building at the University of Illinois at Chicago — unfinished, challenged, but there. It is designed as studios surrounding a baroque walkway enclosing public space that will never be. That was about 1960, and the aesthetic die was cast.

More complete in theory, the Basic Sciences Building at the University of Iowa involved the street, the baroque use of light, structure, and space, an advanced concept of laboratory design, a deliberately "incomplete" building awaiting future accretions. The design, layout and structure enhanced progress on Field Theory.

The building is a form field, assembled as a necklace about another Field Theory building — here the intimate geometry holds the plan, but the larger form dominates. This is at Wells College, Aurora, New York.

My house and studio represent a change in the basic fields — gone is the rotational element in the geometry. The house is a combination of square and triangle within a theoretical cube. The studio, much later, explores the chrysanthemum — a geometry interrelated at two scales with proportional change the keynote in plan, section, and elevation. A maquette for current work in prefab housing — the imaginary landscape for the year 2000.

The Miami Art Museum (Miami University, Oxford, Ohio) carries both the house and the new attitude towards geometry forward. Based upon the medieval platonic square, the basis for Gothic construction, this field is carried into the variables in proportion converting plan, form, and building to sculpture.

Living with Art, Two (1983)

Statement in Miami University Art Museum, Living with Art, Two: The Collection of Walter and Dawn Clark Netsch *(Oxford, OH: Miami University Art Museum, 1983), 7.*

It has been a long time since 1954, when as a young designer, I began living with original art (not just reproductions). Robert Motherwell's *Ile de France* was my first acquisition. By 1971, my collection had grown, and Mr. Ulfert Wilke, the Director of the University of Iowa Museum of Art, asked my wife, Dawn, and me to show selections from our art collection at the Iowa Museum.

In the beginning of my collecting, I bought the works of artists who were about my age. They were, along with me, asserting personal aesthetic ideas. I have continued enjoying and adding later works of these artists, but have also acquired the works of new and younger artists whose attitudes and aesthetic goals have special appeal to me.

The art in our home is not a comprehensive collection of contemporary artists of the period, but rather an expression of my own choice and taste bounded by two rules: the art is selected when produced and the work must be by an American artist who, in a sense, is involved with a cultural struggle similar to my own. This may seem to suggest that the selections have a particular architectural interest, but I believe they reflect a broader range of aesthetic sensibilities.

Dawn and I live with some art that is not contemporary American — Middle Eastern rugs, pottery, dishes, and fabrics — products of other cultures, cultures which I learned to appreciate in my travels. And as a result, a few of these objects — the Haniwa head, the Buddhist head, the Japanese tea ceremony cold water vessel — represent travel acquisitions.

Since living in our own house, the art has had a dialogue with my aesthetic viewpoints, each enhancing the other in friendly confrontation. I cannot imagine living without art, music, books and film. Creativity is a continual conversation with yesterday, today, and tomorrow. For Dawn, living with art has complemented her political career, and as a result, she has grown fond and even protective of the works.

The art in the house is visually noisy and vibrant but the interior volumes provide a support of quiet contrast. Both the Miami University Art Museum, for which the house is a precedent, and the Snite Museum of Art at the University of Notre Dame, designed by my old friend and boss, A. M. Richardson, should find the art, the span of time, and the aesthetics compatible. *Living with Art, Two* can only lead to *Living with Art, Three.*

Notes for a Speech (c. 1984)

Every architect likes to talk about his work. Chicago architects are happy to have this show in Paris about our city and its architectural history. Born in Chicago, one block from a Barry Byrne (a student of Wright) building, and not far from the Robie House, I have always been around renegade Chicago architecture.

Although an intimate part of SOM for 32 years, I almost always wanted to be an architect, and with the Air Force Academy and the Chapel decided on the need to be a renegade Chicago architect — in the tradition.

In 1960, a new fad in style was affecting America. I called it "sweetness and light," an architecture of Yamasaki and Ed Stone, far from the modern movement and the Chicago tradition.

My search started on my study trip to England, France, and Italy after the first design for the [U.S. Air Force Academy] chapel was turned down. There and then I relived and relearned both the geometric base and the qualities of Gothic, Romanesque, and Renaissance architecture. But it was the first two that convinced me that modern geometry and modern materials could for me be a way out of a style I did not like and a continuation of the goals of Chicago and the modern movement. As you see, this evening, others also searched their separate ways.

On Nathaniel Owings (1984)

Letter of condolence to Margaret Wentworth Owings,* in remembrance of her husband, Nathaniel Owings, July 17, 1984.

Dear Margaret,

Although I know you know I called when the word came, but I fear you may misunderstand why this letter has taken so long. It has taken so long because I don't want to believe that Nat and I will not continue to share joys and concerns. I have had a letter framed on my desk — a copy is enclosed — of a letter Nat sent after the SOM retirement party for him in New York. He spoke of the team as family and I guess I believed him. So now see my sense of loss — much different albeit than yours — but a true loss, for we had maintained our communication — our friendship had grown.

In the beginning was Oak Ridge — and the first time I met Nat in 1947 was in the Design Room in Oak Ridge, with A. M. Richardson, Tallie Maule, Carl Russell, John Weese, and myself — the latest hire. We were preparing the design presentation drawings for the Garden Apartments. I had heard stories, I was afraid of him — though I remember his humor special to the project directed the day.

All of us, except A. M., who was a boss, became Nat's first protégés, and we followed him like the Pied Piper from Oak Ridge to Chicago to Tokyo to San Francisco, and of all four I remained at SOM — Nat's first protégé partner....

So you can see these weeks of preparation have been done with my sense of loss. I talked to Dawn about my lonesomeness, which she shared.

We all know what Nat has accomplished, we surmise the special relationship you and he shared. I have seen him in so many roles — in SOM fighting for the firm, on a project fighting for good design, in planning fighting for principles even above design. I have seen him enjoy beauty — in Japan, in New Mexico, in Big Sur. I have heeded his advice, tried to make him take mine, shared our special image of SOM, and shared some great successes — Oak Ridge, the Air Force Academy, Baltimore, David Childs and the Washington Office, and later Pennsylvania Avenue and the Commission on Fine Art.

I hope that you will feel some day like continuing to show, so that the circle is not yet closed. For I remember leaving the sketch of your site for Wild Bird on the blackboard wall at 100 Alta and the pine tree on the terrace — and my naive wedding present. So that we may continue to share a little — for we have so much to hold — our love for Nat.

As always,

Walter Netsch

*Margaret Owings, a noted wildlife conservationist, died in 1999 at Wild Bird, her home in Big Sur, at the age of 95.

Notes on a Field Theory Game (c. 1984)

Notes on a game patented by Netsch.

I have had time on the various trips to synthesize what for me has up till now been a predominately intuitive creation involving the chrysanthemum primarily.

At this moment, I believe that the game succeeds and is operative because it extends creatively basic geometric rules involving proportion, rates of change, sequence, proportional interaction, extrapolation, and most prominently the utilization of the rules involving *both* the solids (the squares or any developed shapes within the squares' boundaries), the voids, the unfilled spaces between the squares that behave mathematically and proportionately between the radial divisions of the circle (360°), and the angles setting the rates of proportional change between the squares. These mathematical "facts" have existed since the evolution of geometry; what is unique about the game is the utilization of these basic geometries to create new forms utilizing the inherent aesthetic and proportional values in the basic system.

Many games have been created using proportional blocks in groups of orthogonal packing systems to form images from the proportional systems. $\sqrt{2}$, $\sqrt{5}$, and the Fibonacci sequence are three proportional number systems, just as triangles, circles, stars, etc. cut out within these systems can be used. The difference between these systems and the game is that these proportional systems involve a fit of the solids (most often squares) without the secondary proportional systems of the spaces in between.

It is the sophisticated overlapping of both the proportional squares, the radial subdivisions, and the angular spaces that allow for the creative extrapolation into the game, and this is what is unique and not done before, to my knowledge and research. It is also the creative transition from abstract forms to anthropomorphic forms.

Since geometry involves arithmetic, geometric, and harmonic progressions or combinations thereof, as well as $\sqrt{2}$, $\sqrt{5}$, Fibonacci, and those progressions, the game seeks to find the basic mathematical and proportional rules of the geometries, especially involving multiple and overlapping systems. One must realize that like growth and rates of change these are infinity systems. It is possible, using the boundaries of radial proportions, to develop other, more spiral-like systems.

I hope this explanation assists in defining the differences of the game, a difference of sophistication in basic geometries and the application of the geometries.

Chicago Park District President's Report (1986)

Preface, Preliminary Reorganization Report *(Chicago: Chicago Park District, 1986), 6.*

Since the inception of my responsibilities as President of the Chicago Park District Board, it has become self-evident that the current management system must change if the heritage of the Chicago Parks, the open space living room of all Chicagoans and their guests, is to survive.

This change requires more than a paper shuffle of people. It requires that a deep sense of responsibility and professional ethics be reestablished for the Chicago parks, both in depth and character, irrespective of the impact of personnel and politics.

The proposed decentralized organization will solicit and nurture local responsibility, improve park quality through coordinated management, improve recreation through responsive management, and will provide, even at the Commission level, a new depth in professional support to prevent the erosion of purpose: Building the finest park system in the United States.

The subject of this report is professional ethics, continuity and review, central and local management, local community participation, and decentralized organization.

Although the organization of recreational management has been changed, the recreation program opportunities and improvements will be the subject of the second management review, after basic reorganization is complete. At this time, the diversity of recreation and cultural programs, quality of performance, fees, community benefits, areas of choice, etc., will be analyzed.

The Commission can now review the changes proposed to the current system and the priorities and programs necessary to begin the new professionalism of the Chicago Park District. The public will join us in this beginning of the renaissance of Chicago's hidden resource — the lakefront and inland parks.

May this review begin so that the national search for professional support can make the ethical change a reality.

Remarks (c. 1987)
Remarks, Chicago Park District presentation.

I was born in 1920 in a new part of town — South Shore — living there because it was the best place near transportation to the Chicago Stockyards (streetcar and roadway) with a new school and middle class and out of the ghetto, like ourselves upwardly mobile.

I have been a part of this change, had to fight for the West Side parks, and if the Park District doesn't train its staff, the horticulture, the path design, and the roadways will make them shadows of their great designs.

I suggest you take the walking trips of downtown and the automobile trips of the neighborhoods in the book by Dominic Pacyga and Ellen Skerrett, *Chicago, City of Neighborhoods: Histories and Tours* [Chicago: Loyola University Press, 1986].

I wish to show you the last opportunity to approach planning at a doable scale, use planning criteria for today and tomorrow, and use green technology.

While grand plans are difficult to achieve, grand ideas at reasonable size can make a difference and perhaps change our attitudes for the 21st century.

Living with Art, Three (1991)

Statement in Living with Art, Three: The Collection of Walter and Dawn Clark Netsch *(Oxford, OH: Miami University Museum of Art, 1991), 6–7.*

Dawn and I are glad to introduce new artists and old friends. Many of the younger artists have yet to have "made it" in the art scene, but that was also true in *Living with Art, One* when Al Held, Kenneth Noland, and Roy Lichtenstein were beginning to be accepted.

The world of art is so complex today — the fresh explorations of ideas and techniques — staining, flooding, optical effects have become neo-events. Ideas like Abstract Expressionism or Pop or Color Field or even realism have turned into anarchic recurrences — the canons of art have given way to individualism. The avant-garde forms of video, television, and performance are ideas seeking form.

It is natural that I should keep an interest in old friends like Held, Tony Delap, Lichtenstein, or Robert Motherwell. For while they have kept their signatures, they have also pursued their canons and produced fresh ideas. Accepted art is now so expensive that new acquisitions are limited for us either in paint or in print form, so that the so-called decorative arts such as pottery, china, the Alan Siegel chairs (which I consider sculpture) — art forms for "arrived artists" — are our opportunity.

As always, there is the search for fine younger artists. Here the traditional forms, sculpture and painting, are still available, but the search is more complex because my responses must be filtered through the diverse forms and neo-statements.

Time will tell which of the younger artists will be recognized for their ideas and whether they continue to develop — many of our old friends from *Living with Art, One* and *Living with Art, Two* have had to settle for personal satisfaction rather than fame, but these artists still speak to us, and we enjoy their company.

Lake Shore Park (1992)

Written remarks read at an open forum on Lake Shore Park and the Museum of Contemporary Art, held at Northwestern University School of Law, May 13, 1992.

My old friend and associate, Don Powell, has asked me to express my thoughts about the future of Lake Shore Park and the new MCA. As I had already have a commitment for an interview in Colorado and am giving a lecture tour of the Air Force Academy for the Denver Art Museum, I cannot be in two places at the same time, but I offered to write these remarks so that they can be added to the dialogue.

Many of you know that my wife, when senator of this district, helped immensely in the evaluation of the proper use for the site of the old armory and supported the use of the site for the MCA as a positive cultural crown for the Magnificent Mile and the land of Streeterville and SOAR [Streeterville Organization of Active Residents].

Many of you also know me as an architect and planner, and as the president of the Chicago Park Board responsible for the reorganization, the soft-surface playlots, and the establishment of the research and planning group so ably headed by Ed Uhlir and his fine staff. You also know that during that time all of us moved the Air Show, worked with Ed Schulman, Commissioner [William] Bartholomay, and the community for the best small urban park in Chicago (Schulman Playground in Seneca Park), began the revitalization of the regional parks, and with Friends of the Parks and groups like SOAR assisted the Chicago Park District in looking ahead and evaluating the future.

You also know me as straightforward, even controversial, when necessary. By giving you my thoughts, I hope to form a framework for this forum and subsequent actions. I know that these thoughts will not please all, but I ask each of you to look five years into the future. I also, in expressing these thoughts, have questions for the trustees of the MCA, who I count as my friends and fellow collectors of modern art. I, with Mrs. [Walter] Paepke and John Entenza, became the first "outside" trustees of the MCA during its exciting beginnings, and wish the best for the MCA in this opportunity.

We need to expand our imaginations, for we have many opportunities — a fine restaurant overlooking the lake and the park, a model yacht basin where children (and adults) can rent sailboats, special traveling food carts, etc. But whatever is done, we can design a park that looks for the sun and accommodates strollers and joggers, families and visitors to this new center.

I hope to make the next meeting. Lake Shore Park and the MCA can create a gem for the Magnificent Mile and the Streeterville community.

The Cadet Chapel (1996)

Remarks on accepting the AIA Twenty-Five-Year Award for the U.S. Air Force Academy
Cadet Chapel at the Accent on Architecture 1996 gala, Washington, D.C., January 30, 1996.

Madam Secretary, Supreme Court Justice Stephen Breyer, members of the Architectural Foundation, officers and members of the AIA and guests: This evening, Accent on Architecture 1996, is celebrating the Twenty-Five-Year Award for the Air Force Academy Chapel. I would like to go back to 1962 when SOM won its first firm award and the chapel was the last building to be completed for the original Air Force Academy corps size of 2,640 cadets. To go back is to remind us of the character of modern architecture created then by SOM. For without that body of work, this evening would not be; SOM would not have had the commission for the Academy and the overall design for the Academy. The chapel in particular would not have happened without the principals in the firm at that time, the design principles at that time, and the times themselves.

The victory of World War II was not alone on the battlefield. Our brilliance of invention, academic participation, industrial might, and overwhelming belief in a just cause gave unbelievable impetus to all of us to make the needs of the postwar period reflect the same enthusiasm.

In architecture and the arts, the infusion of the émigrés from Europe (Gropius, Neutra, Gideion, Aalto, Sert, Mendelsohn, Corbusier, Mies, et al.) gave the aesthetic road map for American modern architecture and architectural education.

The designers in our group made our interpretations of the modern movement as our education and beliefs possessed. We were all spurred on by Nat Owings, who expected SOM to be the best. The historian Henry Russell Hitchcock attributed the aesthetic results to the fact that "fortunately, the looseness of the SOM organization, the importance of designers in its hierarchy, and the inclusion of engineers in the firm have encouraged a greater degree of experimentation than might have been expected."

Needless to say, this accent on design by the firm had its internal tumult, and the chapel was a prize example. Architectural change, as no other art form, is so interdependent on culture, on technology, on human response, and on designer dedication, and therefore so dependent on the times.

In the post–World War II years, the building industry was waiting, hungry for new ideas and products, on extending the available but unused technology. And we as designers were only too willing to participate, as we saw this component as the American addition to the modern movement born in Europe.

My crisis then was not to try to duplicate the impossible, not just to recreate but to invent in modern terms the third Service Academy place of worship. The design would not have happened without the character of the site, without the character of the buildings and site plan already under construction, without Dan Kiley's landscape and gardens, and without the support first and foremost of Nat Owings and Gordon Bunshaft, and then Eero Saarinen and Pietro Belluschi of the Air Force Secretary's Consultant team.

Chicago and Architecture (2002)

Remarks on accepting the Daniel H. Burnham History Maker Award for Distinction in Architecture and Design at the Making History Awards, Chicago Historical Society (now Chicago History Museum), May 9, 2002.

I want to thank Chicago for giving all of us a physical environment that gives every Chicago architect a gift, a dowry, a challenge to see and enjoy, some to love. For me it started with the Kenna Apartments by a staff member of Frank Lloyd Wright. This modern building of 1916, 2214 East 69th Street, taught me modernism, form, and geometry at the age of 11.

Now the search just grew — the Chicago bungalow, the Robie House, the Chicago parks, the first and second Leiter buildings, the Reliance Building, the Auditorium Building, the Singer, the downtown Chicago School buildings — both here still and gone, Oak Park, 860–880, the Fountain of Time, the Japanese Gardens of 1893, the past, the present, and the future.

I often say, "Look, see, enjoy, and love." It's a long way from looking to loving, but it's worth the effort. Enjoy the buildings and parks that make Chicago, and form your own loving list.

2060 (2006)

Introduction, 2060: A Theory for an Environment and for the Future *[unpublished].*

The more I read and see about global warming and energy costs, the more I am convinced that the current living environment is too expensive, too dependent on the automobile, buses, and trains, and too expensive for security. It is goal-less for much of the population and requires new educational standards.

All the money on streets, sidewalks, lighting, and security, with fences and walls for privacy, and a government structure far from democratic. Costs can be reused in a new way because the rise of a social technology is now available.

I can see the land more valuable for food and recreation — new industries for 365-day production for fruits and vegetables and even substitutes for meat. The 2060 mind still wants sports, culture, and education, but on an immediately available time so that Center City will contain a 2060 Center with events worldwide convening at the same time. Of course, it also will be available for personal use. Issues of health, advanced education. Birth rates will be redefined.

It may seem foolish to students, but with 1920 as my birth date, I see the rise of the auto and its form giving in urban design. The rise of the labor movement to counter management, social legislation to try to equalize the playing field, cultural changes with the maturation of man, and more and more.

I use words and rectangles for shopping, for those are useless to predict except for availability. I do see the Center City as a social and electronic center and a major job market. In a way, my master plan at UIC was a modern Greek or Roman model, not a medieval model, and certainly not Renaissance. This time, technology can be a social force — with natural conservation and modern energy, we can have as modern a model as we had in the new world.

Center City Thoughts

I have two attitudes. The first is an enclosed manor form including housing and local parks. The other is a central park with the cultural activities and satellite housing. I am working on the first because it gives me an urban focus for living, and enclosures for large audiences are not that beautiful in a cluster — and besides, with the natural environment community scale, there still is an opportunity for an urban all-weather design. This is the form I must first tackle with a park as the axis. In the procession to large public spaces, my image is a form not of but from Paris — a leisurely walk to shopping and dining and major events.

Personal gardens here would be communal and probably personal-needs-oriented in a high-tech manner as the civic activities would dominate. I am hoping for at least two overlapping fields and new living forms. Perhaps the manor house form could coexist.

Northwestern University Library (2006)

Remarks at the opening of the Walter Netsch and the Northwestern University Library *exhibition, Northwestern University, Evanston, Illinois, March 1, 2006.*

The design and programming of Northwestern University Library was one of the most satisfying experiences of my professional life. Professor Clarence Ver Steeg assembled a brilliant team of colleagues for the original planning committee — a historian, an economist, an author, and a much-admired humanities professor. They came with one goal — how to bring the discipline, the student, and the books together as though each reader had a library of his own. Each discipline would have a home with unique book shelving to aid in searching, surrounded by carrels looking out on the enlarged campus. The committee also began a computer option for searching that would enlarge availability.

This sounds easy to resolve, but each idea had to be defined and defended for each discipline, and the committee developed the concept and added a separate available undergraduate research collection within the library.

It was a devoted activity, and I thought up some bizarre solutions, but the buildings you see are the result.

When library staff members came to me with an already assembled concept of an exhibit, history of my work, and a bibliography, I of course accepted and donated to the library three complete plans of the original library — beautiful, hand-drawn plans, drawn before the days of the computer.

Bibliography

Primary Sources

All primary sources are by Walter Netsch unless otherwise noted.

1943

"Characteristics of the House As Determined by Space-Use and Its Application to Storage." B. Arch. thesis. Massachusetts Institute of Technology. 37 pp.

Netsch's fifth-year undergraduate thesis examines the growth and change of residences in relation to family size and storage needs. His theory was that as families grew, different types of storage units evolved that changed enclosed and open spaces, thus reshaping the volume of the typical domestic family home. Copy in Institute Archives, MIT Libraries.

1954

"Programming the U.S. Naval Postgraduate School of Engineering, Monterey." *Architectural Record* **115, no. 6 (June 1954): 150–57. 11 illustrations, 7 plans, 1 map, 2 charts.**

Netsch discusses the development of the design program for the U.S. Naval Postgraduate School in Monterey, California, for which he was associate partner in charge of design, representing Skidmore, Owings & Merrill (SOM). The design program was created by considering faculty needs and the course catalog, which were used to determine the amount of time spent by students and faculty in different types of facilities and the technical requirements of each department. Based upon their analysis of this information, the design team devised a schematic plan involving a multistory laboratory sciences building; two-story buildings for electrical engineering, mechanical engineering, and aeronautical engineering; a building for classrooms and offices; and an auditorium.

The article includes schematics, design drawings of buildings, and simple floor plans. Reprinted in part in Statements, pages 99–101.

1957

"Die Hochschulanlage der Air Force Academy, Colorado Springs, Colorado: Die Entwicklung eines Gesamtplans." *Bauen + Wohnen* **11, no. 4 (April 1957): 124–28. 3 illustrations, 9 plans, 3 maps.**

Overview of the design of the U.S. Air Force Academy that details programming of the project, site topography, preparation, and development of the master plan. Illustrations, maps, and photographs show the Academy's location, models and elevations of buildings, the chapel surrounded by the Court of Honor, and other buildings. Text by Netsch covers approximately two pages.

Bauen + Wohnen was published in Zurich (1946–47) and Munich (1947–81).

1958

"Objectives in Design Problems." *Journal of Architectural Education* **13, no. 2 (Autumn 1958): 44–46.**

Printed text of a presentation at "The Teaching of Architecture" seminar, sponsored by the Association of Collegiate Schools of Architecture and the American Institute of Architects (AIA). Netsch enumerates eight touchstones for a high-quality architectural education and advocates for lifelong learning. Proposes adding a year to an architect's training toward a professional degree in architecture. According to Netsch, the sixth year "would increase the opportunity to begin the professional phase of education with better prepared and more motivated students" (p. 45). Concludes with a plea for environmentally conscious architecture and criticizes licensing exams that support single solutions that ignore environmental concerns. "Architects have evidently not accepted their responsibility for our physical environment … the opportunity exists for greater fulfillment of the society which must inhabit this environment" (p. 46).

Reprinted in part in Statements, page 101.

1959

"What Architecture Is and Is Not." Convocation address, Grinnell College, Grinnell, IA, October 17, 1959. Typescript. 8 pp.

In this address Netsch emphasizes human components of architecture:

> *I think architecture in all civilizations has been the environmental structure arising out of human need, and utilizing the materials and techniques of the particular era. Today, the multiplicity of human needs, materials, and techniques provides an infinite variety of spatial opportunities. The search for unity in this variety, the search for the nuances of need, and the search for visual order are the primary elements of today's total modern architecture.*

Netsch also discusses individual buildings, such as the Woolworth Building, the Reliance Building, the Guaranty Building (Buffalo), the Seagram Building, the S. C. Johnson and Co. Administration Building, the Robie House, Unité d'habitation, Notre-Dame-du-Haut at Ronchamp, as well as his own Burling Library for Grinnell College. Copy in Grinnell College Archives.

Reprinted in part in Statements, pages 102–03.

1960

"On Political-Economic Horizons." *American Institute of Architects Journal* 66 (June 1960): 82–84.

Text of remarks made at the conclusion of a presentation to an AIA convention in San Francisco by C. Northcote Parkinson (1909–93), the English historian and political scientist famous for satires of bureaucratic institutions, notably *Parkinson's Law and Other Studies in Administration* (1957). Netsch relates Parkinson's remarks to urban life and design by examining societal trends such as greater mobility, longer life spans, more free time and recreation, and accelerated concepts of time, space, and knowledge.

He urges architects in the audience to be open and to explore opportunities to address changing patterns in basic human needs:

> *As architects we should: 1) Intensify our critical values for a personal philosophy. 2) Recognize through personal research the opportunities available through science and technology to give new solutions to human shelter. 3) Recognize that basic research in our field is a requirement now if we are to maintain a mature environment for future civilization.*
> (pp. 83–84)

A caricature of Netsch standing beside two seated speakers (likely Parkinson and Robert E. Alexander) appears in the article.

Reprinted in part in Statements, pages 103–04.

1964

"Background Paper: Educational Concept of Northwestern University's New 'Laboratory' Library." Evanston, IL: Northwestern University, May 1964. 2 pp.

In 1962 Netsch was selected to design a new library for Northwestern University. His design, created in consultation with members of the faculty and staff, had seven major objectives, according to this document:

> To relate the individual to the specialized purposes of the library.
>
> To extend the visual environment possibilities of the book collection.
>
> To reuse and integrate the existing library.
>
> To develop form and scale consistent with the existing campus structures.
>
> To develop a design incorporating the more formal demands of a structure of this size with geometric possibilities of orthogonal and radial patterns and express the different reader-to-book relationships.
>
> To consider the problems of maintenance and economy.
>
> To consider possible future changes in library use.

In the report Netsch summarized his design as follows:

> The new library is therefore conceived as three connecting research pavilions above the unusually large ground floor reference and staff areas. The pavilions permit access from all directions from the campus and provide an intimate, private, single reader–book relation and an architectural scale relating to the existing campus structure.

Copy in University Archives, Northwestern University.

1966

"University of Illinois at Chicago Circle — Revisited." In *Architecture and the College: Proceedings of North American Conference to Consider the Critical Issues in Campus Planning and College Building Design, April 17–21, 1966*, 84–93. Urbana, IL: University of Illinois, Urbana, 1966.

Text of Netsch's presentation about designing the University of Illinois Circle Campus (UIC) in Chicago. Discusses the history of its conception, phase I criteria and designs, and the 27 early schemes the design team created. Details problems of designing an undergraduate campus for 20,000 students on an urban site confined to 106 acres adjacent to slums. Explains elements of the project's final model, including overall layout, walkways, buildings, lecture halls, classrooms, laboratories, and offices. Refers to slides, diagrams, charts, and documents shown during the presentation. Moves to phase II of the design process, which was under way in 1966, and envisions plans for further expansion. Demonstrates Netsch's concept of Field Theory and shows how it begins with central, core designs that rotate out into surrounding areas, including into the greater urban environment.

Reprinted in part in Statements, pages 104–06.

"The Philosophy." In "Comprehensive Building Systems: Threat or Promise?" Special issue, *Building Research* 3, no. 5 (September–October 1966): 8–11.

Netsch's essay — a philosophical discourse on structuralism and systems theory in contemporary architecture — begins with an outline of building systems and evolves into an introduction and evaluation of an environmental planning strategy. Netsch closes with a utopian consideration of the future of urban systems. The essay is the introduction to a 10-part exploration of the individual architect's role in comprehensive building systems by 10 different authors (mostly architects) that makes up the entire issue.

Reprinted in part in Statements, pages 106–08.

1967

"Architecture." In "Impact '67: The University of Illinois after 100 Years." Special supplement, *Chicago Tribune*, February 26, 1967, R40. 1 photograph.

Netsch comments on the design program of the UIC campus and touches on building techniques and materials, air-conditioning, window glass, walkways, and landscaping. He concludes by saying, "Chicago Circle is a forerunner of many other campuses throughout the world. It is, therefore, an early full-scale urban model that can aid in future models…. But the campus is more than a model for an academic institution: it is a microcosm of issues and answers for a new urban environment." The article includes a photograph of an upper-level walkway to the library at UIC.

1974

"EE-RLE Fairchild Building at MIT, Cambridge, Massachusetts." *Design Quarterly*, nos. 90–91 (1974): 60–61. 2 illustrations, 1 plan.

Netsch discusses his Sherman Fairchild Electrical Engineering and Electronics Complex of the Research Laboratory of Electronics. His design differentiates between highly specialized technical spaces and more public areas like staircases, hallways, and classrooms. The facility allows the electrical engineering program to be housed in a single building and allows a reorientation of undergraduate teaching toward a more personalized approach. He concludes:

> Yet in many ways such a world as MIT represents the continuum of change, the domination of content over form. The conflict between aesthetics and utility, and the awareness of institutional and technological change, controls the concept of the environment as a working and educational tool. (p. 61)

1976

Parker, Alfred Browning, Walter A. Netsch, and Gordon Bunshaft. "Proposal to Office of County Manager, Metropolitan Dade County, for the Urban Library–Museum Complex, Metropolitan Dade County, Dade, Florida." Chicago: Skidmore, Owings & Merrill, 1976. Unpaged.

1978

"Postmodernism in Context." In "The Search for a Postmodern Architecture." Special issue, *CRIT*, no. 4 (Fall 1978): 17.

Here Netsch discusses the revolutionary underpinnings of some postmodernist architectural theories, suggesting that, in practice, postmodernist works "flaw theory." He maintains that the philosophical motives behind the movement provide little guidance in practice and that architects should pursue their own individual ideas rather than those of a movement. He concludes, "I prefer a more personal way, or as Lou Kahn would say, 'the existence-will.' The reality of commitment for the architect or the artist must always be the lonely individual pursuit of idea; for each of us it should be different — both the pursuit and the idea." Other architects who address similar topics in the issue include Gordon Bunshaft, Serge Chermaneff, Bertrand Goldberg, I. M. Pei, and Paul Rudolph.

Reprinted in part in Statements, pages 109–10.

1979

"Creativity: A Personal View." In *Perspectives on Creativity and the Unconscious: Proceedings of the Jungian Conference, Miami University, Oxford, Ohio,* **edited by Donald W. Fritz, 9–37. Oxford, OH: Old Northwest Publications, 1979.**

Text of an address delivered June 2–4, 1979. Netsch concentrates on the development of Field Theory aesthetics, beginning with its early manifestations in the U.S. Air Force Academy and continuing to the UIC campus. He defines architecture as a "semi-solitary art" and explains that a new synthesis comes to the individual architect alone. Netsch describes working on Field Theory designs at SOM and credits several architects on his team with helping him to discover and refine the theory. He also cites the importance of problem solving, conflicts, and opportunities in advancing and nurturing creativity.

Other speakers included psychoanalyst Silvano Arieti, artist and critic Walter Darby Bannard, lexicographer Richard Howard, and Jungian analyst June Singer.

Reprinted in part in Statements, pages 110–15.

"Designing in the Third World: Work in Algeria." George A. Miller Lecture, Center for Advanced Study, University of Illinois at Urbana-Champaign, March 27, 1980. Unpaged.

Text of Netsch's lecture that pays tribute to Louis Sullivan, Frank Lloyd Wright, and Le Corbusier. Presents Netsch's involvement with the U.S. Air Force Academy, his computer-generated design for *Late Entries to the Chicago Tribune Tower Competition,* and Field Theory designs for Sophia University Library in Tokyo. Opens: "If I have a guardian, it is Louis Sullivan, who gave the transcendental war cry for effort, faith,

and conviction. Wright, the iconoclast, was every student's secret friend, for he espoused Sullivan, fought the system, and argued for a native architecture."

Reprinted in Statements, pages 115–16.

1980

"Case Study: The University of Blida in Algeria." In *Places of Public Gathering in Islam: Proceedings of Seminar Five in the Series Architectural Transformations in the Islamic World, Held in Amman, Jordan, May 4–7, 1980,* **edited by Linda Safran, 29–37. Philadelphia: Aga Khan Award for Architecture, 1980. 9 illustrations, 5 plans.**

Text of Netsch's address summarizing the basic nature of shelter and its relationship to technology and available building materials. He mentions SOM projects in Algeria and other Muslim countries and emphasizes the firm's sensitivity to cultural interpretations. He defines Field Theory as a "contemporary search for proportional patterns, scales, and forms that can be logically incorporated into shelter. These forms are abstract and highly personal, but they are still responses to the culture and society in which they exist" (p. 30).

Netsch concentrates on the development of designs for the University of Blida complex and cultural differences in designing for universities in the United States and Europe. He says three major factors informed Blida's design: 1) reflecting the goals and aspirations of Algeria; 2) incorporation of Islam's rich heritage and history; and 3) modern yet affordable facilities, in recognition of the nation's goals for improvements to housing, industry, health care, and education. SOM's commission included the creation of not only a comprehensive master plan and design for individual facilities but also the academic program, curriculum design, and selection of major equipment. Netsch explains SOM's solutions to various design challenges and opportunities to apply Field Theory geometry to Muslim culture. Includes photographs of the model site plan, drawings and diagrams of various buildings, and floor plans for the Teaching Hospital, a decidedly Field Theory conception.

Netsch's presentation was the first of five in the seminar's "Educational Buildings" session.

1984

"Remembering Nat Owings." *Inland Architect* **28, no. 5 (September–October 1984): 9. 1 illustration.**
Part of a tribute to Nathaniel A. Owings, a founding partner of SOM and Netsch's mentor and advocate, published shortly after Owings's death on June 13, 1984. Netsch writes:

It is difficult for me to write about Nat, for despite his foibles, he gave me my first opportunity and ended up my friend.

I have known Nat since 1947, so there are many Nats in my memory. During these recent years, I moved from protégé to friend, and Nat from boss to confrere, from partner to national conscience for architects.

Nat was always mercurial, a tough fighter with major victories in Baltimore, Washington, D.C., and Big Sur — victories always won others, for he was a leader, tenacious and devoted to a cause as he saw it.

In the early days he espoused compromise, a factor that would send me back to the boards to do a whole new solution. He developed a sense of loyalty for his stands on planning and design, perhaps because he gave all young designers a chance. He had no competitive ego, but fed your ego to make you do your best.

After I left SOM, we still shared the issue of Pennsylvania Avenue and the Mall. His devotion to the environment, built and unbuilt, continued to the end.

In the beginning, Nat was the dominant partner/leader, the primary force of SOM. But for me, finally, he was a beloved and trusted friend.

Netsch, Walter, and Lawrence B. Anderson. "Conversation between Lawrence B. Anderson and Walter Netsch, Lois Craig Attending." Chicago, 1984. Typescript, 30 pp.
Transcript of a candid conversation on April 7, 1984, at Netsch's Chicago residence. Anderson was one of Netsch's favorite professors at MIT, and the conversation begins with Netsch's decision in 1939 to study architecture there. He credits MIT — and Anderson's tutelage in particular — with preparing him for his career: "My training allowed me to be a maverick architect all my life. You allowed me to be a maverick student. That was one of the delights of your teaching; you didn't make all of us in your image" (p. 6).

Netsch recounts his early years with SOM, including projects in Oak Ridge, Tennessee, San Francisco, and Japan, before transferring to the Chicago office in 1954. He discusses programming the designs for the U.S. Naval Postgraduate School and the U.S. Air Force Academy; the Cadet Chapel receives considerable attention (pp. 19–23). Netsch then moves on to his SOM career and design studio in Chicago, conflicts within the firm, the Pruitt-Igoe public housing project in St. Louis, and Netsch's philosophy of architecture and architectural education. Craig, author of *The Federal Presence: Architecture, Politics, and Symbolism in U.S. Government Buildings* (MIT Press, 1978), was also in attendance.

Copy in University Archives, Northwestern University.

1986

Chicago Park District. *Preliminary Reorganization Report.* **Chicago: Chicago Park District, 1986. 157 pp. Illustrated.**

In this plan Netsch lays out his agenda as president of the Board of Commissioners of the Chicago Park District, an office he held from June 1986 through 1987. (Netsch continued as a commissioner until 1989.) In the report preface, he states his mission:

> Since the inception of my responsibilities as President of the Chicago Park District Board, it has become self-evident that the current management system must change if the heritage of the Chicago Parks, the open space living room of all Chicagoans and their guests, is to survive.
>
> This change requires more than a paper shuffle of people. It requires that a deep sense of responsibility and professional ethics be reestablished for the Chicago parks both in depth and character, irrespective of the impact of personnel and politics.
>
> The proposed decentralized organization will solicit and nurture local responsibility, improve park quality through coordinated management, improve recreation through responsive management, and will provide, even at the Commission level, a new depth in professional support to prevent the erosion of purpose: Building the finest park system in the United States.
>
> The subject of this report is professional ethics, continuity and review, central and local management, local community participation, and decentralized organization. (p. 6)

After reviewing results of the reorganization program and enumerating goals and priorities for 1986–87, the report is divided into two parts: the first describes the current organization and host park areas, while the second contains job descriptions and addresses miscellaneous issues, such as playground safety and concessions.

For an overview of Netsch's ambitious program for the Park District, see Nevin Hedlund's article, "Netsch Takes on the Parks," *Inland Architect* 31, no. 1 (January–February 1987): 79–85. Netsch's preface to the report is reprinted in Statements, pages 122–23.

1987

Division of Landscape Architecture, University of Virginia. *Classic Parks — How Can They Live Today?* **Charlottesville, VA: University of Virginia, 1987. 12 pp. 1 illustration.**

Contains the text, with accompanying illustration, of the third annual Benjamin C. Howland Memorial Lecture at the University of Virginia, delivered by Netsch on April 10, 1987. Following introductory remarks by Jaquelin T. Robertson, dean of the School of Architecture, Netsch reviews the history and importance of parks in Chicago and presents the challenges for their future. In his remarks he pays homage to such visionaries as Daniel Burnham, Frederick Law Olmsted, William Le Baron Jenney, Jens Jensen, A. Montgomery Ward, and Alfred Caldwell. He concludes:

> We continue to seek ways to bring people to the lakefront and to the parks in an atmosphere of camaraderie and in beautiful surroundings which have typified our classic parks and which are Chicago's natural and cultural legacy. It is quite possible we can revive Olmsted's methods of creating informal and open spaces, and again combine [them] with formal promenades ... and very formal plantings, as exemplified in Jensen's rose garden, and high technology to rival the beauty of the bridges of the past, and techniques of restoration of the Refectory in Lincoln Park.
>
> These parks of Chicago should again become, like the Chicago skyscrapers, major events in the city scene. The cities — all cities, including Chicago — will only survive

if their parks survive, and only if the missions and responsibilities in the professional areas of landscape architecture and architecture and planning continue to take a positive interest. (p. 12)

Johnson, Al, Mary Decker, and Walter Netsch. *Final Report of Mayor Washington's Stadium Review Committee.* **Chicago: Stadium Review Committee. 1987. 24 pp.**

1996

Netsch, Walter, and Dawn Clark Netsch. "Myron Goldsmith." In *Myron Goldsmith.* **Chicago: Illinois Institute of Technology, 1996. 24.**

A tribute to Goldsmith (1918–96), who taught at the Illinois Institute of Technology (IIT) for 35 years and worked at SOM. The Netsches' contribution reads:

> *Education and architecture, whether at IIT or SOM, were Myron's philosophy and love. His creative talents provided SOM with memorable architectural contributions. His methodology, whether as an architect at SOM or a professor at IIT, imbued his life and work with that special quality that talent gives to few architects — love and integrity, patience, and caring; his work and teaching attest to these qualities.*

1997

"Oral History of Walter Netsch." Interview by Betty J. Blum. May 10, 1985; June 5–28, 1995. Transcript. Chicago: Art Institute of Chicago, 1997. 474 pp.

A rich and remarkable combination of history and memories drawn from interviews conducted over 12 sessions and 24 hours of tape. The transcript — "compiled under the auspices of the Chicago Architects Oral History Project, the Ernest R. Graham Study Center for Architectural Drawings, Department of Architecture, the Art Institute of Chicago" — includes bibliographical references (pp. 464–67) and an index and is available at www.artic.edu/aic /libraries/caohp/netsch.html.

2001

"Walter Netsch Interviewed by Detlef Mertins." By Detlef Mertins. *SOM Journal* **1 (2007): 136–51. 16 illustrations, 14 plans and diagrams.**

A wide-ranging interview conducted on May 21, 2001, at Netsch's residence in Chicago by Mertins, an architectural historian at the University of Toronto. The article summarizes Netsch's life and career, touching on major commissions such as the U.S. Air Force Academy. Netsch explains the development and experimentation of Field Theory and discusses individual contributions by his design team and engineers at SOM as well as working relations and interactions within the firm. He explains reasons behind his early retirement in 1979 and various projects he has been involved with since then. The interview explores the importance of art in his work and life and how he seeks design sources in nature, in particular the gingko leaf and the chrysanthemum. Netsch mentions books and architects who influenced him and why and how he collected art. He cites the Louis Jefferson Long Library at Wells College in Aurora, New York, as his best building. The article includes images of his home, the U.S. Air Force Academy, and assorted Field Theory studies and diagrams.

1947

Goodman, Percival, and Paul Goodman. *Communitas: Means of Livelihood and Ways of Life.* **Chicago: University of Chicago Press, 1947. 141 pp. 11 plans, maps.**

Netsch on *Communitas*:

> *I also had a book that inspired me — this is 1947 — called* Communitas *by Percival and Paul Goodman. Percival Goodman was the architect, and Paul Goodman was the writer and leftist. And this came out of the University of Chicago — part of the leftist bit of the University of Chicago. And it was the idea of a brave new world in which it had a ring of high-rise units. But you see, here is discussed Gropius, and this had Mies and this had Corbu. And Bucky Fuller is in it. So this is part of my being — unlike Gordon [Bunshaft], I read and I bought books.* (Walter Netsch, "Oral History of Walter Netsch," interview by Betty Blum, May 10, 1985; June 5–28, 1995, p. 130)

1948

Horne, Louther S. "Price Cut Doubted by Meat Executive." *New York Times,* **June 14, 1948.**

Quotes Walter Netsch Sr., "Vice President of Armour & Co. in charge of livestock purchasing," regarding consumer demand for price cuts. He explains that Armour is "'very much concerned' with three fundamental problems: high meat prices, declining livestock production, and failure of the per capita meat supply to keep pace with other foods."

1949

"Progressive Architecture Jay-Cee Competition Honorable Mentions and Special Prizes." *Progressive Architecture* **30, no. 9 (September 1949): 62–63.**

Netsch — then of Burleigh, Adams, Netsch & Dinkerloo — listed in "other honorable mentions."

1950

"Skidmore, Owings & Merrill Architects, U.S.A." Special issue, *Bulletin of the Museum of Modern Art* **18, no. 1 (Fall 1950), 20 pp. Illustrated.**

Catalogue of the museum's first exhibition of work by a contemporary architectural firm. The introduction explains:

> *When the Museum invited Skidmore, Owings, and Merrill to exhibit its recent buildings, it did so because this firm, composed of a group of single designers working exclusively in the modern idiom, produces imaginative, serviceable, and sophisticated architecture deserving of special attention. The single designers who function within this organization have no fear of a loss of individuality.* (p. 5)

The catalogue includes descriptions, images, and plans for several projects on which Netsch worked, including Lake Meadows Shopping Center in Chicago (pp. 8–9); Del Monte Shopping Center in Del Monte, California (pp. 14–15); and Garden Apartments in Oak Ridge, Tennessee (pp. 18–19). Sections on Netsch's designs are illustrated by four photos and four plans.

1951

Sanderson, George A. "America's No. 1 Defense Community: Oak Ridge, Tennessee." *Progressive Architecture* 32 (June 1951): 63–84. 37 illustrations, 16 plans.

Traces the history of Oak Ridge and SOM's involvement in it from the town's secret beginning in 1942 as a Manhattan Project research center and its original design for 3,000 families, its expansion into a city with a population of 40,000 to 50,000, and finally its evolution into a permanent city after the end of World War II. SOM's staff of six in 1942 had increased to about 450 by 1944. The master plan, neighborhoods, housing, and schools are profiled.

"Who's News — Management Personnel Notes." *Wall Street Journal*, November 26, 1951.

Announces election of Netsch to associate partnership of the San Francisco office of SOM.

1954

"Bus Maintenance Center." *Progressive Architecture* 35, no. 9 (September 1954): 102–03. 4 illustrations, 1 plan.

Profiles Netsch's Greyhound Service Garage in San Francisco. The maintenance depot is recognized as a new building type made necessary by an increase in bus ridership. The project occupies an entire city block, with a main service area work floor with no columns to obstruct movement of the buses. Netsch is particularly proud of its enormous interior open spans. After extensive renovations, the building later became part of the California College of the Arts.

Gutheim, Frederick. "Washington Perspective." *Progressive Architecture* 35, no. 9 (September 1954): 4.

An editorial concerning the new method of selecting architects for federal projects. The appointment of SOM — in association with Welton Becket, Wallace Harrison, and Eero Saarinen — to design the U.S. Air Force Academy was determined by anonymous architectural selection boards. Gutheim questions whether this process results in the best decisions:

> *The selection board method, as distinguished from other and more traditional forms of competition, makes it more difficult for the man of talent to break through the perimeter of seniority, arbitrary specialization, and precedent. In the name of administrative convenience and a safe political policy, attention is diverted from elusive and often controversial factors of design, and concentrated upon issues which may be relevant to the execution of design but have little to do with its creation or its recognition.*

1955

"Air Academy Design Brawl." *Architectural Forum* 103, no. 2 (August 1955): 9, 13. 4 illustrations.

Charts behind-the-scenes political wranglings regarding design of the U.S. Air Force Academy. Subtitled "Backstage manipulations, strange alliances put [Frank Lloyd] Wright in camp with modern-design foes, commercial lobbyists; except for Legion, Wright may have been designer." Text quotes principal players and includes excerpts from congressional hearings and debates. Notes, "Rare was the subcommittee witness without some motivation beyond architectural design" (p. 13).

Carr, J. R. "The Air Force Academy: A First Report." *Engineering News-Record* 154, no. 18 (May 5, 1955): 21–23. 3 illustrations, 1 map.

Details site preparation for the U.S. Air Force Academy. Earthmoving equipment began clearing the site in early June 1955 for the $125 million project. Gives an overview of the project, basic facilities, airfield construction, appropriations, land acquisition, contracts and procedures, architects, field office, and history of the project to 1949.

"Debate Over Air Force Academy Design Concept?" *Architectural Record* **118, no. 8 (August 1955): 17–18.**
Companion piece to "Air Academy Design Brawl" (above). Reports that construction funds for the U.S. Air Force Academy were rescinded by the House of Representatives until the design was more firmly established. States that professional views from the AIA, the president of the Producer's Council, an architecture professor, and the director of the Society of Architectural Historians support the project, while architect Frank Lloyd Wright protested against the plans.

"Grown Up at Last." *ARTnews* **54, no. 4 (Summer 1955): 23. 1 illustration.**
The buildings for the U. S. Air Force Academy are hailed as a significant moment in American history, the first important example of architecture of the 1950s erected by the federal government within the United States.

"The Navy's Graduate Engineering School at the U.S. Naval Postgraduate School, Monterey, California." *Architectural Record* **117, no. 4 (April 1955): 159–71. 30 illustrations, 14 plans.**
Describes the U.S. Naval Postgraduate School designed by SOM, mainly through pictures and plans. Netsch was associate partner in charge of design for the project. The article discusses the considerations of space, interdepartmental relationships, budget, and site considerations in programming the project. It also describes and illustrates the campus's six buildings.

"19 Office Floors without Columns." *Architectural Forum* **102, no. 5 (May 1955): 114–18. 4 illustrations, 6 plans.**
Reviews the plans for the Inland Steel Building, the first major building to be constructed in Chicago's Loop since the Field Building in 1934. Designed by a team of architects, beginning with Walter Netsch and completed by Bruce Graham, the Inland Steel Building constitutes the "longest clear spans of any tall building ever built" by isolating utilities into a windowless annex tower and moving all columns to the exterior of the building. Compares the design to SOM's Lever House in New York City and comments briefly on the Inland Steel Building's unique structural elements.

Sanderson, George A. "Air Academy: U.S. Air Force Exhibits Plans at Colorado Springs." *Progressive Architecture* **36, no. 6 (June 1955): 89–92. 7 illustrations, 1 plan.**
The author attended the ceremony and exhibit at which the U.S. Air Force Academy models and plans were first displayed. The grandeur of the site clearly impressed the author, who describes in detail its landscape. Discussion of the buildings is minimal.

"The United States Air Force Academy." *Architectural Forum* **102, no. 6 (June 1955): 100–09. 8 illustrations, 10 plans and maps.**
Provides an overview of plans for the U.S. Air Force Academy, which is described as "the first U.S. national shrine to be designed in the modern style." Architects at SOM, having spent only eight months on the project, present no complete design at this point. Nat Owings explains that the designers "were attempting an architecture with a national, not a regional character, the direct simple way of life, as styleless as the most modern guided missile … timeless" (p. 102). Buildings in the cadet area, the airfield, housing, and the town of Colorado Springs are profiled with plans.

"United States Air Force Academy, El Paso County, Colorado." *Architectural Record* 117, no. 6 (June 1955): 172 (triple-fold sheet). 9 illustrations, 1 plan.

Covers the planning stages of the U.S. Air Force Academy. A special exhibition and tour of the site were arranged by the Air Force for members of Congress, the press, and invited individuals. Project drawings and four models of the site, each measuring 10 x 15 feet, provided a sense of the conceptual scheme. The chapel design is "still under study," conceived as a "space frame of thin strips of aluminum filled with narrow slabs of marble, giving the facade something of a mosaic affect [sic]."

"What Kind of Criticism Has Congress Heeded in the Debate over Air Force Academy Design Concept?" *Architectural Record* 118, no. 8 (August 1955): 16, 304, 308, 314, 318.

Reprints the remarks of Rep. John E. Fogarty (D-Rhode Island) to the U.S. House of Representatives on June 20, 1955. Fogarty protests the design of the new Air Force Academy and calls for Congress to halt progress on the present plans. The presentation of plans and models caused "considerable consternation," according to Fogarty. He also notes that "a spontaneous protest by churchmen throughout the Nation caused the Air Force to withdraw almost immediately the design for the Chapel" (p. 16). Frank Lloyd Wright is quoted as saying that if the Air Force Academy is built as planned, it would be known "not as the national shrine it should and must be — but as Talbott's aviary and a factory for birdmen" (p. 16) — reference to Secretary of the Air Force Harold Talbott. Fogarty considers the design un-American in conception, unworthy of the tradition of the nation, and a burden to maintain.

1956

"Final Schematics for Air Force Academy." *Architectural Record* 120, no. 7 (July 1956): 192–96. 4 illustrations, 5 plans.

Final plans for the academic area of the U.S. Air Force Academy are discussed in this article. The "much-argued" Cadet Chapel is established in size and location only. The academic building and library are also examined.

"Glass Tower Planned for San Francisco." *Progressive Architecture* 37, no. 6 (June 1956): 93. 1 illustrations, 1 map.

Brief announcement of the 22-story headquarters of the Crown-Zellerbach Corporation, a paper manufacturer, located on the corner of Market and Bush Streets in San Francisco. Netsch designed the preliminary concept drawings, often called "the West Coast Lever House." The 320,000 square-foot building was completed by Charles Bassett in 1959.

"Section technique de l'Ecole Navale des U.S.A. à Monterey." *L'Architecture d'aujourd'hui* 27, no. 67–68 (October 1956): 36–41. 15 illustrations, 16 plans.

Comprehensive, detailed overview of exteriors, interiors, floor plans, and elevations of the main buildings and campus of the U.S. Naval Postgraduate School, with lengthy captions.

Credits Netsch along with SOM architects M. Alexander, W. E. Dunlap, and I. Montgomery and engineers D. Fitzroy, Gannon, Keller, Ch. M. Lee, and I. Thompson with the school's design and engineering.

"The U.S. Air Force Academy, El Paso County, Colorado." *Architectural Record* 119, no. 3 (March 1956): 163–66. 7 illustrations.

Presents the first photographs of the revised design of the U.S. Air Force Academy. Side-by-side comparisons of the original and revised plans show little change in the basic plan, except for a reduction in the use of glass throughout.

1957

"Academy Design Director to Talk to Stockholders." *Colorado Springs Gazette-Telegraph*, September 30, 1957.

Short announcement of Netsch's address to the Colorado Springs Chamber of Commerce on October 8, 1957.

"Academy Designed to Fit Site, Says Local Architect." *Colorado Springs Gazette-Telegraph*, September 14, 1957.

Positive article on the U.S. Air Force Academy site that quotes supportive statements from leading architects such as Eero Saarinen.

"Air Academy Chapel May Look like 'Row of Tepees' After All." *Colorado Springs Free Press*, March 20, 1957.

Short reaction to design plans for the Cadet Chapel on exhibit in *Buildings for Business and Government* at the Museum of Modern Art, New York.

"Air Academy Chapel: New Design, Old Controversy." *Architectural Record* 122, no. 3 (September 1957): 9–12. 7 illustrations, 2 plans.

The new design for the U.S. Air Force Academy Cadet Chapel is discussed, along with a review of the Congressional debate that preceded the approval of $3 million in funds for the chapel. Materials, square footage, and building dimensions are noted, and images of the original and redesigned models are compared.

"Auditorium in Monterey, Kalifornien." *Bauen + Wohnen* 11, no. 4 (April 1957): 134–35. 7 illustrations.

Highlights the auditorium of the U.S. Naval Postgraduate School. Photographs, floor plans, and elevations show the completed complex (exterior and interior), classrooms, the ground floor, and an exterior view of the auditorium, with the Laboratory Sciences Building in the background.

Brown, Andrew J., and Wayne Teng. "How Foundations for the Air Force Academy Were Designed." *Engineering News-Record* 158, no. 16 (April 18, 1957): 50–52, 56. 5 illustrations, 1 diagram.

Technical article on engineering and design of foundations for the U.S. Air Force Academy buildings. Explains various tests and wall reinforcements. Teng was SOM's assistant chief structural engineer for the project.

"Chapel–Air Force Academy." *Engineering News off the Record* (December 1957): 1–2. 2 illustrations.

Announces Netsch's address to the Chicago Engineers Club on December 10, 1957. Includes a photo of a model of the Cadet Chapel and a short biography of Netsch.

"Chapel of the Air." *Architectural Forum* 107, no. 3 (September 1957): 136–37. 1 illustration, 2 plans.

Color preview of the U.S. Air Force Academy Cadet Chapel, designed by Netsch in 1956–57. Includes a full-page color photo of the model, a floor plan, and an elevation.

Favre, George H. "Clergymen Back Air Chapel Design." *Christian Science Monitor*, November 9, 1957.

Records comments by clergy who visited a small exhibition of drawings, designs, plans, and models for Netsch's U.S. Air Force Academy Cadet Chapel, on display in the main foyer of the administrative building at MIT. Quotes Pietro Belluschi, dean of MIT's School of Architecture, as saying it is a "brilliant solution of a very difficult subject." Clergymen who viewed the designs favorably included Rabbi Aryeh Lev, the Very Rev. Darby W. Betts, the Very Rev. Joseph Marbach, and the Rev. Edward Fry, among others. Includes a front-page photo of the Chapel's design.

Giedion, S[igfried]. "Das Experiment SOM = L'Experience SOM = The Experiment of SOM." *Bauen + Wohnen* **11, no. 4 (April 1957): 109–14. 11 illustrations. In German, French, and English.**

Introductory article of an issue devoted to SOM and featuring partners and major projects. Describes various design teams:

> Small groups of architects work together so that both individual design and large-scale planning can coincide within one organization. The herbarium of styles is replaced by living people, each with the responsibilities of artistic freedom.... It is characteristic of current problems that they tend to expand beyond the confines of architecture. Walter Netsch, who is about thirty-five, is currently involved in designing not only the individual academic buildings for the large program for the Air Force Academy, but also the community supported by it, and the entire surrounding terrain. (p. 114)

Photograph of members of the "Air Force Academy Design Group" studying a site model on p. 111.

Guevrekian, Gabriel. "Jeunes architectes aux Etats-Unis." *L'Architecture d'aujourd'hui,* **no. 73 (September 1957): 80–83. 10 illustrations, 4 plans.**

Part of an issue largely devoted to discussing prominent young American architects, this four-page section on Netsch includes illustrations of a model of the Inland Steel Building, a model of the U.S. Air Force Academy, and photos of the U.S. Naval Postgraduate School. The profile suggests that Netsch is one of the young American architects who benefits from working under the auspices of a large firm.

"Inland Steel Builds a New Home." *Engineering News-Record* **158, no. 2 (January 10, 1957): 43–48. 6 illustrations, 2 diagrams.**

Feature on the Inland Steel Building. Netsch designed the initial concept and model in 1954, and the project was completed by Bruce Graham. Discusses construction details and procedures, as well as innovative features such as "complete air conditioning."

Kaufmann, Edgar Jr. "The Inland Steel Building and Its Art." *Art in America* **45, no. 4 (Winter 1957–58): 22–27. 6 illustrations, 1 map.**

Previews the Inland Steel Building and its art collection. "American sculptors Richard Lippold and Seymour Lipton were commissioned to do major works for important spaces, and two dozen paintings and smaller sculptural pieces were individually selected and acquired as part of a splendid program for equipping the interiors" (pp. 22–23). Photos show works by Lipton, Georgia O'Keeffe, Niles Spencer, and Fred Farr. Credit for the collection goes to Mr. and Mrs. Leigh B. Block. Leigh Block was a senior vice president at Inland Steel, and the Blocks were ardent collectors who in 1980 endowed the Mary and Leigh Block Gallery (later Museum of Art) at Northwestern University. Of the building, for which Netsch designed the original model, Kaufmann writes: "The Inland Steel Building is a triumph; a number of its features go beyond the best practice of the day" (p. 25).

Museum of Modern Art. *Buildings for Business and Government.* **New York: Museum of Modern Art, 1957. 36 pp. Illustrated.**

This exhibition catalogue includes reproductions of four plans for the U.S. Air Force Academy (pp. 12–15).

"Perspectives: Air Force Chapel: Professional Opinion." *Architectural Record* 122, no. 12 (December 1957): 9, 266, 272, 278. 1 illustration.

This article compiles quotes from notable architects, critics, writers, and architectural historians about the U.S. Air Force Academy Cadet Chapel. Project consultants Welton Becket and Roy F. Larson along with several others support the chapel. Becket observes, "Architecture should harmonize, if possible, with geographic surroundings and the pinnacles symbolize architecturally the sharp mountains which serve as the Academy's backdrop" (p. 9).

"Projekt einer Siedlung innerhalb der Air Force Academy." *Bauen + Wohnen* 11, no. 4 (April 1957): 129–30. 3 illustrations, 2 plans.

Publishes and critiques designs for officer and cadet housing at the U.S. Air Force Academy. Illustrations show floor plans and photos of models of neighborhoods, "court houses," and cadet quarters (exterior and interior).

"United States Air Force Academy." *Engineering News off the Record* (May 1957): 1–2. 2 illustrations.

Short feature on the U.S. Air Force Academy commission. A sidebar, "Air Force Academy Colorado Springs Luncheon," includes a photo and biography of Netsch, who addressed the Chicago Engineers Club (the publisher of the newsletter) on April 21, 1957.

"Verwaltungsgebäude der Inland Steel Company in Chicago." *Bauen + Wohnen* 11, no. 4 (April 1957): 118. 1 illustration, 1 plan.

Photograph of the Inland Steel Building under construction, with a floor plan that identifies rooms, elevators, utilities, garages, and other spaces on the ground floor and in a typical layout.

1958

"Accent on the Vertical: The Inland Steel Building." *Inland Architect* (March 1958): 7–10. 7 illustrations, 2 plans and diagrams.

Concentrates on the Inland Steel Building's unique design and engineering features. Also describes interior spaces and color schemes. The building was Chicago's first air-conditioned office building.

"The Architects from 'Skid's Row.'" Pt. 1. *Fortune* 57, (January 1958): 137–40, 210, 215. 14 illustrations.

This profile of SOM focuses on the unique financial aspects of the firm. Its four regional offices operate autonomously in their own areas but have the ability to join forces when needed for national or international projects. The firm's distinctive structure — by which a board of general partners divide the workload — is unlike many architectural firms. The formula to expand the base of partnership is a variation of one widely used by law firms and is nearly unheard of in the architecture world. A substantial account of Louis Skidmore, Nathaniel Owings, John O. Merrill, and the creation of the firm is included along with an overview of its accomplishments and noted buildings. Netsch is recognized as a design partner who heads a group of young architects doing design work. His contribution to the U.S. Air Force Academy is also noted.

Brown, Andrew J., and Wayne Teng. "Jacks on Columns Erect Two-Acre Roof at AF Academy." *Engineering News-Record* 160, no. 4 (January 23, 1958): 26–28. 5 illustrations, 1 diagram.

Explains equipment and techniques used in raising precast concrete floors by the lift-slab method for the Cadet Dining Hall roof. The entire 308-square-foot, 1,150-ton V roof is supported by only 16 columns. Lifting frames were set under the roof trusses, and hydraulic jacks raised the trusses in two stages. The roof framing was assembled and welded at ground level.

Bush-Brown, Albert. "Aloft with the Landless Gull." *Journal of Architectural Education* **13, no. 2 (Autumn 1958): 5–11.**

Report on the third annual seminar on the teaching of architecture, held on Nantucket Island in summer 1958. Summarizes conference proceedings, events, speakers' presentations, and significant ideas and trends in architectural education. The seminar was sponsored by the AIA and the Graham Foundation for Advanced Studies in the Fine Arts in Chicago. The author found Netsch's presentation one of the most impressive:

> *Those who think of Skidmore, Owings & Merrill as 'The Three Blind Mies' will surely be caught short by the leadership displayed by a principal designer in that firm, Walter Netsch, whose quiet, almost buried, remark embraced the theme of the whole Nantucket conference: The aim of architectural education, he said, is to nurture intuitive judgment, sharpen visual perception, and encourage a will to understand and improve the society in which we live — through architecture.* (p. 5)

For other references to Netsch's presentation, including his work on the Illinois Board of Architectural Registration licensing exam, see page 10.

Darby, Kim. "New Air Force Academy." *Modern Metals* **14, no. 11 (December 1958): 36–44. 12 illustrations, 1 diagram.**

Details innovative uses of aluminum cladding in the U.S. Air Force Academy buildings, in particular the Cadet Chapel. Photos show use of aluminum in buildings and furniture.

"The Flexible Formula at Work: Inland Steel Co., Chicago." *Interiors* **118, no. 3 (October 1958): 112–21. 25 illustrations, 8 plans and diagrams.**

Describes the Inland Steel Building and shows its exterior and interior spaces in numerous photos. Although Netsch designed the concept and first model, Bruce Graham is named as project designer. Includes details of office spaces, furniture, color schemes, acoustical ceilings, air-conditioning, windows, and the dining area. Includes a list of contractors and suppliers.

"Furnishing for Fifty Years." *Industrial Design* **5, no. 4 (April 1958): 28–37. 20 illustrations, 2 plans.**

Discusses the job of "equipping an academic city of over 12,000 people" at the U.S. Air Force Academy by Walter Dorwin Teague Associates, considered the largest assignment an industrial design firm has ever tackled. The planning of space was done concurrently with the designs of the buildings. Consultation with Netsch on basic floor plans determined the location of equipment in the plan. The article details the process of planning such a large project.

"The Inland Steel Building." *Products Council Incorporated* **(June 1958): 17–20. Illustrated.**

"Inland Steel: Skidmore, Owings & Merrill, Architects and Engineers." *Architectural Record* **123, no. 4 (April 1958): 169–78. 14 illustrations, 9 plans and diagrams.**

Overview of the newly completed Inland Steel Building. Describes the building's design, engineering, creative uses of new materials, and innovative air-conditioning system. Includes several full-page black-and-white photos.

> *This 19-story office building, which has an exterior of approximately one-third stainless steel and two-thirds glass, is framed by seven slender steel columns on each of the broad sides, spanned by uninterrupted 60-ft plate*

girders. This, it is believed, give the widest clear span of floorspace ever designed for a multi-story building. (p. 170)

"Inland's Steel Showcase." *Architectural Forum* 108, no. 4 (April 1958): 88–93. 11 illustrations, 4 plans.

This article draws parallels between the Inland Steel Building and William Le Baron Jenney's Fair Store (1890–91) and Louis Sullivan's Carson, Pirie, Scott, and Co. Building (1899–1904), situating the Inland Steel Building as a true descendant of the Chicago School. These comparisons are fitting in that the Inland Steel Company supplied the steel for Chicago's architectural masterworks. The Inland Steel Building thus fulfills dual roles as an impressive work of modern design and as a potent advertisement for steel-frame construction. The article illustrates the interiors and highlights the efficiency and savings afforded to Inland Steel by the building's open floors.

"New Way to Raise the Roof." *Architectural Forum* 108, no. 3 (March 1958): 126–28. 7 illustrations, 1 plan.

Details lifting the huge steel-grid roof frame of the U.S. Air Force Academy's Cadet Dining Hall, using hydraulic jacks.

> *The square roof measures 308 feet on a side, covers just over two acres, weighs 1,150 tons, has a clear span of 266 feet yet rests on only 16 columns. It is the first structure of this type to be jacked into place. The largest known concrete slab ever lifted weighed more, 1,466 tons, but covered only about one-third the area of the Air Academy roof: 32,000 square feet versus 94,864 square feet. And of course, concrete slab construction would require many more columns, with consequently less free span.*
>
> *The roof frame is a grid-truss system, in which trusses run both length-wise and crosswise, intersecting at right angles.* (p. 127)

Photos show the six-hour process of hoisting the roof frame into place.

Sachs, Samuel. "Air Condition New Building via Cellular Steel Floor." *Heating, Piping & Air Conditioning* 30, no. 6 (June 1958): 97–100. 3 illustrations.

Trade journal report on construction and engineering details and air-conditioning mechanics of the Inland Steel Building. Sachs was SOM's chief mechanical engineer and worked closely with Netsch on several projects.

1959

"Académie de l'armée de l'air américaine, Colorado Springs, Etats-Unis." *L'Architecture d'aujourd'hui*, no. 85 (September 1959): [1]–9. 22 illustrations, 3 plans.

This article highlighting current American architecture is the second from this publication to praise the U.S. Air Force Academy, and it affirms the recognition that Netsch's work received in Europe. The text comprises short critical remarks and a synopsis of each building at the Air Force Academy. The text is accompanied by several photographs and renderings.

"The Air-Age Acropolis." *Architectural Forum* 110, no. 6 (June 1959): 158–65. 12 illustrations, 2 plans.

Abundantly illustrated article on the U.S. Air Force Academy includes photographs showing cadets at the newly opened grounds but no chapel, as it had not yet been constructed. However, its completion is noted as crucial to the entire design's success.

Kenney, Nathaniel T. "Where Falcons Wear Air Force Blue." *National Geographic* 115, no. 6 (June 1959): 844–73. Illustrated.

Lavish overview (with photographs by William Belknap Jr.) of the U.S. Air Force Academy that highlights buildings, site, and aspects of cadet life. The class of 1959 was the first to graduate from the Academy. Page 852 shows Lt. Gen. Hubert R. Harmon, the Academy's first superintendent, next to an architect's early aerial drawing of the site.

Koeper, H. F. "At the Summit."
Journal of Architectural Education
14, no. 2 (Autumn 1959): 5–9.
Report on the fourth annual seminar
on teaching architecture, sponsored
by the Association of Collegiate Schools
of Architecture and the AIA and held
in northern Wisconsin at the Williams
Grindstone Lake Lodge. Netsch, the
final speaker, addressed grading licensing exams for the Illinois State Board
of Registration for Architects (p. 9).

"Luftwaffen-Akademie bei
Colorado Springs." *Bauen +
Wohnen* 13, no. 12 (December 1959):
443–54. 23 illustrations, 4 plans.
Feature article on the U.S. Air Force
Academy with particular attention
to engineering and construction
details. Includes numerous photos
of the site, buildings, and interiors.
Captions are in German and English.

McQuade, Walter. "Acropolis of
the Air." *Think* 25, no. 9 (September
1959): 30–33. 7 illustrations.
Positive critique of the U.S. Air
Force Academy that emphasizes how
the buildings characterize the Air
Force's modern image. Concludes:

*In picking a physical site for their
Academy, the Air Force aimed high.
They selected a part of the country
where the mountains rear up like an
opponent, a forbidding barrier to
mankind. Then they picked architects
who would surely oppose the mountains with a highly logical portrayal
of the modern mind at work, without
sentiment or emotionalism.*

*The real meaning of the architec-
ture of the Air Force Academy may be
that the men who are being trained
there are not going to be concerned
primarily in years to come with getting into planes and taking to the air,
but with pushing the right buttons at
the right time and sending metal up
into the air to do abstract battle with
other metal. They will have to oversee*

*what may be the most intricate and
enormously technical mechanism in
our technical culture — the defense
system....*

*Such a realization, spoken or
unspoken, was the basis of the design
now growing in Colorado. Final
judgment as to the complete success
of the group must fairly await the
completion of the chapel; the design
for this building is a real piece of
architectural courage, which will
make or break the entire composition.
But so far the choice of technique for
this gleaming group of structures
represents a coming of age of the
newest independent service, the
Air Force.* (p. 33)

"New Look: Air-Age Buildings for
Air Cadets." *Engineering News-
Record* 162, no. 5 (February 5, 1959):
36–39, 42, 44. 5 illustrations.
Presents the basic design approach to the
U.S. Air Force Academy structures and
grounds and showcases its major buildings. Explains how cadets live, eat, study,
and exercise. Credits Netsch as director
of design for SOM. Photos show the
sprawling site and individual buildings.

San Francisco Museum of Art.
Two Buildings San Francisco 1959.
San Francisco: San Francisco Museum
of Art, 1959. 51 pp. Illustrated.
Catalogue to an exhibition of drawings
and models for the Crown-Zellerbach
Headquarters Building and the John
Hancock Western Home Office
Building. Netsch began designing
the Crown-Zellerbach Headquarters
Building in 1954, before he was trans-
ferred to SOM's Chicago office; the
project was completed by architect
Charles Bassett.

"United States Air Force Academy in Colorado." *Architects' Journal* 130 (October 1959): 383–85. 4 illustrations.

Heavily illustrated feature on the U.S. Air Force Academy that includes an aerial photograph of the site and exterior photographs of buildings and one classroom.

"U.S. Air Force Academy." *Architectural Record* 125, no. 6 (June 1959): 151–62. 17 illustrations, 4 plans.

Generously illustrated article written to commemorate the dedication of the U.S. Air Force Academy. Questions are raised concerning the architecture, but the author points out that a visit to the site is necessary to grasp the overall effect. The Cadet Academic Area, Cadet Quarters Complex, Cadet Dining Hall, and academic complex are described and illustrated.

1960

"Crown Zellerbach." *Architectural Review* 128, no. 766 (December 1960): 392. 2 illustrations, 1 plan.

"The Crown Zellerbach Building." *Architectural Record* 127, no. 4 (April 1960): 197–204. 22 illustrations, 4 plans and diagrams.

Doms, Keith, and Howard Rovelstad, eds. *Guidelines for Library Planners: Proceedings of the Library Buildings and Equipment Institute.* **Chicago: American Library Association, 1960. 128 pp. 3 plans.**

Lt. Col. George V. Fagan, director of the U.S. Air Force Academy, and Donald C. Davidson, librarian at the University of California, Santa Barbara, discuss the Academy's library (pp. 43–50, 1 illustration, plans). Fagan describes the makeup of the Academy and the library's functions, while Davidson makes critical remarks on the building. Davidson praises the mezzanine level and the abundance of space and criticizes some of the furniture, lighting, and staff

spaces. In a transcribed conversation, Fagan and Davidson debate the practicality and performance of the circular central staircase (pp. 48–50).

1961

"Air Academy Chapel Shapes Up." *Architectural Forum* 114, no. 5 (May 1961): 128–29. 4 illustrations.

Describes construction of the U.S. Air Force Academy Cadet Chapel:

> *Last month the framework was finished, a lacy skeleton of tubular steel tetrahedrons stacked one on top of the other…. [T]he frame consists of 100 identical tetrahedrons, each 75 feet long and weighing 5 tons. They were fabricated in Missouri, shipped by rail, and hoisted in place by cranes. The tetrahedrons are spaced 2 feet apart creating gaps in the framework which will be filled with 1-inch-thick panels of stained glass.* (p. 128)

Photos show the chapel under construction.

"Campus Design by Function, Not Discipline." *Architectural Record* 130, no. 4 (October 1961): 12–13. 4 illustrations.

Presents SOM's plan for the University of Illinois Circle Campus in Chicago (UIC). The article's title highlights the main innovation of the campus, tailoring buildings not to the subject taught within but rather to their function (i.e., all offices together, all labs together, etc.). The campus was designed to grow with the school in three phases, with the goal of incorporating the varied and changing uses of the university in the most economical manner.

"Chapel of the Air Force Academy, [Colorado] Springs, Colorado." *Kokusai-Kentiku* 28 (November 1961): 37–39. 5 illustrations, 4 plans. In Japanese.

Presents floor plans and photos of the Cadet Chapel during construction. Minimal caption text only.

"Chapelle de l'Académie de l'Armée de l'Air Américaine, Colorado Springs, Etats-Unis." *L'Architecture d'aujourd'hui*, no. 96 (June–July 1961): 78–[79]. 5 illustrations, 2 plans.

Article on the Cadet Chapel summarizes its structural highlights in a brief text.

Northwestern University Trustee Committee on Development. *Northwestern University 1961/1971.* **Evanston, IL: Northwestern University. 14 pp. Illustrated.**

Development brochure on the Lakefill project that details proposed stages of construction and shows concepts for new buildings on the site. According to the report, the Lakefill would add 71 acres to the Evanston campus at a cost of $6.5 million. Netsch helped plan the project and designed several buildings for it; the brochure includes a plan for a library that is a square, fortress-like building with an interior courtyard.

Office Buildings. **New York: McGraw-Hill, 1961. 248 pp. Illustrated.**

The Inland Steel Building is featured in this compendium of office architecture. The entry includes interior and exterior photos and plans illustrating details of structural and framing elements (pp. 43–50, 12 illustrations, 8 plans). While it touts the innovations of the building, the text mainly treats the engineering principles behind the design in highly technical terms.

"P/A Eighth Annual Design Awards." *Progressive Architecture* 42, no. 1 (January 1961): 96–97, 154–56. 7 illustrations, 1 chart.

This article presents the results of *Progressive Architecture*'s annual juried competition, judged by five eminent architects, among them Netsch and Philip Johnson. The jury members note certain tendencies they observed in reviewing the 507 applications and outline their criteria for award selection. Netsch suggests chaos, concrete, and cubism

as the current trends in architecture, and he and Johnson defend the "brutalist" tendencies of Earl Carlin's New Haven Fire Station.

"Space Age Symbol: Air Academy's Chapel." *Engineering News-Record* 166, no. 16 (April 20, 1961), 32–34. 5 illustrations, 1 diagram.

Shows designs and construction of the Cadet Chapel, noting its distinctive modern style. A diagram shows the chapel's spire frame. Concludes: "Completion of the chapel is scheduled for this fall. It is the last major structure in the Air Force Academy's present construction program."

1962

"Campus Expansion on Made Land." *Progressive Architecture* 43, no. 8 (August 1962): 130–35. 2 illustrations, 4 plans.

This article begins with excerpted remarks by Netsch on campus planning, in which he discusses the tenets that determined the plan for UIC and poses questions about the discipline of campus planning. Netsch describes the campus-planning process from preparation to development, and also discusses plans for the U.S. Air Force Academy and Northwestern University. The remainder of the article reviews plans for the Lakefill expansion at Northwestern University, focusing more on the Lakefill itself than the buildings to be constructed there.

"The Chapel, United States Air Force Academy, Colorado." *Architectural Record* 132, no. 12 (December 1962): cover, 87–92. 16 illustrations, 3 plans.

Praises the Cadet Chapel as a "deft fusion of color, form and structure … the visual dominant of the Academy" (p. 85). Includes numerous photos and construction notes, such as details about the use of structural steel pipe in the tetrahedron frames. Notes: "The fuss over weather leakage at joints is being resolved to the satisfaction of all; double glazing (originally called for in the architect's detail and then eliminated for economy's sake) will be provided and should solve the problem" (p. 92). The cover has a color photograph of the chapel.

"Grinnell's Library and Fine Arts Center." *Progressive Architecture* 43, no. 9 (September 1962): 146–53. 13 illustrations, 4 plans.

Presents Netsch's Burling Library and the Fine Arts Center at Grinnell College, the first buildings constructed in SOM's campus development plan for the college. Most of the article details the Roberts Theater in the Fine Arts Center.

Northwestern University Library Planning Committee. *20-Year Planning Program: New Research and Core Library — Integration of Deering Library.* Evanston, IL: Northwestern University, 1962. 186 pp. Illustrated.

Report of the committee of seven Northwestern faculty members, library staff, and SOM representatives that determined the physical and intellectual requirements of the University's new library. Clarence L. Ver Steeg, professor of history, chaired the committee.

"Soaring Pattern — The Air Force Chapel." *New York Times Magazine* (July 22, 1962): 22–23. 7 illustrations.

Feature article on the Cadet Chapel, then nearly completed. Includes a short text by Ada Louise Huxtable on the chapel's "daring" architecture and "dramatic" setting. Photos of the structure are juxtaposed with photos of Le Corbusier's Notre-Dame-du-Haut at Ronchamp, Wright's synagogue in Elkins Park, Pennsylvania, and Marcel Breuer's St. John's Abbey Church in Collegeville, Minnesota.

"Spires That Soar." *Time,* July 27, 1962, 34–39. 6 illustrations.

Showcases the Cadet Chapel, including its controversial history and design. Quotes Netsch on his design philosophy and inspiration for the chapel. Illustrated by five color photographs by J. Alex Langley, including two full-page photos of exterior and interior spaces.

Temko, Allan. "The Air Academy Chapel: A Critical Appraisal." *Architectural Forum* 117, no. 12 (December 1962): 74–79. 8 illustrations, 1 plan.

Criticizes the Cadet Chapel as being "laden with Gothic reminiscence and ravaged internally by the official taste of the clergy and the Air Force.... [It] is in truth our first militant monument to Mass Cult" (p. 75). Temko also finds fault with the "unwieldy tetrahedrons" and stained glass: "Have we not had enough of these cloying yellows, sickening pinks, and vile purples and violets which are a travesty of the medieval glassmaker's art?" (p. 78).

"Those Towering Spires." *Monsanto Magazine* (Summer 1962): 13–15. 4 illustrations.

Complimentary article about the Cadet Chapel that details design features of "this modern masterpiece of point-and-counterpoint." Covers artwork elements in the Catholic, Jewish, and Protestant worship areas and notes religious symbolism. Regarding the Jewish area: "Here, as in the soaring beauty of the Protestant nave and the modern artistic richness of the Catholic chapel, the architects' aim has become reality: 'A chapel of the future for an Air Force of the future'" (p. 15). Predicts that "those spires of the Cadet Chapel will be the USAFA symbol best remembered by millions of visitors who stroll across the beautiful academy campus in coming years" (p. 13).

1963

"The ACSA Committee Reports."
Journal of Architectural Education
18, no. 2 (September 1963): 19–21.

Lists Netsch as one of seven members
of the Committee on the Advancement
of Architectural Education responsible
for this report on professional training and licensing examinations. The
report was accepted by the ACSA at
its annual meeting in May 1963.

**"Chapelle de l'Académie de l'Armée
de l'Air Américaine, Colorado Springs,
Etats-Unis."** *L'Architecture d'aujourd'hui*
**34, no. 108 (June–July 1963): 10–16.
11 illustrations, 4 plans.**

Overview and description of the U.S.
Air Force Academy, replete with critical
praise, 11 photographs of exteriors and
interiors, floor plans, elevations, and captions. The Cadet Chapel's revolutionary
aesthetics, engineering, and innovative
uses of new materials receive the most
attention and appreciation. Photos (one
of them a full page) capture the chapel
from many angles and highlight its
distinctive location on campus. "This
chapel is certainly one of the most
important in the world today that merits
continued attention" (p. 12). One photo
shows a long series of tetrahedron
frames loaded onto railway cars.

Danz, Ernst. *Architecture of Skidmore,
Owings & Merrill, 1950–1962.*
**New York: Praeger, 1963. 232 pp.
Illustrated. In English and German.**

This book gives an overview of 38 major
SOM projects, with an introduction
to and history of the firm. It includes
descriptions, plans, elevations, and
photographs of several of Netsch's early
works: the U.S. Naval Postgraduate
School (pp. 48–53), the Inland Steel
Building (pp. 74–81); the U.S. Air
Force Academy (pp. 102–17), and UIC
campus (pp. 212–15). Introduction
by Henry Russell Hitchcock.

1964

**"Bold Library Plan for Total User
Experience."** *American School &
University* **37, no. 1 (September 1964):
cover, 48, 50. 4 illustrations.**

Summarizes plans for the Northwestern
University Library and includes this
quote by Netsch:

> By developing an individual-
> centered use, the concept reflects the
> direction toward self-study; and by
> maintaining a vertical control section
> with the circulation desk, and by
> developing radial centers, flexibility
> of current use is assured and any
> future changes and electronic
> equipment installations can be
> conveniently accommodated.

**Buck, Thomas. "Upside-Down U.
of I. Building Takes Shape."** *Chicago
Tribune,* **August 2, 1964. 2 illustrations.**

Article about construction of the 28-story
University Hall at UIC, "one of 14
structures being rushed toward completion for the scheduled opening of the
new Chicago Circle campus in February
under the initial building program costing approximately $60 million." Reprints
an architect's sketch of the structure.

**"Concepts behind New Library
Design Discussed by Architect."**
Daily Northwestern, **June 1, 1964.**

An issue of the *Daily Northwestern* is
dedicated to articles about the library.
See other article below. Here Netsch
explains concepts behind the design
of the new library at Northwestern.

"Editorial: Buildings." *Daily Northwestern,* **June 1, 1964. 1 illustration.**

Includes an artist's rendering of one
of the floors of a research tower of
Northwestern University Library.

"Institutions Get Modern Look."
Chicago Tribune, May 25, 1964.

Katz, William A., and Roderick G. Swartz, eds. *Problems in Planning Library Facilities: Consultants, Architects, Plans, and Critiques; Proceedings of the Library Buildings Institute, conducted at Chicago, July 12–13, 1963.* Chicago: American Library Association, 208 pp. Illustrated.
In a section on the library at UIC, the university's librarian Edward Heiliger and Netsch discuss the building and its planning (pp. 46–56, 1 illustrations, 5 plans). In a written section and a transcribed interview, Netsch considers the library building and its relation to the larger plan for campus expansion. He looks at the prominent features of the space, discusses intended use as a foundation for design, and outlines provisions for future additions to the building. Five floor plans are illustrated.

"Map Pictures Layout of 'New' Northwestern." *Daily Northwestern,* June 1, 1964. 1 illustration, 1 map.
A detailed map of the Lakefill and how areas will be designated in the future.

"New Library Plan Approved." *Northwestern Alumni News* 43, no. 6 (May 1964): [1].

"New Northwestern Laboratory Library." *Antiquarian Bookman* (June 29, 1964): cover, 2815–17. 3 illustrations.
Describes the features of the library, on which construction had not yet begun, and the nearly completed "Lake campus," or Lakefill project. The author pays particular attention to the innovations of the library design, including its attention to technology such as telephone and television communications, the Core Library, and research towers, and "radial rather than linear arrangements of books and resources, spreading like sunbursts from central information centers."

"NU to Build $9 Million Library, Triple Book Capacity of School." *Chicago Tribune,* May 31, 1964. 2 illustrations, 1 plan.
This article outlines the funding, timeline, and increased space of the new Northwestern library. Netsch is photographed at a press conference with University representatives.

"NU Plans a $10 Million 'Living' Library." *Chicago American,* May 31, 1964.

"President Miller Announces Plans Set for Library: $10 Million Complex to Extend on Lakefill." *Daily Northwestern,* June 1, 1964. 1 illustration.
Outlines the improved features of the new Northwestern library and includes three paragraphs on the "architect's concept," including the belief that the building must harmonize with existing architecture and complement what will become the architectural mood of the new campus in decades ahead.

Terte, Robert H. "Out of the Lake: A Library." *New York Times,* May 31, 1964.
Short piece on Northwestern University's Lakefill and library projects.

"Unique Library Planned as 'Intellectual Capitol.'" *Northwestern University Alumni News* 43, no. 7 (July 1964): 3–5. 5 illustrations.
Highlights the benefits of the new library. John E. Burchard, dean of the social sciences and humanities at MIT, is quoted: "This building is innovative within the bounds of reason; it is focused on the life of the user; it is thoughtfully conceived and beautifully detailed."

"University Library Employs Radial Plan." *Architectural Record* 136, no. 1 (July 1964): 15, 3 illustrations.

Article on the library at Northwestern notes that Netsch's design accommodates flexibility of space and privacy for self-study. It also notes that the design program takes a large facility and breaks it down to a scale that relates architecturally to existing campus structures and supports the intimate relation between the individual and the library's special functions.

"University to Start Work in Spring on $10 million Addition to Library." *Evanston Review*, June 4, 1964.

This article discusses the library at Northwestern, its new amenities, and its radial plan for book stacks.

Ver Steeg, Clarence L. "Ver Steeg's Concept of Complex: Library — 1st Step in Long-Range Plans." *Daily Northwestern*, June 1, 1964. 1 illustration.

Ver Steeg, chair of the Library Planning Committee, wrote this article on the educational concepts underlying Northwestern's new library design.

1965

Banham, Reyner. "A Walk in the Loop." *Chicago* 2, no. 2 (Spring 1965): 24–27. 1 illustration.

Banham — who coined the term the "New Brutalism" — lays out a walking tour of the Loop that includes two structures on which Netsch worked: the Harris Trust Building and the Inland Steel Building. Banham dubs the latter "one of the few modern buildings in the Loop that can even claim to be in the same league as Mies." Richard Lippold's sculpture in the lobby is illustrated.

"Chicago Circle Opens." *UIC News*, February 23, 1965. 5 illustrations.

Collage of photographs of the construction of and dedication ceremony for the UIC campus. The campus was dedicated on February 22, 1965. Includes a photo of Netsch at the construction site.

"Civic University: Functional Hierarchy." *Architectural Review* 138, no. 826 (December 1965): 391–92. 9 illustrations, 4 plans.

Evaluates and describes Netsch's UIC campus. The article suggests that it is the first new university that is thoroughly urban in setting. Argues that the scheme is the most successful architectural attempt at implementing a functional order of civic life rather than a hierarchical one.

Dixon, John Morris. "Campus City, Chicago: University of Illinois' New Urban Campus." *Architectural Forum* 123, no. 2 (September 1965): cover, 21–45. 38 illustrations, 16 plans, 2 maps.

Describes Netsch's UIC campus in great detail. Sections of the article describe the general concept, the evolution of the plan, the rules governing the design, and the prominent features of the campus. These include the second-story walkways, the Lecture Center quad, the Science and Engineering Building, University Hall, and plans for future expansion, including the Art and Architecture Building. The article concludes with an evaluation of the project, which argues that its strength is in its lack of conformity within design rules. It also argues that the functional design might prove problematic to faculty and students and that the organization risks creating an alienating atmosphere with little room for expansion. The author urges the university to make an effort to become integrated into the surrounding community.

"Grinnell's Social Geometry."
Progressive Architecture 46,
no. 12 (December 1965): 118–25.
13 illustrations, 8 plans.

Guides the reader through the Forum
at Grinnell College, designed by SOM
with Netsch as partner in charge of
architectural design. The building was
designed as the primary social space on
campus, with interiors inviting to students. It features an open plan with many
levels and interior and exterior windows
that allow students to observe activities
throughout the building as they pass by
and through it. SOM also designed all of
the fixtures and furniture for the interior
to ensure that they are appropriate for the
overall function of the building. Article
discusses the building's function and
architectural elements. Quotes Netsch
on the project's "strong geometry."

"Interiors Irresistible to Students."
Contract Interiors 125, no. 5 (December
1965): [74]–[79]. 9 illustrations, 5 plans.

Describes the Forum at Grinnell College.

Moholy-Nagy, Sibyl. "Nouveau campus
de l'université d'Illinois à Chicago."
L'Architecture d'aujourd'hui, no. 122
(September–November 1965): 10–13.
9 illustrations, 1 plan.

Evaluates the UIC campus soon after
its completion. The author is generally
enthusiastic about the project's overall
conception and its high level of craftsmanship and detail. She finds fault,
however, with the fact that all of the
windows in the buildings are fixed and
fenestrated because the buildings are
air-conditioned. She finds this contradic-
tory to the idea of the campus having an
"open door" to all who want to learn.

"NU Development Plan Ready."
Chicago Tribune, December 13, 1965.

"NU Expects Library Plans in Winter."
Daily Northwestern, September 30, 1965.

Siegel, Arthur, ed. *Chicago's Famous
Buildings: A Photographic Guide to
the City's Architectural Landmarks
and Other Notable Buildings.* Chicago
and London: University of Chicago
Press; Toronto: University of Toronto
Press, 1965. 272 pp. Illustrated.

This book includes short entries on
the IIT campus (pp. 150–53), the Lake
Meadows Shopping Center (p. 164),
and the Inland Steel Building (pp.
160–63). None of the entries mention Netsch's involvement with these
projects. Includes illustrations and plans
of the Inland Steel Building. Other
editions appeared in 1969 and 1980.

"$2.5 Million Gift Given NU for
New Three-Tower Library." *Evanston
Review*, March 18, 1965. 1 plan.

Focuses on a large gift of Grover M.
Hermann, which was to be used to build
one of the three principal research towers
in the University library as a memorial
to his son, Grover M. Hermann Jr.,
who attended Northwestern before
being killed in World War II.

"University of Illinois, Chicago
Campus: Transition, Tradition,
or New Approach?" *Progressive
Architecture* 46, no. 10 (October 1965):
222–31. 16 illustrations, 2 plans.

Reprints highlights of a discussion between Netsch, *Progressive Architecture* senior editor James Burns, Edward Dart of
Loebl, Schlossman, Bennet & Dart, and
Leonard Currie, dean of the School of
Architecture and Art at UIC. The article
discusses specific problems faced in conceiving the campus and its architecture,
as well as the larger problem of new university design. Dart is the most critical
of the project, suggesting that it does not
go far enough to innovate, and he wishes

it were more compact and compatible with Chicago weather. Dart subsequently worked with Netsch on expansion projects at Northwestern University.

Von Eckardt, Wolf. "Chicago's No-Nonsense Design for a True Urban Campus." *Providence [RI] Journal Bulletin,* **June 20, 1965. 1 illustration.**

Feature article on the new UIC campus. "The campus was designed by Skidmore, Owings & Merrill, with lanky, scientific minded Walter Netsch the designer in charge…. Mr. Netsch has designed each building to serve a function rather than a department." Favorably reviews both the overall plan and individual buildings. Concludes, "As at the Air Force Academy, which Walter Netsch also designed, we have visual order."

Webster, J. Carson. *Architecture of Chicago and Vicinity.* **Chicago: Society of Architectural Historians, 1965. 69 pp. Illustrated.**

This architectural guide contains an entry on the UIC campus (pp. 19–23).

1966

Gueft, Olga. "From Roads to Lockers: SOM Designs New Campus for Illinois University." *Contract Interiors* **125, no. 10 (May 1966): 130–41. 34 illustrations, 2 plans.**

Discusses the UIC campus as "total design," in which all aspects of the project are considered together and executed according to guiding principles. The article describes the overall organization of the campus and many of its custom details. It includes plans of the Lecture Center and the top floor of University Hall and lists material sources for the interiors. Photos show everything from outdoor walkways to classrooms, furniture, and chalkboards.

Heyer, Paul. *Architects on Architecture.* **New York: Walker & Co, 1966. 415 pp. Illustrated.**

Survey of major architectural firms. The section on SOM (pp. 363–77) lists Netsch as partner. Highlights the firm's major commissions, including the U.S. Naval Postgraduate School, the U.S. Air Force Academy, the UIC campus, and Northwestern University Library (see pp. 371–75).

> *If SOM's design leaders do not act as disciples of one another — Netsch, for example, seem[s] interested in exploring different avenues, while [Bruce] Graham seems more concerned with the evolution and refinement of an approach — they do seem to have found the freedom in teamwork to concentrate their attentions appropriately.* (p. 376)

"La nuova città universitaria di Chicago." *L'Architettura* **11 (February 1966): 668–69. 9 illustrations, 4 plans.**

Illustrations show designs for Netsch's UIC campus with one caption.

Mendini, A. "I grandi organismi di progettazione negli Stati Uniti." *Casabella* **30, no. 309 (September 1966): 28–29, 43–41. 12 illustrations, 5 plans.**

Extensive presentation of the U.S. Air Force Academy, supplemented by aerial photos of the site and of individual buildings. Devotes several pages to the Cadet Chapel.

Moholy-Nagy, Sibyl. "Chicago Circle: Grosstadt Campus der Universität von Illinois." *Der Baumeister* **63 (May 1966): 525–36.**

"Netsch of SOM Honored." *Interiors* **125, no. 12 (July 1966): 10.**

Netsch was awarded the National Society of Interior Designers Total Design Award for the UIC campus, which is cited as an outstanding example of total environmental design.

"University of Illinois, Chicago Circle by SOM; W. Netsch Partner in Charge." *Architectural Forum* 124, no. 4 (May 1966): 50–51.

Part of a section on university planning, this article evaluates Netsch's scheme for the UIC campus. It suggests that the functional organization is problematic and that the circulation system is not conducive to social life on campus.

1967

"First Plan for the Seventies." *Northwestern Review* (Winter 1967): 2–7. 6 illustrations.

Reveals campus planning and new building projects for the University's Lakefill, including Northwestern University Library.

"Universität von Illinois: Chicago Circle Campus." *Deutsche Bauzeitung* 101, no. 7 (July 1967): 533–34. 1 illustration, 1 plan.

Brief overview of the UIC campus, illustrated by a photo of the outdoor amphitheater and a site plan.

1968

"Cold Can't Cool Construction." *Daily Northwestern,* January 24, 1968. 1 illustration.

A photo of the new library during construction. The caption notes that the cold weather and snow are not hampering the project.

"Dedication Tomorrow: Library Creator to Speak." *Wells Courier,* October 17, 1968. 1 illustration.

Article discussing the dedication ceremony of the Louis Jefferson Long Library at Wells College in Aurora, New York. Netsch is listed as the primary speaker; his speech is titled "Architecture — Spaces Between." The story notes that the Netsches plan to donate some felt banners that were on display for the opening of the library; students are encouraged to vote on which banners they would like to have.

Dixon, John Morris. **"Campus City Continued."** *Architectural Forum* 129, no. 5 (December 1968): cover, 28–43. 16 illustrations, 13 plates and diagrams.

Assesses buildings — in particular the Art and Architecture Building — and public spaces that were part of phase I of construction of the UIC campus. Reports on controversial elements, such as a widespread perception of a shortage of windows, the campus's "impersonal environment," and complex interior circulation patterns, that make finding classrooms and offices difficult. Studios in the Art and Architecture Building are deemed too small. Ends on a positive note, however, with comments on its intriguing geometric spatial arrangement:

> A&A is, after all, one part of a much larger work of architecture — the campus. Starting with a blank site barely five years ago, Walter Netsch and his co-workers at SOM have turned it into a place with strong identity. To the students who come here each day, most of them from homes in the anonymous sprawl that separates the Chicago Loop from the prairies, this sense of place is the most valuable gift an architect can offer. (p. 42)

"'First Plan' Progress." *Northwestern Review* 3, no. 2 (Winter 1968): 1. 1 illustration.

An aerial photo shows construction of the Northwestern library in progress. The cost of the library is now cited as $11.6 million, as opposed to an initial figure of $10 million.

"Infirmary Permit, NU Library Top Building Volume." *Evanston Review*, May 16, 1968. 1 illustration.

Koeper, Frederick. *Illinois Architecture from Territorial Times to the Present: A Selective Guide.* Chicago and London: University of Chicago Press, 1968. 304 pp. Illustrated.

Includes sections on the UIC campus (pp. 94–95) and the Lindheimer Astronomical Research Center at Northwestern (pp. 120–21).

Lublin, Joann. "Library on Its Way, But...." *Daily Northwestern*, November 21, 1968. 5 illustrations.

This update on construction of the new library at Northwestern indicates that the towers have been completely enclosed and that plaster work has begun. The article states that the $12 million library is expected to open in March 1970.

Moore, Patricia. "The Arty Life of Walter Netsch." *Chicago Daily News*, April 20, 1968. 3 illustrations.

Feature on Netsch's art collection, then housed at his apartment at 20 East Cedar Street in Chicago. Reviews major pieces in the collection and mentions Dawn Clark Netsch, who since their marriage in 1963 "has been given veto power over his art purchases."

1969

Fisher, Dennis. "New NU Library Is an 'Architect's Dream.'" *Chicago Sun-Times*, December 26, 1969. 3 illustrations.

States that the Northwestern library is scheduled to open on January 19, 1970. Robert D. Kleinschmidt, an interior designer and a colleague of Netsch's, is quoted: "This project is an architect's dream. We've designed everything according to a detailed program of what the university wanted ... from landscaping to furniture."

Grigg, Steven. "Chicago Circle Campus: A Student's Questioning View." *Inland Architect* 13, no. 4 (April 1969): 18–21.

Appraisal of the UIC campus by an architecture student. Grigg acknowledges the challenges involved in planning the site and complains about uncovered walkways, poor circulation patterns, and changes to the original "rectilinear system of reinforced concrete buildings" (p. 20). Criticizes rotated-square designs, finding "the new geometry, even if valid on itself (and there is controversy about that), has produced a chaotic visual effect" (p. 20). Concludes:

Although there are many basic problems with the Circle Campus as it exists today, it should be noted that only a fraction of the total campus has been built. If future planning and construction take these problems into account, there are great possibilities for a great campus. If some of the problems are not remedied, then the Circle Campus will become a monument to man's inhumanity to architecture.

Owings, Nathaniel Alexander. *The American Aesthetic.* New York: Harper & Row, 1969. 198 pp. Illustrated.

Monograph on beautification, environmental preservation and protection, and city planning in the United States, illustrated by sweeping photos by William Garnett of landscapes and urban sprawl. Includes photos of the U.S. Air Force Academy's Cadet Chapel (pp. 169–71) and the UIC campus (pp. 176–80). Introduction by S. Dillon Ripley.

Scully, Vincent. *American Architecture and Urbanism.* London: Thames and Hudson, 1969. 275 pp. Illustrated.

Brief mentions of the U.S. Air Force Academy (p. 190, 2 photos) and the "mechanistic" UIC campus (pp. 236–37, 1 photo). Calls the Cadet Chapel "wigwammy": "[It] seeks to invoke, a little like late Wright at Elkins Park or at Taliesin itself, the Rocky Mountains' serrated forms" (p. 190). A second edition appeared in 1988.

Smith, C. Ray. "Forms as Process: An In-depth Study of Field Theory." *Progressive Architecture* **50, no. 3 (March 1969): 94–115. 18 illustrations, 29 plans and diagrams.**

Detailed explanation of Netsch's Field Theory. Includes illustrations and diagrams, quotes from Netsch on the theory and its use in planning, stills from an animated color film by Netsch (pp. 96–96), and examples of Field Theory buildings. Projects include the Art and Architecture Building, the Behavioral Sciences Building, and the Science and Engineering South Building at UIC; Northwestern University Library, Lindheimer Astronomical Research Center, and the O. T. Hogan Biological Sciences Building at Northwestern University; Long Library at Wells College; St. Matthew United Methodist Church in Chicago; and the Basic Sciences Building at the University of Iowa. Includes several full-page color photos. According to Netsch:

> *Field Theory, as a system and of a way of looking, assumes that all actions are not linear, that all forms must be additive, that plans need not be orthogonal (straight-lined) to be useful or active. Field Theory is network oriented rather than structure oriented. It is iconic, volumetric, and spatial.* (p. 94)

1970

"Critics Praise Wells Library." *Syracuse Herald-American,* **July 26, 1970. 1 illustration.**

Concerns Netsch's Long Library at Wells College in Aurora, New York.

"Dedicate Library at NU." *Chicago Tribune,* **October 22, 1970. 6 illustrations.**

Dixon, John Morris. "New Galaxies at Chicago Circle." *Architectural Forum* **133, no. 4 (November 1970): 24–33. 25 illustrations, 6 plans.**

This review describes and evaluates Netsch's Behavioral Sciences and Science and Engineering South Buildings, both of which were added to the UIC campus during later phases of development. Both buildings represent what the author calls the "high" phase of Netsch's Field Theory. Both are large and complex, composed as systems of repeated modules in a range of sizes. The buildings are not functionally distinct like the other buildings on campus but instead integrate offices, labs, lecture halls, and libraries. This organization, says the author, has proved to be even more appropriate for the graduate population than was originally anticipated.

"Galaxis–symmetrisch." *Deutsche Bauzeitung* **104, no. 1 (January 1970): 26–27. 2 illustrations, 1 plan.**

Presents Field Theory–inspired designs and photos of the Behavioral Sciences Building at UIC.

"Die Glorifizierung des Korridors." *Deutsche Bauzeitung* **104, no. 1 (January 1970): 18–21. 3 illustrations, 3 plans.**

Short piece on the Art and Architecture Building at UIC, with an emphasis on the building's interior corridors. Includes a sweeping aerial view of the campus under construction.

Green, Peter M. "Astronomisches Gestell." *Deutsche Bauzeitung* **104, no. 1 (January 1970): 16–17. 2 illustrations, 2 plans.**

Details Netsch's Lindheimer Astronomical Research Center at Northwestern, constructed at the northeast corner of the Lakefill in 1966. It was demolished in 1995.

Haas, Joseph. "A Library Programmed for People." *Chicago Daily News,* January 10–11, 1970. 3 illustrations.

Concentrates on the "human program" behind the new library at Northwestern. According to Netsch, "All we've done is relook at an age-old idea and extrapolate it into 20th-century forms, needs and materials. It's very contemporary, and yet we hope it hasn't lost the traditional quality a library should have of quiet dignity and of privacy" (p. 4). The second half of the article walks the reader through the library's different components, including service, study, and collection areas. Also discusses the library's color scheme and furnishings.

Harsh, Bonita. "If Books Ever Become Obsolete, Library Ready." *Evanston Review,* February 16, 1970. 6 illustrations.

Describes the Northwestern University Library, designed with an eye toward automation. The design included a single computer station in the Core Library.

"The Libes." *Northwestern Engineer* (March 1970): 18–19. 5 illustrations.

"A Library Built on Research." *Environmental Planning and Design* 8, no. 4 (July–August 1970): cover, 17–27. 22 illustrations, 3 plans.

Previews the new library at Northwestern. Examines the library's programming and design challenges with particular attention to collection space in the book towers: "[T]he provision for an overlapping rectangular grid enabling increased numbers of books to be stored does give the building's carefully structured environment a flexibility that similar institutions would be grateful to have" (p. 26). Includes numerous photographs and floor plans that illustrate service areas and furnishings.

"A Library for People." *Northwestern Report* 1, no. 3 (spring 1970): 26–[35]. 15 illustrations.

Heavily illustrated with photographs by George Bangs, this article on the new library at Northwestern University focuses on student and faculty uses. Includes many interior photos with captions of the faculty.

Marlin, William, and Anne Patterson. "Celebrating Art in Life and Life in Art: Four Architects' Own Designs for Living." *Inland Architect* 14, no. 8 (December 1970): 8–11. 7 illustrations.

Describes Walter and Dawn Clark Netsch's Chicago condominium, with an emphasis on their collection of modern art. Narrative proceeds room by room, beginning at the entrance hall and continuing to the two-story living room, library-dining room, and master bedroom. Photos show art works from the collection, as arranged in the home, and includes a small photo of Walter Netsch.

Mount, Charles. "NU Library Integrates People, Books." *Chicago Tribune,* January 11, 1970. 4 illustrations

"Northwestern Planned a Living Library." *College & University Business* 48, no. 5 (May 1970): 67–70. 5 illustrations.

Selected as the "College Building of the Month," the new library at Northwestern is the subject of this feature. It explains the library's radical contemporary style and its radial book stacks, as well as elements of various service and study areas. Concludes with a caption that shows "Construction Details" and a list of "What Makes This Building Different."

"The Northwestern University Library by Walter Netsch of SOM." *Architectural Record* 148, no. 1 (July 1970): cover, 89–96. 14 illustrations, 5 plans.

This review describes the Northwestern University Library and discusses its principal design goals. The library was designed to put readers into a close and intimate relationship with the books. The design also sought to maximize exterior wall surface and windows to give light to as many readers as possible and to accommodate a large portion of the University's population simultaneously. The author cites the library as an immediate precursor to Netsch's Field Theory and a major work of 20th-century architecture.

Northwestern University Library Dedication, October 21, 1970. **Evanston, IL: Northwestern University Library, 1970. 8 pp. Illustrated.**

Program for the dedication of the Northwestern University Library; includes a section on the concept and programming of the library, photos of the building, donor tributes, and illustrations based on the library's radial stack arrangement. Gives a short history of the Library Planning and Building Committee, which worked closely with Netsch from 1962 to 1970.

"Passage à la Milano." *Deutsche Bauzeitung* 104, no. 1 (January 1970): 24–25. 4 plans.

Concerns designs for the Basic Sciences Building (now Bowen Sciences Building) at the University of Iowa.

Shields, Gerald R. "Northwestern's New Library." *American Libraries* 1, no. 5 (May 1970): cover, 442–45. 10 illustrations, 2 plans.

Heavily illustrated with photographs by James Biery, this discussion of the new library at Northwestern begins:

> Most librarians are not going to like Northwestern University's new $12 million library that sits on stilts on a thrust of land-fill edging Lake Michigan. The rough grey cement

> exterior at a distance looks like corrugated boxes on their sides. Yet, as you approach the building and step onto its stone plaza, your eye is pleased and delighted by the variety of forms, spatial relationships, thrusts, and indentations. It is a giant piece of sculpture that changes with the light of day and the angle of the seasonal sun. (p. 444)

Examines service and collection areas and comments favorably on design features and aesthetics. Speculates on challenges for the library staff in operating the facility, but concludes: "They have a library that is a pleasure to be in, inviting to use, and stimulating to the mind. There aren't too many around that can say that" (p. 445). Includes photos of the exterior and interior and simple floor plans of a tower and "cultural center" (Core Library). Also includes size, cost, and construction details.

Skidmore, Owings & Merrill. **New York: Simon and Schuster, 1970. 136 pp. Illustrated.**

This book, first published in Japan in 1968, details several of Netsch's projects: the Inland Steel Building (pp. 12–14, 125), the UIC campus (pp. 18, 92–95, 129), and the U.S. Air Force Academy (pp. 18–25, 125). The book features an introduction and notes by Christopher Woodward and photographs by Yukio Futagawa.

Smith, C. Ray. "Environment für Bücher." *Deutsche Bauzeitung* 104, no. 1 (January 1970): 28–31. 3 illustrations, 4 plans.

Netsch's Long Library at Wells College is showcased. Smith states that it was Netsch's first Field Theory project and one of his favorite commissions. Includes exterior and interior photos, elevations, and base-plate shoe-and-beam connection detail diagrams.

———. "Formen als Prozess: Die Feldtheorie von Walter Netsch." *Deutsche Bauzeitung* 104, no. 1 (January 1970): 11–15. 11 illustrations, 1 plan.

Presents Netsch's Field Theory and shows it at work in various buildings, including the Art and Architecture Building, the Behavioral Sciences Building, and the Science and Engineering South Building at UIC; Northwestern University Library, Lindheimer Astronomical Research Center, and the O. T. Hogan Biological Sciences Building at Northwestern; Long Library at Wells College; St. Matthew United Methodist Church in Chicago; and the Basic Sciences Building (now Bowen Sciences Building) at the University of Iowa. Many of these projects are individually featured in other articles in this issue. Includes a small photo of Netsch.

A German translation of excerpts from an article originally published in *Progressive Architecture* (see above, 1969: Smith, C. Ray, "Forms as Process: An In-depth Study of Field Theory").

"Vierstern mit Anhang." *Deutsche Bauzeitung* 104, no. 1 (January 1970): 22–23. 2 illustrations, 2 plans.

Highlights the Science and Engineering South Building at UIC. Includes floor plans and photos of the model.

"Walter A. Netsch: Welcoming Groves of Academe Beside the Lake" *Interiors* 130, no. 4 (November 1970): 110–15, 169–70. 14 illustrations, 1 plan.

Describes and discusses the Northwestern University Library, emphasizing its relationship to Field Theory. The library's faceted surface, lack of façade, avoidance of masses, and compatibility with the surrounding landscape are all elements that became important in Field Theory.

> For in a sense Netsch is the victim of his own orderliness of mind. He has been so successful at pinning down Field Theory principles that he has made some of us lose sight of the

> psychic raison d'être of the approach, and the wonderful environmental results which can be achieved with it by a designer of his talent. (p. 110)

Includes a floor plan, exterior and interior views, photos of furniture and decorative elements, and a list of suppliers.

Zevi, Bruno. "La biblioteca universitaria di Walter Netsch: Un albergo foderato con milioni di libri." *L'Espresso*, August 30, 1970. 2 illustrations.

Brief note on the Northwestern University Library.

Zotti, Ed. "Library Dedicated: Minow Urges Moderation." *Daily Northwestern*, October 22, 1970. 1 illustration.

1971

"Centro di scienze comportamentali e Facoltà di scienze ed ingegneria sud per l'Università di Chicago." *L'Architettura* 16 (April 1971): 815–19. 14 illustrations, 6 plans.

Features Netsch's Science and Engineering Building and the Art and Architecture Building at UIC. Illustrations include exterior and interior views and a full-page floor plan of the Science Center (p. 815).

Elsen, Patricia. "College Museum Notes." *Art Journal* 31, no. 2 (Winter 1971–72): 186.

Mentions two paintings by Richard Smith given by the Netsches to the University of Iowa Museum of Art.

Francis, Simon. "A Traveling Librarian in the United States." *Assistant Librarian: Journal of the Association of Assistant Librarians* 64, no. 8 (August 1971): 114–18. 3 illustrations.

Mentions UIC campus and the Northwestern University Library:

> At Northwestern the library was designed by a committee consisting of a professor of history as chairman and Netsch, with an elderly librarian

who, I was told elsewhere, resigned
in frustration at his inability to
put over his views. From the basic
premise that the design came first
and cost second emerged a building
that cost $12 million, which no other
librarian I met felt was a success in
spite of costing "$3 million too much."
Architecturally, it looks superb and
prizes have been won, but as a
library even a short visit raised many
doubts. (p. 117)

Includes a photo of the exterior of the
library.

**Horny, Karen. "Building
Northwestern's Core."** *Library
Journal* **96, no. 9 (May 1, 1971):
1580–83. Illustrated.**

Article about Northwestern
University Library by a librarian.

Metropolitan Fund Inc. *Regional
New-Town Design: A Paired Community
for Southeast Michigan.* **Detroit:
Metropolitan Fund Inc., 1971. 161 pp.
Illustrated.**

Netsch's SOM design team prepared
schematics for this project, located near
Detroit. The document explains the concept, introduces the design team (see p.
xviii for a group photo with Netsch), and
presents the physical plan, social impera-
tives, economic model, and town government. The project was not completed.

**Miller, Nory. "Two Libraries Miles
Apart Yet Sharing a Family Origin."**
Inland Architect **15, no. 4 (November
1971): [7]–13. 8 illustrations, 2 plans.**

Compares two contemporaneous Netsch
projects: Northwestern University
Library and the Joseph Regenstein
Library at the University of Chicago. The
article outlines the schemes underlying
both libraries and articulates the differences between the two. The author
concludes that Northwestern University
Library is generally a more successful
building, although Regenstein Library
suits its research-centered function.

**"Northwestern University Utilized
New Methods."** *Chicago Tribune,*
December 5, 1971. 1 illustration.

Describes construction of the
Northwestern University Library,
with reference to comments by John
Skanderup, president of Pepper
Construction Co. Details challenges
such as the difficulty of connecting concrete columns, beams, and
slabs at tight precision angles.

**Osman, Mary E. "City and Suburb
in Tandem."** *AIA Journal* **55, no. 6
(June 1971): 43–44. 1 illustration.**

Discusses the report *Regional New-Town
Design: A Paired Community for Southeast
Michigan* (see above), which, according
to the author, proposes to reconcile the
polarization of inner city and suburb by
creating a common bond uniting the two.
Hubert Locke of Wayne State University
sees the report as an attempt to "make
certain that future urban growth — both
physical and economic — takes into account the needs of both city and suburb,
so that one is not expanded and enhanced at the expense of the other." The
planning team for the project consists
of "a multifaceted group of architects
and planners under the overall supervision of Skidmore, Owings & Merrill."
Structure, governance, and economics
of the proposed community are detailed.
Illustration of the design concept
incorporates Field Theory elements.

University of Iowa Museum of Art.
*Living with Art: Selected Loans from
the Collection of Mr. and Mrs. Walter A.
Netsch.* **Introduction by Walter Netsch.
Iowa City: University of Iowa Museum
of Art, 1971. 20 pp. 18 illustrations.**

Catalogue of the show, curated by
Ulfert Wilke, that first showcased
the Netsch collection at a college art
museum. Contains photos of the Netsch
home and works from the exhibition accompanied by corresponding
catalogue numbers. Brief descriptive
text is provided for each of the 79 pieces
of painting, sculpture, rugs, and glass.

An introduction by Netsch discusses why he collects art and how it informs his architectural designs. Review: *Art Journal* 31, no. 4 (summer 1972): 446. "Statement" reprinted in Statements, pages 108–09.

1972

"The Labor of Love That Created a New Church in a Wasted Ghetto." *Inland Architect* 16, no. 10 (December 1972): 22–24. 3 illustrations, 1 plan.

Discusses St. Matthew United Methodist Church in Chicago, designed by Netsch in hopes of helping spur urban renewal in the poor neighborhood near the Cabrini-Green housing project. While the church is a successful multifunction structure, other planned initiatives, such as adding housing, were not completed due to a lack of funding. The parish was plagued by social problems that the building alone could not solve.

"New Form for Therapy [Winnebago Children's Home Near Neillsville, Wisconsin]." *Architectural Forum* 136, no. 5 (June 1972): 62–64. 4 illustrations, 2 plans.

Describes Netsch's houses at the Winnebago Children's Home (also known as the Sunburst Youth Home) for emotionally disturbed children. The houses are built in a radial design centered around a large two-story structure for community activities. The design encourages a community atmosphere while also allowing easy supervision and is conducive to the interaction and stability necessary for the children's therapy.

"A New Geometry for the Library Inside the Neo-Classic Dome at MIT." *Architectural Record* 152, no. 3 (September 1972): 119–24. 14 illustrations, 4 plans.

Describes and evaluates Netsch's redesigned interior for the dome of the James Madison Barker Library of Engineering at MIT. Netsch's interior juxtaposes his own geometric forms, based on a system of intersecting diagonals, with the neoclassical form of the dome.

Netsch solved the problems presented by the space through specially designed furniture and lighting and the selection of sculpture, plants, and colors. He also addressed acoustical problems by installing carpet, removing a hanging light fixture, and installing acoustic panels in the coffers of the dome.

Schramm, Peter. "A Study of Walter A. Netsch's Field Theory of Design." Kent, OH: College of Architecture and Environmental Design, Kent State University, 1972. 18 pp. 4 diagrams.

Student paper prepared for a class ("AR 448") at Kent State University's School of Architecture and Environmental Design in May 1972. Schramm examines Field Theory, citing examples of its use in such projects as the U.S. Air Force Academy Cadet Chapel, Northwestern University Library, the Forum at Grinnell College, the UIC campus, and Long Library at Wells College. Includes a diagram of the radial floor plan at Northwestern University Library (p. 12), schematics of various lattice systems employed in Field Theory (p. 13), and schematics of the Art and Architecture Building and the proposed Pahlovi Building (never completed) at UIC (pp. 14–15).

Wille, Lois. *Forever Open, Clear and Free: The Historic Struggle for Chicago's Lakefront.* **Chicago: Regnery, 1972. 175 pp. Illustrated.**

Describes Netsch's volunteer work on a Chicago metropolitan housing and planning project in the late 1960s:

> *The council's plan was prepared by a task force headed by Walter Netsch, a top architect and designer of the striking Chicago Circle Campus of the University of Illinois. He recommended that high-intensity development, both residential and commercial, be restricted to the areas adjacent to mile streets, with medium-intensity development at half-mile streets and low-intensity development, restricted to low-rise buildings, at quarter-mile streets.*

At two-block intervals there would be park strips, open vistas with easy access to the lakefront parks and beaches. (p. 172)

1973

McCue, George. "$57 Million Later: An Interdisciplinary Effort Is Being Made to Put Pruitt-Igoe Together Again." *Architectural Forum* 138, no. 4 (May 1973): 42–45. 8 illustrations, 2 plans.

Discusses an "interdisciplinary effort" to put Pruitt-Igoe, St. Louis's notorious 1950s public housing project, "together again." Pruitt-Igoe housed 13,000 people in 33 buildings of 11 stories each when it opened in 1955. Netsch (shown in a group photo) was part of this ultimately unsuccessful enterprise. The St. Louis Public Housing Authority began demolition of the complex in 1972.

Murphy, James A. "Iowa's Fields." *Progressive Architecture* 54, no. 4 (April 1973): 82–91. 9 illustrations.

Features three new buildings at the University of Iowa that were designed according to Netsch's Field Theory: the Basic Sciences Building (now the Bowen Sciences Building; pp. 84–87), the Health Sciences Library (now the Hardin Library for Health Sciences; pp. 88–89), and the Medical Education and Research Facility (pp. 90–91). Begins with an introduction to Field Theory and Netsch's "new approach to technology." Quotes Netsch: "Technological architecture, which is different from Mies, was leading to some very mundane and aggressively ugly buildings. We do not start with the material as the demigod, but with ordering as the demigod" (p. 82). Sections on individual buildings detail their design and include floor plans, sketches, engineering elements, and exteriors. Concludes:

One thing is clear from discussions with Walter Netsch: he will not remain within the relative comfort of rules from past field theory

experience. In addition to using field theory as a way of looking at things, he constantly looks for new ways of looking at fields. Geometric ordering of architecture is not unique to Netsch, but the extent and steady change of field theory set it apart. "You see, to be able to work on a building, find its form and then suddenly get its field later — that would be intuitive to me," he says. "I'm sure, however, that some people think of that as highly inventive." Almost all design begins, consciously or unconsciously, with a learned body of knowledge. The Golden Mean, Le Modulor, observations and past experiences — all can have bearing on how a designer orders his creative process, and its result. So can field theory. (p. 90)

"Netsch in biblioteca [Joseph Regenstein Library, l'Università di Chicago]." *L'Architettura* 19 (October 1973): 324–25. 7 illustrations, 5 plans.

This brief article includes small photographs of exteriors and interiors of the University of Chicago's Regenstein Library, floor plans, and one caption.

Owings, Nathaniel Alexander. *The Spaces in Between: An Architect's Journey.* Boston: Houghton Mifflin, 1973. 303 pp. Illustrated.

Autobiography of Nat Owings (1915–84), a founding partner of SOM and Netsch's mentor and advocate at the firm. According to the foreword, "What follows is a very personal recording. I have selected only things that make me laugh or swear or cry" (vii). Includes reminiscences and anecdotes about Netsch, some of which are excerpted below:

In Chicago we had brilliant young designers — like Ambrose Richardson, Harry Weese, Charles Dornbusch — who came and went. It would be five years before Chicago had a third partner: William Hartmann, and another five before Walter Netsch, the first of the youngsters to stick, joined the partnership. (p. 67)

…

We learned slowly to adjust to things Japanese [in 1953]. I watched fish-allergic Walter Netsch turn green as he settled his six-foot-six frame into the approved Buddha squat, eyeing a very dead, unblinking fish on a plate before him at our first official Japanese dinner in Tokyo. I have often wondered what would have happened if that fish had blinked. (p. 129)

…

Monterey's luxuriously beautiful old Hotel Del Monte, built in 1887, was bought by the United States Navy in 1943. With the money [real estate tycoon Sam] Morse made from this sale, he hired Gardner Dailey, just famous for his "Bay Area houses," and me to expand the more profitable Del Monte Lodge. When this job was completed I offered SOM's services to the navy direct for the [U.S. Naval Postgraduate School] which they proposed to build and they handed us standard barracks plans which, if applied to that beautiful site, would have required the destruction of its dozens of ancient oaks. At this point young Walter Netsch, fresh from Oak Ridge, faced with his first important architectural opportunity in SOM, simply refused to proceed with the barracks plans; and, aware that he was committing an architectural form of mutiny punishable with termina-tion of the contract by the client if the plan for change was unsuccessful, asked for and got permission to appeal this monstrous plan to the admirals in Washington, D.C. I agreed in principle, but from a practical point of view, how were we to crack this one?… Netsch made a model.

[Rear Adm. Ernest Edward Herrmann], a man of ships and guns, was transfixed with amazement as Netsch cleared the model's terrain of

oak and eucalyptus trees and covered the flattened surface with standard-plan barracks — and then, in swift sleight of hand, resurrected the trees from destruction, neatly fitted between the gleaming pavilions, leaving the reincarnated countryside intact. At that time not just navy men but most educators were doing their academic planning by the seat of their pants. Not Netsch! He won over Admiral [Herrmann] and gained a thirty-day period of grace in which to put up or shut up.

Netsch moved his San Francisco crew to Annapolis, Maryland. At night the admiral would come over to their barracks work-shop-bedrooms and share in this first taste — for him — of research and programming. (pp. 140–41)

…

At the heart of our interest in the Air Force Academy project lay a kernel of old-fashioned, sentimental idealism framed in history. Louis Skidmore not only had begun to look something like Churchill but also shared some of his sense of history. This sense of history in its essence was epitomized in the problem posed in designing a chapel. Since no one felt very deeply about religion anymore, and since the Air Force Academy chapel must house all principal religions under one roof, what did one do? SOM would rise to the heights just this once and build to the Virgin instead of the Dynamo — even if she was a warlike Virgin — and we would raise a house to God with a passion and a meaning of its own. It turned out that our avenging angel in this case was Walter Netsch.

One day Jim Douglas, by then secretary of air in his own right, called me and said, "I've been on the Hill for five hours before the Senate Finance Committee. One hour and forty-five minutes were spent on next year's entire budget for the air force, about four and a half billion dollars, and the other three and a half hours on your damn chapel. I got it approved just as you fellows have it designed." (p. 158)

…

The fruit of the SOM tree, by the laws of pure genetics, had to have some resemblance to the tree, no matter how exotic that fruit might be. Like steel filings drawn to a magnet, the result would be in orderly rows: straight, stiff and rigid. The Air Force Academy had to be an impersonal derivative of the conscious and subconscious rule of our order. When we refer philosophically to humanity, to warmth, we think of soft, pliable surfaces, of depths, of things that give, have texture. These were things we couldn't do — yet. But in the evolution of people as well as architecture, in the development of Walter Netsch or Chuck Bassett, we can see later on the widening of the vision, the enriching of the palette. (p. 160)

…

When the University of Illinois decided to experiment with their Chicago campus, which had no dormitories and was centered in the heart of an enormous freeway interchange that would bring students from every segment of Chicago, Walter Netsch would draw on the rich compost resulting from his work on the Air Force Academy. The result — the university's Circle Campus — is the plastic and concrete yang to the academy's steel and glass yin; the one for twenty-five hundred cadets, the other for twenty-five thousand Chicago youths — richer for the work done at Colorado Springs. (p. 161)

…

As a light breeze stirred the leaves of the banyan tree I thought of Ambrose Richardson, Walter Netsch, Tallie Maule and a good many other young men who had come our way — gold nuggets of pure design talent discovered at Oak Ridge. Returnees from military service, these youngsters thrilled to the instant results possible

there and helped develop unique techniques of research, programming and design. Freed of worrisome client headaches, budgetary squeezes and hemming and hawing, each new project they designed went up fast. Under these conditions their designs proved not only the boys' worth to us, but the system's benefit to them. They were potential partners, yet some had left us. Some didn't like our ideas. Some simply wanted to squeeze SOM dry. Some thought that anonymity was for the birds. Some couldn't stand the hard-driving tactics. (p. 178)

…

One trademark of our profession is "great architecture designed by great architects," and by the early 1960s I felt that SOM could claim five of the dozen or so famous names generally acclaimed as such in the United States. A substantial part of the success of each of these five could be attributed to the workings of our own system — Gordon Bunshaft, Walter Netsch, Bruce Graham, Charles Bassett and Myron Goldsmith, their geniuses surfacing from a neutral start within our firm. (pp. 268–69)

…

Days later a phone call from Walter Netsch reached me at Big Sur. I found him tackling one of the toughest sections of St. Louis [ed.: the Pruitt-Igoe housing project] in a total effort to resolve the repressions of a depressed area; to mount an on-site self-renewal of the blacks in the central core. I heard him say all this in a voice filled with excitement and emotion. "But, Nat, this job cannot be charged on a commercial basis. How can we accomplish it within the fabric of SOM?" "We will discuss this as a research project when the partners next meet," I told Walter. And at the meeting I heard them say, the partners, "We wish to give, not take, fees here. Profits from conventional work will be reinvested in such sensitive areas." (pp. 284–85)

A photo section between pages 146 and 147 shows Netsch in 1957 with other SOM partners, two photos of the U.S. Air Force Academy, and a double-spread of the UIC campus under construction with Netsch at the site.

"People in P/A." *Progressive Architecture* **54, no. 4 (April 1973): 7. 2 illustrations.**

Editorial introduction to the issue that devotes several paragraphs to Netsch. Three of Netsch's new buildings at the University of Iowa are featured in the issue (pp. 82–91; see above, Murphy, James A. "Iowa's Fields."). States:

> Walter Netsch's field theory is only one facet of SOM/Chicago, involving only 10 of the 475 employees. "We began looking for modes outside the box in 1959, while working on the Air Force Academy Chapel," Netsch recalls. "We went through stages of increased formality (of field applications) leading to increasing familiarity of field's properties." To him, the field theory has matured as an organizing device.

Includes a photo of Netsch.

1974

***Architecture of Skidmore, Owings & Merrill, 1963–1973.* London: Architectural Press, 1974. 283 pp. Illustrated. In English and German.**

This book features 77 major SOM projects completed between 1963 and 1973, including nine by Netsch. It highlights Netsch's designs for Miami University Art Museum, Oxford, Ohio (pp. 174–77), including a double-spread color photograph of the museum's exterior. Also featured are Regenstein Library at the University of Chicago (pp. 202–07), Long Library at Wells College (pp. 208–15), campus and buildings at UIC (pp. 224–29), Lindheimer Astronomical Research Center at Northwestern (pp. 248–51), and housing units at the Winnebago Children's Home (also known as the Sunburst Youth Home), Neillsville, Wisconsin (pp. 260–63).

Moore, Patricia. "Top Architect Builds His Dream Home." *Chicago Daily News,* **October 25, 1974.**

Moore praises the newly completed Netsch home in Chicago's Old Town neighborhood. Describes the neighborhood, the Netsches' art collection, and the interior of the home. Briefly mentions Dawn Clark Netsch's contributions to its planning and Walter's career highlights. Concludes, "Netsch termed all of this 'the field theory — a developing series of geometric views, the esthetics of what you look at.'"

"1974 Honor Awards, Merit Awards, Special Mentions." *Wisconsin Architect* **(June 1974): 21–31. Illustrated.**

Part of a larger article listing individual winning buildings that include Netsch's Sunburst Youth Homes (also known as the Winnebago Children's Home) in Neillsville, Wisconsin (pp. 24–25), winner of an Honor Award. The project's problem, solutions devised by the architect, and jury comments are accompanied by plans and illustrations. Concludes:

> These buildings are very intimate and friendly in scale and imaginative in structure. The architect expanded beyond the normal ordering system of rectilinear or a straightline structural square. There is a sense of fun, with a lot of ups and downs and around the corners. This low, small scale residential solution is very appropriate and well detailed.

Powers, Richard Gid. "The Cold War in the Rockies: American Ideology and the Air Force Academy Design." *Art Journal* **33, no. 4 (Summer 1974): 304–13. 5 illustrations.**

Analysis of the U.S. Air Force Academy, which the author views as a technocratic example of 1950s' military establishment International Style. Places the Academy's architecture in the Cold War era and reviews the predominance of International Style in the 1950s. Photos show the site, the Cadet Chapel, and cadets marching. Concludes:

A visit to the Air Force Academy is a melancholy experience. It is one stop on the American grand tour of the West, sharing the itinerary with the Grand Canyon, the Rocky Mountains, and Yellowstone, a journey along expressways, with stops at motels, and food at dude ranches. Everywhere there is the contrast between what America once was and what it has become. Behind the Academy the Rockies tower; the approach road circles the prodigious grounds; the school is a cluster of tinny boxes barking their littleness at the snowy peaks. The grounds are immaculate: not a blade of grass, not a leaf is out of place; the gridiron lines on the football field are as precise and ordered as a mathematician's demonstration that, given determination, money, and men enough, the universe will yet confirm Euclid's geometry.
(p. 313)

Powers was an associate professor of American studies at Richmond College, City University of New York, when the article was published.

1975

"In Progress." *Progressive Architecture* **56, no. 3 (March 1975): 33. 2 illustrations.**
Brief report on progress of the 216,500-square-foot East Wing addition to the Art Institute of Chicago and the 46,000-square-foot remodeling project at the museum to be completed in 1976. Netsch's design is praised for keeping heights lower than the existing structures and for bridging the railroad tracks. Notes that some School of the Art Institute faculty members are unhappy about the size of the space for the school.

1976

Cohen, Stuart E. *Chicago Architects.* **Chicago: Swallow Press, 1973. 120 pp. Illustrated.**
Catalogue of the traveling exhibition organized by Laurence Booth, Stuart E. Cohen, Stanley Tigerman, and Benjamin Weese that presented a revisionist history of Chicago architecture since 1900, concentrating on the work of the "Second Chicago School" of architecture. Cohen's essay outlines Netsch's Field Theory, touches on the influence of the shingle style and of Wright's early work on Netsch, and describes the Netsch home (p. 17). It features photos and a plan of the Netsch home (p. 60) and photos of the Sunburst Youth Home (also known as the Winnebago Children's Home; p. 59) and the Frances Searle Building at Northwestern University (p. 62). A short biography and portrait of Netsch is included (pp. 116–17).

Harrison, Jacquelyn Ann, and Donald Rue Kingman. "Inside and Outside the New School." *New Art Examiner* **4, no. 3 (December 1976): 1, 4, 19. 4 illustrations.**
Purports to reveal inner workings and politics of decisions behind the East Wing of the Art Institute of Chicago, housing (in part) the School of the Art Institute. Netsch's design solutions are addressed, in a mostly positive light:

What Walter Netsch has done here, aside from [wielding] a very skillful shoehorn, is to provide the School with a very arresting presence. (The reflective glass was a part of that intention.) The building does have character both inside and out. And it has a high quality look about it. In our opinion, Walter Netsch's architectural signature is as distinctive and culturally valuable as those of Frank Lloyd Wright, Mies van der Rohe, le Corbusier and Louis I. Kahn and this is a great big free bonus for the School. There's no reason why this kind of high quality visibility cannot be made to serve many positive purposes. The Board of Trustees and the Committee on the School are each to be congratulated on their choice of architect. (p. 4)

Morton, David, and Suzanne Stephens. "The House as a Relevant Object." *Progressive Architecture* **57, no. 8 (August 1976): 37–41. 23 illustrations, 7 plans.**
Introduction to feature articles on five contemporary houses published in the same issue. Mentions the Netsch home briefly: "Walter Netsch creates a 20th-century free house" (p. 38).

Orne, Jerrold. "Academic Library Buildings: A Century in Review." *College & Research Libraries* **37, no. 4 (July 1976): 316–31. 10 illustrations.**
History of academic library buildings from 1876 to 1976 that includes photos and brief mentions of Northwestern's Orrington Lunt Library (built 1894; now Lunt Hall), Charles Deering Library (1932), and Netsch's Northwestern University Library (p. 319), as well as Netsch's contributions to academic library designs: "We continue to have a liberal infusion of design modes coming from other cultures, in buildings of Breuer, Aalto, Pereira, Netsch, Yamasaki" (p. 328).

Stephens, Suzanne, and John Dixon. "Netsch House, Chicago, Ill." *Progressive Architecture* **57, no. 8 (August 1976): 46–49. 12 illustrations, 4 plans.**
Subhead: "Architect's house in Chicago provides a personal proving ground to test his design theories on a small scale." Presents the Netsch home constructed in 1974. Explains Netsch's experimentation with Field Theory: "The interior of the volume is essentially an open loft with living levels spiraling partially around a kitchen-bathroom core. The house, in Netsch's words, becomes an 'event' in which the sequence of spaces is three-dimensional along a strong organizing diagonal" (p. 47). Details the search for and selection of the site (it had to be located in State Sen. Dawn Clark

Netsch's district) and development of the program. Includes comments by Netsch on design elements and solutions, such as, "Asked for his reactions to the house, Netsch points out that the heat load through the skylights was greater than anticipated: corrugated plastic shields had to be installed outside" (p. 47).
In their overview, the authors are critical of exterior façades and window placement and heap praise on the high, open interior space:

> *Inside, on the other hand, the spaces are lovely, dynamic, and rather dramatic. The spiral tree house had taken over from the rotated squares.... It becomes a diagram of the field theory construct that now explains the configuration of the house's exterior envelope. The skylights work exceptionally well in illuminating the art, plus providing lots of natural light with privacy.* (pp. 47–48)

Concludes that the house successfully reflects the architect's individuality as an expression of Field Theory aesthetics. Includes interior and exterior photographs (some in color), floor plans, and elevations.

1977

"Architect's House in Lincoln Park." *Architectural Review* **162, no. 968 (October 1977): 234. 3 illustrations, 1 plan.**
Part of a special section on Chicago architecture, this article describes Netsch's home in a neighborhood on the North Side of Chicago that was rundown when the house was built. The house is a large cube, with its "very stimulating interior" space divided by a system of diagonal walls radiating from the center. The use of multiple levels to divide space allows a feeling of openness and flow. "The broad effect is to dramatize in an extraordinary way the functions of a house.... Here, there are virtually no doors and therefore no sealing off of space from space." Photos show exterior and two interior views.

"Art Institute of Chicago." *Architectural Review* **162, no. 968 (October 1977): 233. 2 illustrations, 2 plans.**

Part of a special section on Chicago architecture, this article discusses Netsch's East Wing addition to the Art Institute of Chicago. Using characteristic diagonals, Netsch added space for the School of the Art Institute, integrated the Sullivan and Adler Stock Exchange Trading Room, and added additional exhibition spaces. Notes that some spaces are awkward, in particular stairs on the diagonal, and states that the series of linked pavilions deliberately contradicts the symmetry of the museum's older buildings.

Goldberger, Paul. "A Sullivan Room Is Created in Chicago." *New York Times,* **April 7, 1977. 1 illustration.**

Critiques the reconstruction of the trading room from Dankmar Adler and Louis Sullivan's Chicago Stock Exchange (1893) in the East Wing addition to the Art Institute of Chicago. Praises the restoration project and preservation of the room's decorative elements. Criticizes Netsch's glass-enclosed corridor and new entrance arch as well as the displacement of Sullivan's original arch in a small garden beside the museum.

Miller, Nory. "Evaluation: The University of Illinois' Chicago Circle Campus as Urban Design." *AIA Journal* **66, no. 1 (January 1977): 24–31. 12 illustrations.**

Evaluates the UIC campus 11 years after completion. Describes the many problems the campus poses for users, including a lack of flexibility, a functional separation of spaces that undermines community building, and an alienating, futuristic appearance.

> *Circle campus was built with ambition and a sense of adventure by both client and architect. Its disfavor today almost mirrors the disfavor in which the general planning implements and goals of the mid-century are held....*

> *The disillusionment is not so much with technology ... but with an environment that calls up the image of the machine.* (p. 31)

Includes 12 photos of the campus walkways and buildings.

Pran, Peter C. "The Diversity of Design among Chicago Architects Today." *L'Architettura* **23, no. 8 (December 1977): 434–[74].**

Discusses the rise of a pluralistic, postmodern architecture in Chicago in the 1970s following the death of Mies van der Rohe and the subsequent diminishing influence of the "heroes" of the Second Chicago School of architecture. The Inland Steel Building is mentioned as one of the foremost buildings designed between 1945 and 1970, when modernism dominated Chicago architecture. Includes images of and captions describing 33 innovative works by Chicago architects designed since 1970. Entry on Netsch's home discusses the use of Field Theory in its design (pp. 454–55; 4 illustrations and 2 plans).

"Science-Engineering Library Feted." *Northwestern Alumni News* **(November 1977): 4. 5 illustrations.**

Coverage of the October 14, 1977, dedication of the Seeley G. Mudd Library for Science and Engineering at Northwestern. Photos show the building and dignitaries at the ceremony.

"Seeley Mudd Library Preview." *Northwestern Alumni News* **(September 1977): 1. 3 illustrations.**

Announcement of a reception for donors and committee members held upon the completion of the Seeley G. Mudd Library for Science and Engineering at Northwestern on October 14, 1977. Includes a photo of Netsch and John McGowan, University librarian.

Smith, C. Ray. *Supermannerism: New Attitudes in Post-Modern Architecture.* New York: E. P. Dutton, 1977. 354 pp. Illustrated.

Smith interprets the architecture of Netsch and other modernists as influences on the next generation of "supermannerist" architects through their postmodern uses of wit, camp, and ambiguity. He discusses the process of designing with Field Theory at some length.

1978

Craig, Louis. *The Federal Presence: Architecture, Politics, and Symbols in United States Government Building.* Cambridge, MA: MIT Press, 1978. 580 pp. Illustrated.

Extensive historical and thematic survey of federal buildings, prepared by Craig and the staff of the Federal Architecture Project. Covers the U.S. Air Force Academy (pp. 477–79), including mentions of Netsch and photos of the Cadet Chapel. Reprints excerpts from the architectural and popular press about each project. "Perhaps no architectural debate over government building in the 1950s equaled the discussion about the design for the new U.S. Air Force Academy" (p. 474). A paperback edition was issued in 1984. Review: Bates Lowry, *Journal of the Society of Architectural Historians* 40, no. 2 (May 1981): 146–47.

"A Handsome Library in a Resort Town (Selby Public Library, Sarasota, Fla.)" *Architectural Record* 164, no. 1 (July 1978): 96–98. 6 illustrations, 2 plans.

Describes Netsch's William G. and Marie Selby Public Library in Sarasota, Florida. Netsch endeavored to bring an intimate scale to library patrons while providing interesting and energy-efficient spaces. The plan is composed of interlocking hexagonals within a square grid. The 30,000-square-foot library accommodates 200,000 volumes. Includes photos of exterior and interior views and two floor plans.

1979

"The Baldwin Community Medicine Building of the Mayo Clinic, by Skidmore, Owings & Merrill." *Architectural Record* 166, no. 5 (October 1979): 112–19, 10 illustrations, 5 plans.

Describes and evaluates Netsch's design for the Baldwin Building at the Mayo Clinic in Rochester, Minnesota. Based on Field Theory, the building's design is based on human and functional relationships, creating an arrangement that is clear and easy to follow. All appointment, reception, and administrative activities take place in a central core with V-shaped hallways of exam rooms and offices extending from the core. The building was conceived in close collaboration with doctors and other staff, which contributed greatly to its success. Also notes how well it fits into its surroundings. Concludes:

> *Of course, the Mayo has had the demand that has required it to develop increasingly efficient methods for helping people. That it is doing so without sacrificing the humanity, harmony, and handsomeness of the physical setting makes Baldwin all the more important a model — a model of form in attitude, and in architecture.* (p. 117)

Drexler, Arthur. *Transformations in Modern Architecture.* New York: Museum of Modern Art, 1979. 168 pp. Illustrated.

Exhibition catalogue mentions the U.S. Air Force Academy (pp. 14–15; 2 photos) and the Long Library at Wells College (p. 138, 1 photo). Of the latter project, the author notes: "Walter Netsch's library is particularly interesting in its use of an overhanging roof as if it were a starched handkerchief draped over the walls."

Miller, Ross. "Chicago Architecture after Mies." *Critical Inquiry* **6, no. 2 (Winter 1979): 271–89.**

Casts a critical eye on Netsch, fellow Chicago architects Bertrand Goldberg and Harry Weese, and other "post-Miesians" in light of how they challenged Mies van der Rohe's revolutionary steel-frame and glass-curtain designs that dominated postwar Chicago architecture. Miller contends that the innovation of the first and second generation of Mies's successors lies in their unique design processes, in contrast to the systematic, anonymous architecture of Mies's International Style. Miller praises Netsch's early work, especially the U.S. Air Force Academy Cadet Chapel, for its unorthodox design based on multifarious geometries. Miller goes on to criticize Netsch's Field Theory for being programmatic, overly complex, and academic à la Mies. Designs of the UIC campus and the East Wing of the Art Institute of Chicago are thought to "work better in plan than in execution" (p. 280). The second half of the article considers the work of the "Chicago Seven" architects: Tom Beeby, Larry Booth, Stuart Cohen, James Ingo Freed, James Nagle, Stanley Tigerman, and Ben Weese.

1980

Bach, Ira J., ed. *Chicago's Famous Buildings: A Photographic Guide to the City's Architectural Landmarks and Other Notable Buildings.* **3rd ed. Chicago and London: University of Chicago Press, 1980. 267 pp. Illustrated.**

Includes short entries on the Inland Steel Building (pp. 74–75), the UIC campus (pp. 162–63), the IIT campus (pp. 182–83), the University of Chicago campus (pp. 207–10), and the Northwestern University campus (pp. 232–34). None of the entries mentions Netsch's involvement with the projects. Illustrations feature in the entries for the Inland Steel Building, multiple buildings at UIC,

Regenstein Library at the University of Chicago, and Northwestern University Library and Lindheimer Astronomical Research Center at Northwestern.

Cohen, Stuart. "Late Entries." *Progressive Architecture* **61, no. 6 (June 1980): 94–99. 23 illustrations.**

The traveling exhibition *Late Entries to the Chicago Tribune Tower Competition* is discussed; includes images of some of the entries and a brief summation of the drawings. "Walter Netsch's sinuous glass tower" is featured (p. 96).

Dreyfuss, John. "1922 Tribune Tower: Late Entries in an Architecture Contest." Arts, *Los Angeles Times,* **September 24, 1980. 5 illustrations.**

Review of the *Late Entries to the Chicago Tribune Tower Competition* exhibition, on display at the La Jolla Museum of Contemporary Art. Illustrates Netsch's entry (called "Netschurally" in the caption) and comments:

> For a combination of delicacy, strength and beauty, there is no beating Chicago architect Netsch's computer-drawn entry. Its fine blue lines on a silver nylon field depict an abstract structure that appears light enough to float on mist, resilient enough to defy the most violent storm.

"Miami University Art Museum." *Space Design* **8, no. 191 (August 1980): 3–22. 25 illustrations, 18 plans. Text in Japanese and English.**

Discusses Netsch's Miami University Art Museum (1978). The building contains a number of galleries of different sizes yet all proportionate to one another and arranged in an unfolding sequence suited to exhibiting various types of art. Begins with five evocative full-page photographs of the museum's exterior, taken at different times of the day and from different angles. Explains conceptual criteria, design solutions, interior and exterior spaces, the importance of its placement on the site, galleries, classrooms, and other features. Notes the design's sensitivity to light and atmosphere, as well as its multipurpose flexibility. Included are more exterior photos and gallery and auditorium interiors, floor plans, elevations, and Field Theory designs; smaller illustrations show some of Netsch's other buildings, such as the U.S. Air Force Academy Cadet Chapel, Northwestern University Library, Long Library at Wells College, the UIC campus, and the Central Library at Sophia University, Tokyo.

Schmertz, Mildred F. "New Museum by Walter Netsch of SOM Given Order by his Field Theory." *Architectural Record* **167, no. 1 (January 1980): 111–20. 16 illustrations, 12 plans and diagrams.**

Article on the Miami University Art Museum discusses Field Theory in general, tracing its development and including illustrations of the Behavioral Sciences Building at UIC, the Basic Sciences Building at the University of Iowa, and Long Library at Wells College. Schmertz argues that Field Theory is as significant as other preeminent modernist theories: It is "as important as Corbu's Modulor or Bucky's dome. Netsch makes beautiful buildings with it" (p. 111). Offers several reasons why Field Theory is neither widely known nor practiced. Color photos show museum exteriors, interiors, and site.

Tigerman, Stanley. *Late Entries to the Chicago Tribune Tower Competition,* **2 vols. New York: Rizzoli, 1980. 1: 189 pp.; 2: 113 pp. Illustrated.**

Catalogue documents a traveling exhibition organized by Stuart E. Cohen, Rhona Hoffman, and Tigerman that revisited the 1922 Tribune Tower competition, giving select contemporary architects and artists an opportunity to design the famous Chicago landmark. Seventy architects participated, with Netsch contributing an elegant, futuristic, computer-aided design for a tower based on Field Theory (2: p. 54, 1 plan).

Netsch's statement on his design is reprinted in Statements, page 116.

1981

"Architect Netsch Sculpts New Career." *Chicago,* **April 1981, 18. 1 illustration.**

References exhibition of Netsch's art (mostly watercolrs inspired by Field Theory) at the Zolla/Lieberman Gallery in Chicago. Netsch explains his passion for art, both as a collector and as a designer. Mentions his career at SOM and his design for the Miami University Art Museum.

Comerio, Mary C. "Pruitt-Igoe and Other Stories." *JAE: Journal of Architectural Education* **34, no. 4 (Summer 1981): 26–31. 3 illustrations.**

Examines St. Louis's Pruitt-Igoe public housing project. Traces the project's problems and failures against the backdrop of the decline of St. Louis's inner city in the 1960s. Pruitt-Igoe was demolished in 1972. Notes, "a blue ribbon task force of architects and urban planners worked through 1972 on design schemes to save the project" (p. 27). Netsch's SOM design team formed part of that effort. While maintaining that Pruitt-Igoe's failure was not caused by modern architecture, Comerio faults the complex's design on many points, including architects' and urban planners' failure to understand underlying community and social forces.

JAE was published by the Association of Collegiate Schools of Architecture from 1975 to 1983.

Perkins, Bradford. "Preserving Our Landmarks of the Modern Movement." *Architectural Record* **169, no. 7 (July 1981): 108–09. 7 plans.**

Objects to proposed expansion plans for the U.S. Air Force Academy Cadet Chapel, which included a western addition.

> *The design of the entire Air Force Academy — and the chapel, in particular — is based on a very strong geometry. To break the chapel's podium to introduce another geometry at the very center of this complex is*

a case of architectural bad manners.
A much more sensitive addition was
that proposed by Netsch. This addi-
tion does not make the mistake of the
other podium leaving the building's
original concept unscathed. Luckily,
this project has received a reprieve
since the Air Force has deferred
the addition. This should give the
profession time to focus on it and the
growing number of other modern
landmarks jeopardized by a lack of
concern for this large, essential part of
our architectural heritage. (p. 109)

Uses the example of the Cadet Chapel
as indicative of other modernist
buildings from the 1950s in need
of protection and preservation.

Smith, G. E. Kidder. *The Architecture*
of the United States.* Vol. 2. *The South
***and Midwest.* Garden City, NY:**
Anchor Press/Doubleday, 1981.
749 pp. Illustrated.

State-by-state compendium of noteworthy architecture contains an entry
on the UIC campus. Smith outlines
the plan of the campus and the various
theories that Netsch employed in the
layout of the buildings. He also discusses
both the strengths and the weaknesses
of the architecture, attributing many of
the weaknesses to "broad changes" in the
role of the campus since its conception.
The entry includes a brief discussion
of individual buildings, such as the
central core of lecture halls, library,
and student union, the Science and
Engineering Laboratories, University
Hall, the Art and Architecture Building, and the Behavioral Sciences
Building. (pp. 184–88, 2 illustrations).

Stephens, Suzanne. "SOM at Midlife."
***Progressive Architecture* 62, no. 5 (May**
1981): 139–49. 58 illustrations, 6 plans.

History of SOM that concentrates on
the firm's organization, management
practices, growth, major commissions,
original partners, and succeeding
generations of partners. Mentions
Netsch (pp. 138–39) and highlights

several of his buildings, including the
U.S. Air Force Academy Cadet Chapel
(p. 139) and the Inland Steel Building
(p. 141). The second half of the article
is a photographic "SOM Portfolio"
of current projects (pp. 142–49).

Stoller, Ezra. *Ezra Stoller: Photographs*
***of Architecture, 1939–1980.* New York:**
Max Protech Gallery, 1981. 20 pp.
Illustrated.

Catalogue to an exhibition of architectural photographs by Ezra Stoller
(1915–2004), a favorite photographer
of SOM projects. Stoller was born
in Chicago and studied architecture
at New York University. During his
career he worked closely with leading architects. Netsch recalls:

Of course, there was Ezra Stoller,
who was Gordon's [Bunshaft]
favorite. They were the sort of leaders
in the field. Occasionally, I would get
a photograph. Someone was going to
photograph my building and would
send me one. That happened at
Northwestern, and I have a photo-
graph of one of my buildings that I
really like. He never was able to do
any more because he did it with a red
filter, and it was such a separate kind
of thing that it didn't say as much
about the building as it said about
photography. So you had to be careful
that people wouldn't try to entice you.
I met a lot of photographers, and they
would try, but we really would just
rather fall back on people we knew.
Ezra was especially good on models.
You could work with Ezra Stoller.
He would say, "Make some clouds for
me," or "Do a backdrop." We would
do it, and we would shift it around,
and he could make it look real.
(Walter Netsch, "Oral History,"
1995, p. 413)

1982

Giovannini, Joseph. "Architecture of Information." *UCLA Architecture and Planning* 3 (Winter 1982): 2–7. 5 illustrations, 1 plan.

Article on the use of computer technology in architectural designs that opens with Netsch's computer-generated drawing for the *Late Entries to the Chicago Tribune Tower Competition* (1980, see above).

> There was, however, one drawing, by Walter Netsch — formerly of the Chicago office of Skidmore, Owings and Merrill — that was both different and unsettling. No one knew quite what to make of it; the drawing did not share the assumptions implicit in the others. It was a computer drawing of a new Tribune Tower drawn by SOM computer PDP 1170, and it depicted a vertical, spider-web building spun from logic foreign to the other hand-drawn buildings. The drawing had a cool, calculated look to it, unlike the other sensitively rendered entries, yet Netsch's was no less sensitive in its way: it had a delicacy and a rhythmic regularity, and it looked like a subtle mathematical construct that could be built.

> The entry was disquieting because no one really wanted to be nettled by computers in a show that was cast as art. Many of the drawings were done in traditional, frequently Beaux Arts, materials — inks, colored pencil, charcoal, washes. But the Netsch drawings did not really fade, either in the show, or in one's memory. There was a strength, based not only in the building depicted, but also in its powerful computer origins. Was the computer the new future? The computer would certainly disturb the direction that new architecture, as seen in the Chicago show, was taking.

Miller, Nory. "Staying on Top, or Just Staying Alive?" *Chicago*, May 1982, 156–57. 4 illustrations.

Subtitled, "A critic's view of Skidmore, Owings & Merrill," this article criticizes what the author perceives as the uneven qualities of design and lack of artistic sensitivities in recent high-rise commissions. Blames SOM's diminishing reputation on its large corporate structure and slick marketing machine that spawns "a patchwork of shards from scavenged imaginations" (p. 157). Continues, "Handsome designs are still emerging from the firm, but for the first time oafish clunkers are not the aberration." Wistfully recalls SOM's glory days in the 1950s and 1960s and its founders' vision. Mentions "the controversial but widely published institutional work of Walter Netsch" (p. 156).

Rottenberg, Dan. "SOM: The Big, the Bad, and the Beautiful." *Chicago*, May 1982, 150–55, 196–202. 13 illustrations.

Attributes SOM's success to its ability to form large, cohesive design teams that include members with wide disciplinary knowledge. SOM's success is also indebted to its use of computer technology. Netsch is quoted in regards to the firm's recent inability to win design awards: "The firm's problem, according to another retired partner, Walter Netsch, is that 'success breeds patterns that get replicated.' SOM's performance in design competition would seem to bear him out…" (p. 155, photo p. 154). Includes a photo of the Inland Steel Building.

Tracey, Elizabeth. "Artless Architecture: NU Has Concrete Examples." *Daily Northwestern*, May 28, 1982. 1 illustration.

One-page article in Northwestern's student newspaper that laments the lack of cohesive campus architecture. History of campus buildings from the early 1900s is presented with comments by Northwestern art history professors Carl Condit and Oland Rand, who both criticize the lack of campus planning and resultant hodgepodge of building styles. Maintains that while Northwestern has hired some of the most prestigious architecture firms in the country, the firms did their best work elsewhere. Critiques Netsch's Lakefill plan of the early 1960s and is particularly negative about Edward Dart's campus buildings (Norris University Center, Andersen and Leverone Halls). Quotes Hans Friedman, an architect with A. M. Kinney Associates: "The sad part is that the university could be a real architectural resource for Evanston. It's not. It's a cultural resource, but people don't come to Northwestern to look at the architecture." David Van Zanten, professor of art history, says that lack of communication between the University and outside architects has contributed to mediocre, even ugly buildings. Includes a photo of Northwestern University Library and the Charles Deering Library.

1983

Bush-Brown, Albert. *Skidmore, Owings & Merrill: Architecture and Urbanism, 1973–1983*. New York: Van Nostrand Reinhold, 1983. 393 pp. Illustrated. In English and German.

Heavily illustrated overview of a decade of SOM commissions. Features the reorganization and expansion of the Art Institute of Chicago with Netsch's East Wing addition (pp. 174–77, 2 illustrations, 1 plan), including a magnificent full-color double spread of the museum's exterior.

Miami University Art Museum. *Living with Art, Two: The Collection of Walter and Dawn Clark Netsch*. Oxford, OH: Miami University Art Museum, 1983. 138 pp. 174 illustrations.

Second presentation of the Netsches' art collection at a university art museum, this exhibition took its title from the earlier exhibition at the University of Iowa in 1971. This exhibition contained more art than the first, displaying almost the entire collection from the couple's Chicago home. Fittingly, the art moved

from one Netsch building to another for the exhibition — Netsch designed both his home and the Miami University Art Museum. The book includes 167 entries (most with illustrations), along with exhibition views and short essays by Netsch and Sterling Cook, the exhibition curator. A portion of the collection on display was donated to the museum.

Netsch's statement is reprinted in Statements, pages 119–20.

1984

Berkovich, Gary. "Scaling the Hong Kong Peak." *Inland Architect* 28, no. 6 (November–December 1984): 28–31. 8 illustrations, 3 plans.

Examines and critiques entries to the international competition for the Peak Residential Club in Hong Kong, seven of which were exhibited at Chicago's ArchiCenter in 1983. Of 539 competitors, eight came from Chicago (though none were winners). First prize went to a controversial design by an English team lead by Zaha Hadid. Although Chicago entries were not selected, Berkovich credits them with innovative theoretical designs that tested new ideas. Seven Chicago designers are published, including a "leaping playful dragon fish" — a multidimensional, geometric, and wildly creative interactive design by the "Netsch Team": Netsch, Christopher Goode, Scott Coates, George Madras, and Tess Shire; model by Anthony Berent and Netsch (p. 30).

1985

Glibota, Ante, and Frédéric Edelmann. *Chicago, 150 ans d'architecture, 1833–1983 / 150 Years of Chicago Architecture, 1833–1983.* **Paris: Paris Art Center, Musée-Galerie de la SEITA, and L'Institut français d'architecture, 1985. 383 pp. Illustrated. In French and English.**

This catalogue records the exhibition of prominent Chicago architecture shown at various locations between October 1983 and January 1984. It includes photographs of the U.S. Air Force Academy Cadet Chapel (p. 109), the UIC campus (pp. 176–77), Northwestern University Library (pp. 196–97), Miami University Art Museum (pp. 210–11), and the Netsches' home (p. 293). A separate section on Netsch (pp. 286–93) includes a biography, a definition of Field Theory by Netsch, a tribute and appreciation of his work by journalist and art historian Gilles Plazy, and a list of major projects (p. 289) supplemented by 26 illustrations, plans, and designs. Other references to Netsch: pp. 28, 184, 226, 252, and 261.

Exhibition reviews: P. Hill, *Crain's Chicago Business*, October 3, 1983; J. Audouin, *Inland Architect* 27, no. 6 (November–December 1983): 2.

Hill, Timothy W. "The End of the Rainbow." *Inland Architect* 29, no. 6 (November–December 1985): 10, 13. 1 illustration.**

Examines the controversy surrounding the brightly colored 32-by-12-foot canopy that was added to the entrance of Netsch's Paul V. Galvin Library at IIT (1962), a building of strong Miesian character in keeping with the design of the campus as a whole. Robert Nevel of Chicago-based design firm Mekus/Johnson Inc. designed and installed the canopy to shelter the entrance, to establish a focal point, and to integrate the building with the plaza in front of it. However, its bright colors, guide wires, and perforated steel elements were judged by some as inappropriate for the building, and the canopy was soon removed.

Netsch, who retired five years ago, was totally unaware of the canopy controversy until he read about it and the rest of the library upgrading in his morning edition of the New York Times. *Since then he has been contacted repeatedly by the press, and has steadfastly reaffirmed that the Mies vocabulary of the IIT campus must not be altered or abridged for the sake of renovation. When asked if the rainbow-colored canopy would have been acceptable had it been painted black, he replied that the canopy design, with guide wires and perforated steel members, was in an entirely different vernacular from Mies and therefore inappropriate for the library and unacceptable for the IIT campus.*

"Postmodernists," Netsch said, "should preach contextualism and actually do it."

Photo shows the multicolored canopy at the library's entrance.

Malcolm, Andrew H. "Chicago School to Dismantle Its New Canopy as Un-Mies-Like." *New York Times*, **September 11, 1985.**

Concerns rededication of the renovated Galvin Library at IIT and the dismantling of the entrance canopy installed earlier in the summer. The canopy was considered inappropriate and disrespectful to the memory of Ludwig Mies van der Rohe, whose somber style dominates the 120-acre campus.

Museum of Science and Industry. *A Guide to 150 Years of Chicago Architecture.* **Prepared by Robert Bruegmann, Sabra Clark, Paul Florian, Douglas Stoker, and Cynthia Weese. Chicago: Chicago Review Press, 1985. 151 pp. Illustrated.**

In 1985 the Museum of Science and Industry in Chicago presented an updated version of the comprehensive Paris exhibition *150 Years of Chicago Architecture, 1833–1983,* curated by Ante Glibota (see above). This publication is both an overview of and visitor guide to the new exhibition. Albert Bush-Brown authored the section on Netsch (pp. 106–15), which includes numerous photographs of major projects and a list of buildings designed by Netsch. Bush-Brown reviews Netsch's life, career, and accomplishments, calling him "a sensitive, thoughtful man whose brilliant intellect seeks meaning and order" (p. 106).

> *Over a professional lifetime of hard, intensive work against deadlines, budgets and conventions, Netsch had gained his own aesthetic development within a great architectural firm. It will ever be questioned whether the achievement might have arrived without the resources and opportunities of SOM, but it is equally to be debated whether, as various honors and awards attest, it may well have been among SOM's finest accomplishments. He had won international acclaim for his educational and institutional designs and changed the images of a university as it had not been changed since the nineteenth century, and he was revered as a teacher and colleague and friend to those who were intent upon advancing the nation's best environmental and social interests.* (p. 115)

Stanley Tigerman contributed an essay called "Goldberg, Netsch and Weese: In Exile at Home," in which he analyzes how the "hyper-individualism" of the three influenced the "Chicago spirit" in architecture (pp. 126–27). Also discussed the Inland Steel Building (pp. 68–70).

Pastier, John. "A Creature of Its Storied City." *Architecture* **74, no. 8 (August 1985): 46–53. 1 illustrations, 21 plans and diagrams.**
Discusses the strengths and weaknesses of the School of Architecture at UIC. According to the author, some of the school's strengths are its location within the architectural landscape of Chicago and its professional faculty members, many of whom are prominent architects. The program's weaknesses include a lack of resources and Netsch's Art and Architecture Building, where the program is based. Claims that Field Theory–based design is not conducive to the school's need for studio and instructional spaces. Calls Netsch "one of SOM's brightest talents" (p. 48).

Patterson, James R. "The Chapel That Nearly Wasn't." *Air Force Magazine,* **December 1985, 90–92. 1 illustration.**
Recounts the saga of the U.S. Air Force Academy Cadet Chapel, beginning with President Eisenhower's signing of the bill to authorize the Academy in 1954. Describes the Cadet Chapel, its organ, and gradual public acceptance. Quotes Netsch: "I received a lot of hate mail in those days. I was even called a Communist…. [However] in recent years my heart has been warmed by the many fine letters from parents of cadets who have told me of having been spiritually uplifted in visiting the chapel" (p. 92).

Skidmore, Owings & Merrill. *Cadet Area Master Plan: Executive Summary. United States Air Force Base Comprehensive Plan.* **Colorado Springs, CO: U.S. Air Force Academy, June 1985. 39 pp. Illustrated.**
Updated planning document for buildings and restoration projects in the Cadet Area.

Wolff, Theodore. "Miami University's Art Museum Is Itself a Handsome Work of Art." *Christian Science Monitor,* **April 29, 1985, 27. 1 illustration.**
Highly positive article about the Miami University Art Museum. Observes that the changing geometric scale of the galleries in the "starkly modern" museum is appropriate for showcasing the varied works of art in the permanent collection. "Viewing this museum and its exhibits was a real pleasure. The building itself, its suitability to the display of a very wide variety of art, and its physical location add up to a unique viewing experience."

1986

Cross, Robert. "A Man Who Dreams of Classic Parks: But Architect Walter Netsch Suddenly Finds Himself Recast as a Pivotal Political Player." *Chicago Tribune*, July 6, 1986. 2 illustrations.

Profile of Netsch written shortly after he was appointed president of the Chicago Park District Board of Commissioners by Mayor Harold Washington. Includes personal details about Netsch's childhood dream of being an artist, how he met Dawn Clark, recent health problems, and an assessment of his plans for the Park District. Netsch wanted to restore Chicago's "classic" parks to their late-19th-century designs in order to revitalize the communities in which they are located. He opposed the commercialization of public park areas, having previously served on a panel that recommended against making Navy Pier a commercial entertainment complex. Reprinted in *Friends of the Park Newsletter* 1, no. 17 (Fall 1986): 1–4.

Netsch served as president of the board from June 16, 1986, to May 5, 1987, and was a commissioner of the Chicago Park District from June 19, 1986, to December 19, 1989. His often turbulent tenure with the Park District is chronicled in numerous local newspapers. Among others, see articles in the *Chicago Sun-Times* (May 15, 1986; May 31, 1986; June 27, 1989; and December 19, 1989) and in the *Chicago Tribune* (July 6, 1986; August 29, 1986; March 6, 1987; June 27, 1989; December 19, 1989; and December 21, 1989).

"Army Engineers Fear for Chicago Shore Drive." *New York Times*, December 24, 1986.

Short piece about how the rapid rise of Lake Michigan threatened Chicago's Lake Shore Drive. Quotes Netsch (as Park District president) about the high cost of replacing the sea wall that runs along the drive.

Perkins, Lawrence Bradford. "Oral History of Lawrence Bradford Perkins." Interview by Betty J. Blum, November 8–10 and 17, 1985. Transcript. Chicago: Art Institute of Chicago, 1986. 174 pp.

Includes references to the U.S. Air Force Academy (p. 75) and Netsch and SOM (p. 84). Available at www.artic.edu/aic /libraries/caohp/perkins.html.

Wersich, Carol. "A Building Ahead of Its Time." *Evansville [IN] Press*, March 12, 1986. 4 illustrations.

Feature on the John Wesley Powell Federal Building in the U.S. Geological Survey National Center, a building complex located in Reston, Virginia. The complex, which covers 45 acres, includes the Powell Federal Building, a seven-story, 1 million-square-foot center with triangular wings designed by Netsch and completed in 1974. Sixty picturesque acres of woods surround the center, which houses 2,500 employees. In the article Netsch discusses the design concept and regrets not using more color in the predominantly glass and precast-concrete building. Quotes William A. Schmidt, special assistant for facilities: "Visitors like the design very much. I receive many more favorable comments from them than from the occupants."

Yost, L. Morgan. "Oral History of L. Morgan Yost, F.A.I.A." Interview by Betty J. Blum, May 13–15, 1985. Transcript. Chicago: Art Institute of Chicago, 1986. 128 pp.

Yost (1908–1992) employed Netsch in his small Kenilworth, Illinois, office from April 1946 to November 1947. This transcript includes references to Netsch's involvement in drawing the cabinetwork for the Deno house in Highland Park, Illinois (pp. 72–73), and the Western Homes project in 1946, the working methods of the office (pp. 80–82), and Yost's appraisal of Netsch (pp. 112–13). Available at www.artic.edu/aic/libraries /caohp/yost.html.

1987

Hedlund, Nevin. "Netsch Takes on the Parks." *Inland Architect* 31, no. 1 (January–February 1987): 79–85. 1 illustration.

Drawing on the November 1986 Chicago Park District *Preliminary Reorganization Report* (see Primary Sources, 1986, above), this article outlines Netsch's plans for his five-year term as president of the Park District's Board of Commissioners. Focuses on the crux of Netsch's plan: reorganization of the Park District's human resources and the implementation of accountability measures. Specific projects — such as the revitalization of Garfield Park, the relocation of Lake Shore Drive, and the reaction to rising water levels in Lake Michigan — are discussed. Includes a small photo of Netsch at a board meeting.

Johnson, Sven. "Notes of a lecture on the Miami University Art Museum and Walter Netsch's Field Theory, 1989." 16 pp. 7 illustrations, 16 plans and diagrams.

Notes of a lecture delivered April 10, 1989, at Miami University in Oxford, Ohio. Discusses selection of Netsch for the university's art museum and comments on the museum's design. Includes an explanation of Field Theory (pp. 2–5), illustrated by photos, floor plans, and diagrams of Field Theory buildings at the University of Iowa, Wells College, and Miami University. Held in Miami University Art Museum Archives.

Owen, David. "Writs Fly Round Chicago Architects." *Financial Times* (London), June 26, 1987.

Article about Illinois Attorney General Neil Hartigan suing Murphy Jahn Associates over problems with the State of Illinois Building in downtown Chicago. "In Chicago, we take our architecture seriously," Netsch comments. "The architectural profession is probably as hostile to one another behind backs as any group I am aware of."

1988

Bruegmann, Robert. "The Art Institute Expands: Challenges of Mid-Century." *Museum Studies* 14, no. 1 (1998): 56–81. 23 illustrations, 15 plans and diagrams.

Bruegmann, architectural historian and professor of art at UIC, charts the Art Institute of Chicago's growth and construction projects in the 20th century. Section III (pp. 74–80) highlights East Wing additions of the 1970s designed by Netsch. Bruegmann explores the museum's selection of SOM and Netsch's previous building designs. (Plans for the first phase were announced in December 1972 in a handsome booklet entitled *The Art Institute of Chicago: The Bold and the Prudent*.) Bruegmann enumerates the many design challenges that Netsch faced, in particular the Illinois Central Railroad tracks and issues with the School of the Art Institute.

Regarding the East Wing additions, Bruegmann states:

> Netsch went much further than any of his predecessors in creating a building that broke with the classical tradition. Resolutely modern in its avoidance of applied ornament or specific historical details, it was highly asymmetrical rather than axial and symmetrical; and because it was created as a "Field Theory" building, it was filled with forty-five-degree diagonals rather than the strictly rectilinear lines of the old building. (p. 78)

Discusses incorporation of salvaged elements from the Trading Room of Adler and Sullivan's Chicago Stock Exchange Building (1893). Construction was begun in May 1974 and finished in 1977. The new addition received praise from the press and won a national honor award from the American Institute of Architects. Comments on unresolved problems, mostly minor, and ends with observations about new building programs under way at many major museums in the United States.

"Icons of Modernism or Machine-Age Dinosaurs?" *Architectural Record* **(June 1989): 142–47. 4 illustrations, 9 plans and diagrams.**

Surveys landmark early works of "American Modernism" to determine how they have fared in intervening years. Covers the Philadelphia Savings and Society Building (1932) by William Lescaze and George Howe and two SOM projects: Gordon Bunshaft's Lever House (1952) in New York and the Crown-Zellerbach Headquarters Building in San Francisco. "Though the structures chosen for this article are hardly representative, they do suggest that thoughtful design — even using untried and sometimes risky techniques — can produce buildings of lasting aesthetic and functional value" (p. 147).

Skidmore, Owings & Merrill. *Community Center Master Plan. United States Air Force Academy Base Comprehensive Plan.* **Colorado Springs, CO: U.S. Air Force Academy, August 1988. 70 pp. Illustrated.**

Updated planning document for the Community Center, located in the Cadet Area.

1989

Calloway, Earl. "Chicagoans Make Possible a Public Garden on Oak St." **Entertainment,** *Chicago Defender,* **October 9, 1989. 2 illustrations.**

Dedication ceremony of a 50,000-square-foot public park at the Oak Street Triangle, located on the corner of Lake Shore Drive and Oak Street. Netsch presided at the ceremony as Park District commissioner.

Graham, Bruce. *Bruce Graham of SOM.* **New York: Rizzoli, 1989. 166 pp. Illustrated.**

Overview of Graham's projects, dating from 1956 to 1990. Each project is discussed by Graham, followed by photographs, floor plans, and elevations. Entry for the Inland Steel Building (pp. 16–19, 10 illustrations and floor

plans) fails to mention Netsch's original concept design and model, which Graham completed. In his preface, "Who Is Bruce Graham, Anyway?" (pp. 8–9), Stanley Tigerman notes:

It was at that point in time that I came to know Bruce Graham, who had just been elevated to general partner status in the Chicago office of SOM. I had been hired as a junior designer by his counterpart, Walter A. Netsch, Jr., to work on the Air Force Academy at Colorado Springs, at the closing moments of construction for that immense military complex. The completion of that project coincided with SOM's move to new headquarters in the Inland Steel building, whose authorship both Netsch and Graham share (not without continuing debate as to the extent of each of their roles, I might add). Graham had just become partner-in-charge, and thus, my boss.

Slaton, Deborah, ed. *Wild Onions: A Brief Guide to Landmarks and Lesser-Known Structures in Chicago's Loop.* **Springfield, IL: Association for Preservation Technology International, 1989. 45 pp. Illustrated.**

Contains a short entry on the Inland Steel Building (p. 29), labeling it "an excellent example of 1950s creative architectural expression," with one small black-and-white exterior photo.

1990

Bunshaft, Gordon. "Oral History of Gordon Bunshaft." Interview by Betty J. Blum, April 4–7, 1989. Transcript. Chicago: Art Institute of Chicago, 1990. 333 pp.

Includes references to Netsch's involvement in the Inland Steel Building (pp. 47–49) and SOM (pp. 281, 285). Available at www.artic.edu/aic/libraries/caohp/bunshaft.html.

Davidson, Cynthia Chapin. "In Search of the Avant-Garde." *Inland Architect* 34, no. 3 (May–June 1990): [33]. 1 illustration.

Editorial regarding articles in this issue of *Inland Architect* about Netsch (see Nereim below) and Peter Eisenman. Comments briefly on Netsch's Field Theory and his designs for an addition to the Miami University Art Museum. Includes a color reproduction of one of Netsch's Field Theory–inspired paintings.

Gapp, Paul. "Beauty Treatment: UIC Campus Gets a New Look at Its Old Problems." *Chicago Tribune,* June 10, 1990. 2 illustrations.

Architecture critic examines the architectural history of UIC. The article begins:

> A new chapter is about to be added to the troubled history of the University of Illinois at Chicago, whose campus has long been plagued by poor siting, poor planning and controversial architecture. If anyone loses face in the recently announced program of major campus remodeling and construction, it will probably be Walter A. Netsch, the famous maverick Chicago architect who originally made UIC's most important design decisions.

It concludes: "One can only hope that in the attempt to improve on Netsch's work at UIC, beauty will be of prime consideration. As of now, beauty is nowhere evident in a campus that has been evolving for 25 years."

Goldsmith, Myron. "Oral History of Myron Goldsmith." Interview by Betty J. Blum, July 25–26, September 7, October 5, 1986. Transcript. Chicago: Art Institute of Chicago, 1990. 152 pp.

Includes references to Netsch's participation in the U.S. Air Force Academy project (pp. 97–98), a fountain at Perlstein Hall at IIT (p. 101), and the IIT campus (pp. 118–19). Available at www.artic.edu /aic/libraries/caohp/goldsmith.html.

Harris, Patricia, and David Lyon. "Academy Days." *Adventure Road,* September–October 1990, 22–27. 4 illustrations.

Article on the U.S. Air Force Academy, illustrated with full-page color photos. Discusses the Cadet Chapel (pp. 26–27).

Jones, William Goodrich. "Academic Library Planning: Rationality, Imagination, and Field Theory in the Work of Walter Netsch — A Case Study." *College and Research Libraries* 51 (May 1990): 207–20.

Discusses Field Theory principles in the design of the Northwestern University Library and UIC's Richard J. Daley Library and Behavioral Sciences Building. Also details how Netsch had to compromise Field Theory components in the Seeley G. Mudd Library for Science and Engineering at Northwestern after objections to some design elements from the planning committee. Jones was a librarian at UIC.

Nereim, Anders. "Walter Netsch: Having a Field Day." *Inland Architect* 34, no. 3 (May–June 1990): 60–67. 4 illustrations, 13 plans and diagrams.

Examines the development of Field Theory as a set of artistic principles governing Netsch's work — just as specific artistic principles governed the work of Sullivan and Wright. Suggests that Field Theory evolved over time to become less deterministic and more gestural, especially with the introduction of the "chrysanthemum" field. A sidebar explains Field Theory in more detail. Photos show Long Library at Wells College and the Miami University Art Museum.

Saliga, Pauline A., ed. *The Sky's the Limit: A Century of Chicago Skyscrapers.* New York: Rizzoli, 1990. 304 pp. Illustrated.

This book features two-page entries — with photographs and discussions of historical relevance, influences, and architectural innovations — for the Inland Steel Building (pp. 180–81) and the Harris Trust and Savings Bank addition (pp. 184–85). Includes a further reference to Netsch (p. 298).

Saunders, William S., and Ezra Stoller. *Modern Architecture: Photographs by Ezra Stoller.* New York: Harry N. Abrams, 1990. 216 pp. Illustrated.

Includes photographs of Northwestern University Library (pp. 113, 150). Stoller was a favorite photographer of Netsch and SOM.

Slavin, Maeve, and Davis Brewster Allen. *Davis Allen: Forty Years of Interior Design at Skidmore.* New York: Rizzoli, 1990. 136 pp. Illustrated.

Davis Allen joined SOM in 1950 and was an "Associate Partner, Senior Interior Designer" from 1965 to 1985. Includes references to furnishings and interior decoration of the Inland Steel Building (pp. 26–31, 10 illustrations) and the Crown-Zellerbach Headquarters Building (pp. 32–33, 4 illustrations, 2 plans). Bruce Graham erroneously receives exclusive credit for the design of the Inland Steel Building.

1991

Bristol, Katharine G. "The Pruitt-Igoe Myth." *Journal of Architectural Education* 44, no. 3 (May 1991): 163–71. 3 illustrations, 2 plans and diagrams.

Analyzes St. Louis's notorious public housing project, Pruitt-Igoe, and debunks the myth that the project not only demonstrated an architectural failure but also was a condemnation of high modernism:

By continuing to promote architectural solutions to what are fundamentally problems of class and race, the myth conceals the complete inadequacy of contemporary public housing policy. By furthering this misconception, the myth disguises the causes of the failure of public housing, and also ensures the continued participation of the architectural profession in token and palliative efforts to address the problems of poverty in America. (p. 170)

Netsch's SOM design team worked on renewal plans for Pruitt-Igoe, which were not realized.

Crump, Joseph. "Less Is Skidmore." *Chicago,* February 1991, 76–81, 114.

Discusses a low point in SOM history when both bankruptcy and the dissolution of the firm were under consideration. Examines personalities and conflicts within the firm and chronicles the volatile relationship between Netsch and Bruce Graham while both were partners (pp. 78–79).

Forrey, Roy. "Inland Steel Building: 30 West Monroe Street, Chicago, Illinois: Preliminary Staff Summary of Information." Chicago: Commission on Chicago Landmarks, 1991. 19 pp. Illustrated.

Planning document that assesses the condition and preservation concerns of the Inland Steel Building.

Hartmann, William. "Oral History of William Hartmann." Interview by Betty J. Blum, October 30–31, November 1–2, 1989. Transcript. Chicago: Art Institute of Chicago, 1991. 204 pp.

Includes references to Netsch's relationship with SOM (pp. 81, 103), the Inland Steel Building (pp. 106–09, 134), the IIT campus (pp. 130–31), and the East Wing addition to the Art Institute (pp. 181–83). Available at www.artic.edu/aic/libraries /caohp/hartmann.html.

Miami University Art Museum. *Living with Art, Three: The Collection of Walter and Dawn Clark Netsch.* With a statement by Walter Netsch. Oxford, OH: Miami University Art Museum, 1991. 40 pp. 28 illustrations.

Third installment of the *Living with Art* series of exhibitions presents 34 works of art added to the Netsch collection since the previous exhibition in 1983. Some featured artists, such as Al Held, Roy Lichtenstein, and Robert Motherwell, were staples of the Netsch collection, while many of the acquisitions were works by burgeoning contemporary artists. Highlights of the exhibition include Leon Golub's lithograph *South Africa*, a Lichtenstein tea set from 1984, and Motherwell's silkscreen print *Burning Sun*.

Netsch's statement is reprinted in Statements, page 124.

Weese, Harry Mohr. "Oral History of Harry Mohr Weese." Interview by Betty J. Blum, March 4–24, 1988. Transcript. Chicago: Art Institute of Chicago, 1991. 274 pp.

Includes references to a competition with Netsch for the Seventeenth Church of Christ, Scientist, commission (won by Weese; p. 129) and the East Wing addition to the Art Institute (p. 136). Available at www.artic.edu/aic /libraries/caohp/weese.html.

1992

Bassett, Edward Charles. "Oral History of Edward Charles Bassett." Interview by Betty J. Blum, January 30–31, February 1, 1989. Transcript. Chicago: Art Institute of Chicago, 1992. 159 pp.

Includes references to Netsch's involvement with the Inland Steel Building (pp. 71–72) and the Chicago office of SOM (pp. 79, 88–89, 130). Available at www.artic.edu/aic/libraries/caohp /bassett.html.

Cameron, Robert. *Above Chicago: A New Collection of Historical and Original Aerial Photographs of Chicago.* San Francisco: Cameron, 1992. 159 pp. Illustrated.

This large-format book of aerial photography contains two photos of the Art Institute showing Netsch's East Wing addition (pp. 17 and 25), two photos of the UIC campus (pp. 104–05), and one photo of the Northwestern University campus (pp. 110–11). Highlighted in the accompanying text are the Science and Engineering South Building at UIC and the Lindheimer Astronomical Research Center at Northwestern (pp. 110–11).

Takayma, Masami. *The Structural Architecture of Chicago.* Tokyo: Process Architecture, 1992. 167 pp. Illustrated. In English and Japanese.

Includes references to and illustrations of buildings designed by Netsch in Chicago: Inland Steel (pp. 13, 31–35), the Harris Trust and Savings Bank (p. 57), and other projects (pp. 67, 109, 111–13, 115, 118–19).

1993

Bennett, Julie. "Dawn Clark & Walter Netsch." *Vital Times*, October 1993, cover, 16–17. 2 illustrations.

Feature on the Netsches that highlights Dawn's career in Illinois state government and her historic campaign for governor in 1994. Mentions Walter's career at SOM, his work since retirement in 1979, and his assistance and support of Dawn's campaign, for which he designed pins, posters, and stickers.

Krohe Jr., James. "Altered Visions [UIC]." *Inland Architect* 37, no. 2 (March/April 1993): 52–55. 4 illustrations, 1 plan.

Discusses the proposed redesign of the UIC campus. Netsch's response to the proposed revisions is included and suggests that he was largely left out of the planning process. The article also presents general issues relevant to preserving 1960s-era architecture, concluding that renovations must be undertaken with attention to the logic of the original designs.

Morris, Jack H. *Inland Steel at 100: Beginning A Second Century of Progress.* Chicago: Inland Steel Industries, 1993. 68 pp. Illustrated.

History of Inland Steel Industries, founded in 1893 as Chicago Steel Works by Joseph Block. Mentions the Inland Steel Building (pp. 3, 46).

Rudolph, Paul. "Oral History of Paul Rudolph." Interview by Robert Bruegmann, February 28, 1986. Transcript. Chicago: Art Institute of Chicago, 1993. 66 pp.

Includes references to Netsch's relationship with Rudolph (pp. 52–53). Available at www.artic.edu/aic/libraries/caohp /rudolph.html.

Sinkevitch, Alice, ed. *AIA Guide to Chicago.* New York: Harcourt Brace, 1993. 541 pp. Illustrated.

Includes entries on the Inland Steel Building (pp. 67–68), St. Matthew United Methodist Church (p. 135), Regenstein Library at the University of Chicago (p. 434), the Netsch home (p. 177–78), and the UIC campus (pp. 283–89). (See also 2004: Sinkevitch.)

Zukowsky, John, ed. *Chicago Architecture and Design, 1923–1993: Reconfiguration of an American Metropolis.* Munich: Prestel; Chicago: Art Institute of Chicago, 1993. 479 pp. Illustrated.

Catalogue to an exhibition held at the Art Institute of Chicago. Includes references to Netsch's building designs (pp. 22, 23, 25, 305, 326, 442, and 471).

1994

Brown, Mark. "Dawn's Quixote: A 'Prophet Without Honor,' Architect Walter Netsch Keeps Churning Out Ideas." People Plus, *Chicago Sun-Times,* May 15, 1994. 3 illustrations.

Article written during Dawn Clark Netsch's campaign for governor of Illinois. Walter Netsch talks about his wife's political career, their art collection and home, their love of White Sox baseball and Boston terriers, and his career with SOM. Also comments on the Cabrini-Green housing project, plans for Meigs Field, and his tenure on the Chicago Park District Board of Commissioners. Recalls their courtship ("conducted at Comiskey Park") and designing their home. Mentions controversies that surrounded the U. S. Air Force Academy, the UIC campus, and Field Theory, which he compares to Frank Lloyd Wright's search for innovative designs. Photos show the couple at their home, their art collection, and buildings he designed at Northwestern.

Bruegmann, Robert, ed. *Modernism at Mid-Century: The Architecture of the United States Air Force Academy.* Chicago and London: University of Chicago Press, 1994. 200 pp. Illustrated.

Compilation of essays that document the conception, design, and critical interpretations of the U.S. Air Force Academy. Contributors include Robert Bruegmann, Jory Johnson, Robert Nauman, Sheri Olson, James Russell, and Kristen Schaffer; most are professors or practicing architects.

Part I, "Designing and Building the Academy," deals with the impetus behind building the Academy, the selection of SOM for the commission, the design of the site and buildings, and construction. Part II, "Interpreting the Academy," features analytic essays that explore architectural decisions made at the Academy from sociological, political, aesthetical, and theoretical perspectives. Part III,

"Interviews and Recollections," publishes a 1958 conversation between Netsch and architectural historian John Burchard, recollections by Gordon Bunshaft (from a 1989 oral history), and a 1993 interview with Lt. Gen. Bradley Hosmer, a 1959 graduate of the Academy and Academy superintendent from 1991 to 1994. (Bruegmann credits Hosmer with the idea for this book.)

In Netsch's insightful conversation with John Burchard (pp. 174–89), he discusses studying the site and setting boundaries, conceptualizing the general layout, working with Air Force personnel and the oversight committee, the Academy's symbolic importance, challenges and problem solving, and integrating various elements and buildings into a cohesive spatial organization. Burchard, a well-known architectural scholar and editor, was dean of the School of Social Sciences and Humanities at MIT when the interview took place.

Reviews: C. Kent, *Chicago Tribune*, June 18, 1995; J. Prosser, *Planning for Higher Education* 23 (Summer 1995): 39–40; D. De Long, *Journal of the Society of Architectural Historians* 54, no. 4 (December 1995): 482–83; G. Clancey, *Technology and Culture* 37, no. 3 (July 1996): 646–47.

Mitchell, Dan. "'Hero Architects' Chart a Course." *Inland Architect* 38, no. 2 (Spring 1994): 19.

Summarizes a panel discussion held in May 1994 at the Chicago Cultural Center in which veteran Netsch and Bertrand Goldberg discussed the future of urban design and the role of the architect. Netsch notes the perils of soulless urban designs and urges architects to maintain a sense of community, social consciousness, and humanity in their work.

Pacatte, Marcel. "Illinois' First Spouses: Walter Netsch Thrives Outside His Wife's Shadow." *St. Louis Post-Dispatch*, September 7, 1994. 1 illustration.

Profile of Netsch, written during Dawn Clark Netsch's campaign for governor of Illinois. Discusses the Netsches' home, their art collection (some pieces of which were sold to finance the campaign), their careers, Walter's major commissions at SOM, his study in the early 1970s to redesign St. Louis's Pruitt-Igoe public housing project, his love of Chicago's parks and service on the Park District Board of Commissioners, his youth in South Chicago, Dawn's participation in state government, and their lives since his retirement in 1979. Includes a color photo of Walter.

Webb, Michael. *Architects House Themselves: Breaking New Ground*. Washington, D.C.: The Preservation Press, National Trust for Historic Preservation, 1994. 224 pp. Illustrated.

Profiles the Netsch home (pp. 151–54) along with Netsch's career at SOM and Field Theory aesthetics. Netsch describes selecting the site for his home and describes its design as a "laboratory, built at minimal cost from standard parts" (p. 154). Mentions that he continues to tinker with the residence, in particular "the gazebo above the garage, from which he can enjoy the gingko tree he planted in the courtyard when the house was new" (p. 154). Color photos show Netsch and exterior/interior views. Includes one floor plan/elevation.

1995

Fujikawa, Joseph. "Oral History of Joseph Fujikawa." Interview by Betty J. Blum, September 13, 1983. Transcript. Chicago: Art Institute of Chicago, 1995. 43 pp.

Includes reference to Netsch's UIC campus plan (pp. 28–29). Available at www.artic.edu/aic/libraries/caohp /fujikawa.html.

Hammond, James Wright. "Oral History of James Wright Hammond." Interview by Betty J. Blum. September 23, 1983. Transcript. Chicago: Art Institute of Chicago, 1995. 60 pp.

Interview with SOM architect, 1946–61. Includes references to Netsch's involvement with the IIT campus (p. 20), SOM, the UIC campus, the U.S. Air Force Academy and the U.S. Naval Postgraduate School (pp. 32–35, 42). Available at www.artic.edu/aic/libraries /caohp/hammond.html.

Kamin, Blair. "Air Force Academy Chapel Wins Prestigious AIA Award." *Chicago Tribune*, December 14, 1995.

Announces the selection of the U.S. Air Force Academy Cadet Chapel for the AIA's prestigious Twenty-Five Year Award to be presented January 30, 1996, in Washington, D.C. "The chapel's unusual design made it controversial upon its unveiling, but the building is now one of the most-visited attractions in Colorado."

———. "Air Force Chapel Gets Attention, But Whole Campus Soars." *Chicago Tribune*, December 31, 1995. 1 illustration.

Critique of the U.S. Air Force Academy on the occasion of the selection of the Cadet Chapel for the AIA Twenty-Five Year Award. Finds that the entire Academy is more than the sum of its parts and that the AIA does it a disservice by recognizing only the Cadet Chapel.

———. "The Transformation of UIC; Design Puts Humanity Back in the Equation." *Chicago Tribune*, October 29, 1995. 3 illustrations.

Praises renovations to the UIC campus by Chicago architect Daniel Coffey, who replaced Netsch's original walkways and amphitheater with an open plaza with six seating areas.

Sinisi, J. Sebastian. "Academy Design Was Once a Pinnacle of Controversy." *Denver Post*, November 12, 1995.

Recounts controversies and conflicts over the design of the U.S. Air Force Academy. Claims that today "those attacks have largely run their course," and that the Academy, which was recently proposed for listing in the National Register of Historic Places, has indeed achieved the mantle of "historic." The second half of this short article focuses on the Cadet Chapel. Photos show the chapel's aluminum-clad tetrahedron spires and stained-glass panels.

———. "U.S. Architectural 25-Year Award Won by Academy Chapel." *Denver Post*, December 13, 1995. 1 illustration.

Announces selection of U.S. Air Force Academy Cadet Chapel for the AIA's Twenty-Five Year Award. Explains that the award, conferred each year since 1969, goes to a building 25 to 35 years old designed by an American architect that "exemplifies design of enduring architectural significance." Revisits the chapel's conception and Netsch's designs for the Air Force Academy. Recounts how Netsch's modernistic "Air Age Gothic" chapel met with considerable opposition in Congress and in the popular and professional press, but that the chapel is now one of the nation's most recognizable structures and the "Academy's undisputed centerpiece." Quotes architects Robert Root and Seth Rosenman on their admiration for the Cadet Chapel and how daring it appeared when built. Includes one photo of the chapel's exterior.

1996

"Accent on Architecture."
AIArchitect **3 (March 1996): 5.**

Notes Netsch's acceptance of the Twenty-Five Year Award for the U.S. Air Force Academy Cadet Chapel on January 30, 1996, at the American Institute of Architects/American Architectural Foundation Accent on Architecture gala:

> Netsch spoke fondly of the work on the chapel and how "we were all spurred on by Nat Owings, who expected excellence." He also acknowledged the project's consultants, Eero Saarinen and Pietro Belluschi (both of whom, along with Owings, are AIA Gold Medallists), and said, "It takes many, sometimes, to make a public work succeed."

"A Lasting Treasure." *Air Force Times,* **January 15, 1996, 2. 1 illustration.**

Short notice of the AIA Twenty-Five Year Award for the Cadet Chapel. "The 34-year-old chapel is the first government project to win the award, which will be presented Jan. 30 in Washington, D.C."

Brownson, Jacques Calman. "Oral History of Jacques Calman Brownson." Interview by Betty J. Blum, December 4–9, 1994. Transcript. Chicago: Art Institute of Chicago, 1996. 280 pp.

Includes references to Netsch's involvement with the UIC campus (p. 144) and SOM (p. 155). Available at www.artic .edu/aic/libraries/caohp/brownson.html.

Gill Lui, Elizabeth. *Spirit and Flight: A Photographic Salute to the United States Air Force Academy.* **Colorado Springs, CO: U.S. Air Force Academy, 1996. 133 pp. Illustrated.**

Lavishly illustrated book celebrates both the history of the Air Force Academy and the architecture that molded it. It includes Netsch's 1996 acceptance speech for the AIA Twenty-Five Year Award given to the Cadet Chapel, in which he briefly sketches the character of postwar architecture and the inspirations for his design.

The remainder of the book contains recollections by Netsch in poetry and prose, facts about the institution, and notable quotes.

For a feature article on Lui and this book, see *Colorado Springs Gazette-Telegraph,* November 10, 1996.

Kent, Cheryl. "Softening Brutalism: Is Anything Lost?" *Architectural Record* **184, no. 8 (August 1996): 21–22. 4 illustrations.**

Evaluates plans to "humanize" UIC campus, including reasons why the original project was never fully executed and fell into disrepair. The author argues that some elements of the renovation are incongruous and detract from Netsch's original design, which she defends. Concludes that the solutions devised for the problems with the campus are "very banal." Claims that the campus's "proud air of architectural militance now seems reduced, shriveled, as though it would like nothing more than for some vine to grow over it" (p. 22). Includes photos of the campus and its buildings.

Noel, Tom. "Air Force Academy Captures Its Era." *Denver Post,* **March 31, 1996.**

Reports on a recent visit to the U.S. Air Force Academy, "now perhaps America's purest 1950s architectural period piece."

> Far from ageless, it perfectly captures its time. It epitomizes the international-style dream of buildings as functional machines. The pure, uncompromising plan employs angular glass and aluminum-clad rectangles connected by vast expanses of concrete. The comprehensive international-style design dictates everything, from the Spartan box buildings to the windowless classrooms. Even the desks are made so that cadets have to sit alertly on the front edge, maintaining perfect posture.

1997

Kerbis, Gertrude. "Oral History of Gertrude Kerbis." Interview by Betty J. Blum, May 21–23, 30–31, June 4–5, 1996. Transcript. Chicago: Art Institute of Chicago, 1997. 186 pp.

Includes extensive references to the U.S. Air Force Academy project, for which Netsch hired Kerbis as a designer (pp. 57–60, 63–84), the Inland Steel Building (pp. 118–19), and other recollections about SOM and Netsch (pp. 86, 92, 96, 102, 168). Available at www.artic.edu/aic/libraries/caohp/kerbis.html.

1998

Graham, Bruce John. "Oral History of Bruce John Graham." Interview by Betty J. Blum, May 25–28, 1997. Transcript. Chicago: Art Institute of Chicago, 1998. 333 pp.

Includes references to Netsch's involvement in Oak Ridge, Tennessee (p. 34), and the Inland Steel Building (pp. 100–07), making partner at SOM (pp. 112–13), inclusion on Nat Owings's list of 12 most important designers in America (p. 121), working at SOM (pp. 126, 251, 253), contrasting styles of Netsch and Graham (pp. 135–37), and working methods (p. 155). Available at www.artic.edu/aic/libraries/caohp/graham.html.

Rohan, Tim. "Air-Conditioning Unit." *Wallpaper* 15 (1998): 87–92. 9 illustrations.

Effusive, heavily illustrated feature on the U.S. Air Force Academy ("This top-gun campus stands as America's most formidable complex of modernist architecture.") that lavishes praise on the Cadet Chapel as "the perfect fusion of the spiritual and the technological, the modernist dream come true" (p. 91). Credits "a crack team of America's design talent" under Netsch's leadership and relates how Netsch laid out the stained-glass window designs on his living room rug.

Rotenberk, Lori. "Walter Netsch and Dawn Clark Netsch: Cubelike House Is Hardly Square." *Chicago Sun-Times,* January 2, 1998. 2 illustrations.

Features the Netsch home and the Netsches' art collection. Praises the home's open interior, light, and fluid multilevel spaces that flow uninterrupted. Quotes Netsch's observation that so many architecture buffs — thousands — have toured the home that the wooden floor had to be replaced. Photos show the home's interior and Dawn Clark Netsch with their Boston terriers.

1999

Abercrombie, Stanley. "The Art of Dining." *Interior Design* 70, no. 8 (June 1999): 130–31.

Short piece on the recent redesign of the Restaurant on the Park at the Art Institute of Chicago by the firm of Powell/Kleinschmidt. Notes that the original space was designed by Netsch in 1976 according to Field Theory principles. Powell/Kleinschmidt proposed replacing a solid masonry wall with a window wall to open diners' views to Grant Park and eastward toward Lake Michigan.

Randall, Frank A. *History of the Development of Building Construction in Chicago.* 2nd ed. Revised and expanded by John D. Randall. Urbana and Chicago: University of Illinois Press, 1999. 526 pp.

Includes short entries on SOM (p. 40), the Harris Trust and Savings Bank and its additions (p. 277), the Inland Steel Building (p. 353), and the UIC campus (p. 361). Entries include information on location, physical characteristics, architects, and engineers and a list of photographs. Second edition of a book first published in 1949.

2000

Neal, Steve. "Netsch's Legacy Still Being Written." *Chicago Sun-Times,* **November 25, 2000.**

Editorial tribute to Netsch, "a major American architect … renowned for his bold innovation," wishing him a full recovery from recent health problems. Recounts Netsch's major works, his presidency of the Chicago Park District Board of Commissioners, his farsighted planning for Chicago's waterfront, and his support of his wife's history-making campaign for governor of Illinois in 1994. Concludes, "Of all of Netsch's accomplishments, what I admire most about him is his partnership with his wife…. Because of his unselfishness, she made political history."

2001

Baugher, Shirley. *Our Old Town: The History of a Neighborhood.* **Chicago: The Old Town Triangle Association, 2001. 158 pp. Illustrated.**

Includes short biographical entries on the professional achievements of Walter and Dawn Clark Netsch. Walter is listed as the second vice president of the Old Town Triangle Association in 1980 (pp. 130–31, 141).

Bey, Lee. "Netsch Home Fits; Doesn't Battle Its Neighbors." *Chicago Sun-Times,* **May 6, 2001. 2 illustrations.**

Highlights Netsch's home 27 years after its construction. Compliments its modernist design for blending into the neighborhood and praises it as a "superb design with an open, multilayered interior where bold forms, light and space are properly wed." Netsch responds to questions about the design and flexibility and discusses modifications to accommodate an elevator. Photos show exterior and interior views.

Dupré, Judith. *Churches.* **New York: HarperCollins, 2001. 168 pp. 4 illustrations.**

Includes a two-page spread on the U.S. Air Force Academy Cadet Chapel, illustrated by four color photos and a small floor plan (pp. 132–33). Text highlights the chapel's controversial history, its innovative use of structural technology and prefabrication methods, and its separate chapels.

> *Both praised and derided at the time of its construction as "Air Age Gothic," the chapel and its history present an intriguing study for contemporary church builders who seek to resolve the dilemma of reinterpreting ecclesiastical tradition in a way that reflects their times and yet retains meaning.*

"G. Wiz/Blivas Science and Technology Center, Sarasota, Florida." *Florida/Caribbean Architect* **(Winter 2001): 14, 16. 5 illustrations, 1 plan.**

Credits architect Dale S. Parks (of CC+P Architects) with redesigning the Sarasota County's Selby Public Library, designed by Netsch in 1975 and based on Field Theory. Parks transformed the library into the G. Wiz/Blivas Science and Technology Center in 2000. Details how Parks modified Netsch's original design to accommodate new uses. Concludes, "The building is very respectful of the original architect's design and it provides a dynamic addition to the city's cultural center."

Kamin, Blair. *Why Architecture Matters: Lessons from Chicago.* **Chicago: University of Chicago Press, 2001. 386 pp. Illustrated.**

Compilation of Kamin's architecture criticism that originally appeared in the *Chicago Tribune* from 1994 to 2000. One article, "Masters of Understatement" (originally published February 6, 1998), highlights SOM's outstanding achievements, including the Inland Steel Building (p. 129).

In an article entitled "Grant Park's Double Life" (October 29, 1998) Netsch discusses the "populist status" of Grant Park in Chicago (pp. 323, 328).

2002

Skidmore, Owings & Merrill. *Preserving a Heritage: Executive Summary, the Air Force Academy Design Standards. Prepared for the United States Air Force Academy.* **Chicago: Skidmore, Owings & Merrill, 2002. Unpaged. Illustrated.**

Lengthy document that assesses the present condition of the U.S. Air Force Academy buildings and recommends preservation measures. Publishes design standards used in the original construction phases and cost estimates of various treatment solutions. Strongly urges preservation of this historic site and its unique architecture.

2003

Caldbeck, Elaine, Jeffrey Garrett, Harrie M. Hughes, Robert Michaelson, Joan A. Reyes, James Shedlock, and Christopher Simoni. "Northwestern University Libraries." In *Encyclopedia of Library and Information Science,* **edited by Miriam A. Drake. New York: Marcel Dekker, 2003: 3: 2165–78.**

Entry provides an overview of the history of Northwestern University's libraries, including Netsch's designs for Northwestern University Library and the Seeley G. Mudd Library for Science and Engineering. Includes a list of references.

Diedrich, John. "AFA Chapel Roof Leaking Cash." *Colorado Springs Gazette,* **November 3, 2003.**

Report on water leaks at the U.S. Air Force Academy Cadet Chapel that the author claims will cost $35 million to repair completely. Article states that it costs between $200,000 and $300,000 a year to caulk the chapel's 32 miles of roof joints. States that the building itself is in no danger of major damage.

Glancey, Jonathan. "Architecture: Whose Home Is It Anyway?: NATO Is Finally Getting a New HQ. But Should the US Be Designing It?" Features, *The Guardian* **(London), February 3, 2003.**

Reviews conceptual designs by "that grand old Yankee firm" SOM for the new NATO Headquarters, a complex planned for the King Albert I Royal Air Force base, near the existing NATO Headquarters in Brussels. SOM was awarded the commission in 2002 over 121 other candidates. References Netsch's U.S. Air Force Academy and Cadet Chapel ("One of the world's most magnificent chapels, an aluminum-clad compression of what seems to be 17 vertically stacked jet fighter wings."). Urges SOM to assemble an international team that will safeguard against the overpowering and "terrifying beauty" of multinational corporate megastructures. Postulates that

> *institutions [such as NATO] ought to be housed in buildings that evoke the idea of working together as well as quiet, if firm, resolution. They need to be calm, yet as characterful as the Air Force Academy ... simple, orderly and frills-free as the Air Force Academy, whose buildings are actually quite simple objects, and whose impact derives mainly from its heroic mountainous backdrop and mesmerizing chapel.*

NATO Headquarters is scheduled to open in 2009.

Hein, Rich. "Look Beyond Bottom Line on Selling Thompson Center." *Chicago Sun-Times,* **April 14, 2003. Illustrated.**

Editorial that opposes Governor Rod Blagojevich's plans to sell the James R. Thompson Center (formerly the State of Illinois Building) to a developer who wants to demolish it. Claims that numerous ugly buildings in Chicago have, over time, become accepted as part of the cityscape. Quotes Helmut Jahn, the building's principal architect, defending it as "an important building because it reflects a certain time, the way the state decided how to represent itself." Jahn also points out that the Thompson Center connects to the city's infrastructure. In the opening paragraph Hein rails against "Walter Netsch's famously hideous structures at the University of Illinois at Chicago Campus, buildings so stark and ugly that once a UIC survey of prospective freshmen found that one reason high school students visiting the school chose not to attend was because they hated the buildings." (See also 1987: Owen, David. "Writs Fly Round Chicago Architects.")

O'Gorman, Thomas J. *Chicago — Architecture in Detail.* **London: PRC Publishing, 2003. 96 pp. Illustrated.**
Showcases the Inland Steel Building (pp. 72–75) with three color photos. Credits Netsch and Bruce Graham equally for its design. Notes the building's historical importance and numerous innovative design and engineering features. Discusses how it was immediately embraced by the public and has become a beloved Chicago landmark. "The Inland Steel Building is as bright and fresh as the day it opened forty-three years ago. Its glass curtain and shining stainless steel continue to dazzle" (p. 75).

Schulze, Franz, and Kevin Harrington, eds. *Chicago's Famous Buildings: A Photographic Guide to the City's Architectural Landmarks and Other Notable Buildings.* **4th ed. Chicago and London: University of Chicago Press, 1993. 348 pp. Illustrated.**
Includes short entries on the Art Institute of Chicago (p. 45), the Inland Steel Building (p. 3), the UIC campus (pp. 112, 210–12), the IIT campus (pp. 232–34), the University of Chicago campus (pp. 137, 249), and the Northwestern University campus (pp. 142, 266–67). The fourth edition was the first to credit Netsch's work on these projects. He also is mentioned as the architect of the East Wing of the Art Institute of Chicago and as the design partner behind the UIC campus. Illustrations

are featured in the entries for the Inland Steel Building, multiple buildings at UIC, and the Lindheimer Astronomical Research Center at Northwestern.

Tigerman, Stanley. "Oral History of Stanley Tigerman." Interview by Betty J. Blum, April 10–14, 1998. Transcript. Chicago: Art Institute of Chicago, 2003. 273 pp.
Tigerman (b. 1930) worked as a junior designer under Netsch on the U.S. Air Force Academy commission. In SOM's Chicago office, Tigerman worked with Bruce Graham before opening his own firm in 1964. Discusses his turbulent associations with Netsch (pp. 14, 41–50, 54–55, 64, 65, 69, 103–09, 124, 127, 142–43, 222, and 236). Available at www.artic.edu /aic/libraries/caohp/tigerman.html.

2004

Arnest, Mark. "Academy Created Its Own Classical Style." *Colorado Springs Gazette* **(Spring 2004). 3 illustrations.**
Article on the U.S. Air Force Academy in a commemorative 50th-anniversary section. The Cadet Chapel is featured.

Barber, Joe. "Architect Knows Ins, Outs of Academy." Metro, *Colorado Springs Gazette*, **August 24, 2004. 2 illustrations.**
Feature on the U.S. Air Force Academy, with reference to architect Duane Boyle, chief of program development at the Academy, who is responsible for architectural and planning programs. Boyle previously worked for SOM before joining the Academy staff in 1983. Mentions Netsch's designs and conceptual program for the Academy:

> *Netsch came up with a 7-foot basic unit for the academy's construction and landscape grid…. Netsch liked to travel, and when he was in Japan — before the Academy work began — he took special notice of the tatami, fabric mats roughly 6 feet*

long used for sleeping. "That started him thinking about the proportions of the human body and that relates to the built environment," Boyle said.

Davidson, Cameron, and Magda Nakassis. *Chicago from Above.* **London: Myriad Books, 2004. 32 pp. Illustrated.**

Photographic essay with explanatory text highlights noteworthy Chicago landmarks. East Wing of the Art Institute (p. 14) and the Frances Searle Building at Northwestern University (p. 25) are pictured.

Nauman, Robert Allen. *On the Wings of Modernism: The United States Air Force Academy.* **Urbana: University of Illinois Press, 2004. 173 pp. Illustrated.**

Comprehensive and thoroughly documented history of the Air Force Academy from initial conception to completion of the Cadet Chapel in 1963. Nauman is a professor of art and architecture at the University of Colorado at Boulder. Includes numerous references to and quotations from Netsch. Features design plans, schematics, elevations, and photos of the site and of buildings under construction. Ends with an epilogue about the Academy's future as both a dynamic institution and as a national monument. Appendices include a list of applicants for the Academy competition and text on finalists besides SOM. Includes a selected bibliography (pp. 165–68). Definitive scholarly resource for the Academy's building history. Review: W. Morgan, *Architectural Record* 192, no. 11 (November 2004): 79, 81.

———. "Preserving a Monument: The United States Air Force Academy." *Future Anterior: Journal of Historic Preservation History, Theory and Criticism* **1, no. 2 (Fall 2004): 32–41. 3 illustrations, 2 plans.**

Summarizes efforts by the Air Force Academy and SOM consultants to preserve the Academy's original buildings "within the context of both tradition and continuity, with respect for the past

an eye to the future" (p. 40). Recounts conversations with Duane Boyle, an architect in charge of the Academy's design and planning, as well as SOM consultants Marilyn Jordan Taylor and Mark Leininger. Notes that "Walter Netsch, SOM's architect in charge of the original academy design, also continues to offer advice" (p. 36). Provides a concise overview of the Academy's history, changes and new buildings added in the 1980s (not always in keeping with the original scheme), SOM's new master plan for the Academy (created in 1985), and ramifications and challenges of maintaining the integrity of the Cadet Area since its designation as a National Historic Landmark District.

Randl, Chad Garrett. "The Mania for A-Frames." *Old House Journal Online,* **July 2004. www.oldhousejournal.com /magazine/2004/july/aframes.shtml.**

Brief mention of the U.S. Air Force Academy Cadet Chapel among noteworthy A-frames: "In 1963, Walter Netsch Jr. exploded the typically flat A-frame roof plane into three dimensions with the Air Force Academy Cadet Chapel in Colorado Springs, Colorado" (p. 1).

Sinkevitch, Alice, ed. *AIA Guide to Chicago.* **2nd ed. New York: Harcourt, 2004. 574 pp. Illustrated.**

Contains entries for St. Matthew United Methodist Church (p. 141), a project by Netsch's protegé Wilbert O. Rueter (p. 183), the Netsch home (p. 185), the UIC campus (pp. 297–301), and Regenstein Library at the University of Chicago (p. 451). (See also 1993: Sinkevitch.)

"Walter Netsch Inducted as Life Member of Library Board." *Footnotes* **29, no. 1 (Winter 2004): 6. 2 illustrations.**

One-page biography of Netsch, with a history of the Northwestern University Library and a black-and-white reproduction of a watercolor sketch of the building. Netsch became the Library Board of Governors' first life member in October

2004. Includes a photo of Netsch receiving congratulations, with Dawn Clark Netsch in the background. Publication for donors to and friends of the library.

Zukowsky, John, and Martha Thorne. *Masterpieces of Chicago Architecture.* **New York: Rizzoli; Chicago: Art Institute of Chicago, 2004. 240 pp. Illustrated.**

Publishes more than 200 illustrations drawn from the Art Institute's repository of architectural drawings, models, and building fragments with accompanying text. Includes text on and three color photos of the Inland Steel Building (pp. 122–23); credits Netsch's original all-glass design, which was finished by Bruce Graham in stainless steel to emphasize the owner's corporate image.

2005

Baugher, Shirley. *At Home in Our Old Town: Every House Has a Story.* **Chicago: Old Town Triangle Association, 2005. 172 pp. Illustrated.**

The Netsch home is featured (pp. 125–34), supplemented by seven exterior and interior photos, portraits of Walter and Dawn Clark Netsch, and one floor plan. In the text Walter discusses site selection, design ideas based on Field Theory, engineering a home without interior walls, and the couple's art collection. Includes biographical details about the Netsches (pp. 130–34).

Becker, Robert. "Library Set for Grand New Chapter; U. of C. Facility Will Be Nation's Largest." *Chicago Tribune,* **June 5, 2005. 2 maps.**

Announces plans by the University of Chicago to launch a $42 million expansion of the Joseph Regenstein Library. When completed in 2009, the expansion will make Regenstein the largest research library under a single roof in North America, with a capacity of 8 million volumes. Preserving open access to more than half of the library's print collections is a high priority. Notes Netsch's role in designing the original library.

Clark, Roger H., and Michael Pause. *Precedents in Architecture: Analytic Diagrams, Formative Ideas, and Partis.* **3rd ed. Hoboken, NJ: John Wiley, 2005. 306 pp. Illustrated.**

This book includes a conceptual drawing of Long Library at Wells College (p. 273).

Dickson, William R. "William R. Dickson Oral History Project." Interview by Susan Crowley, February 9, 2005. Transcript. **Cambridge, Massachusetts: MIT Archives and Special Collections. 12 pp.**

Dickson, a former senior vice president of MIT, comments on campus buildings designed during his tenure. Discusses in particular the Center for Materials Science and Engineering Building (Building 13, also called the Vannevar Bush Center for Material Sciences), designed by Netsch in 1963. Mentions foundation problems and the added expense of using reinforced shotcrete concrete for window frames, a solution that Netsch strongly favored:

> So, Walter Netsch, then, fell in love with it [shotcrete] and used it over and over again on all of his other buildings. I think it's adequate, but I never thought it was the cat's meow that I think Walter thought it was. I think the piles [foundation footings] and windows were the most significant things except for one other thing. And that is some pile clusters had to be driven very close to Building 10 — about as close to Building 10 as you could actually get a pile driver in place. And when these were driven — over course we were very cognizant of settlement and stuff of buildings. We found that Building 10 began to rise. It was the building of the campus, and it settled the most over its history, almost ten inches. The concern was that after things stabilized that it would settle.

Felsen, Martin, and Sarah Dunn.
"Walter Netsch: Field Theory."
In *Chicago Architecture: Histories,
Revisions, Alternatives*, edited by
Charles Waldheim and Katrina
Rüedi Ray, 253–60. Chicago and
London: University of Chicago
Press, 2005. 3 illustrations.

Explains and analyzes Field Theory
through text, diagrams, photographs,
and quotations from Netsch.

> *At SOM, Netsch was a maverick.
> He was given little respect from
> his partners, and he had his own
> autonomous studio away from SOM
> headquarters. But he remained
> tightly connected to the SOM estab-
> lishment by way of his general urban
> assumption, even insistence, that any
> project site/context be empty before
> design work begins: field theory can't
> or won't deal with existing context,
> it needs to makes its own fresh start.
> The operative ground condition for
> field theory is tabula rasa.* (p. 254)

Goodman, David. "Systematic Genius:
Walter Netsch and the Architecture of
Bureaucracy." In *Chicago Architecture:
Histories, Revisions, Alternatives*,
edited by Charles Waldheim and
Katrina Rüedi Ray, 261–84. Chicago
and London: University of Chicago
Press, 2005. 3 illustrations, 5 plans
and diagrams.

Lengthy tribute to Netsch, with an
overview of his career, designs, and
theoretical principles. Describes Netsch
as an SOM maverick, idealist, program-
mer, specialist, auteur, and opportunist:
"Netsch is the genius of the bureaucracy,
within the bureaucracy" (p. 263).

> *Netsch pursued an academic market
> that might otherwise reject a firm
> whose clientele consisted largely of
> multinational corporations. Yet,
> unlike executives at GM, the SOM
> partnership was never fully within
> the organization. Although SOM*

*did not pursue this possibility, Netsch
presented them with a model of target
market branding within SOM.*
(p. 284)

Jones, William Goodrich. "Some Fields
Are in the City." Address, Chicago
Literary Club, March 28, 2005. 18 pp.
Typescript.

Text of an address by Jones, a librarian at
UIC, on Netsch's career, major commis-
sions, the UIC campus, and Field Theory.
Focuses on UIC buildings that exemplify
Field Theory. Illuminated with 67 slides.

> *These are beautiful buildings and
> unusual buildings, and they have
> their defenders as well as their critics.
> But the control of space that is readily
> apparent in the architectural draw-
> ings is less evident to those working
> inside those buildings.*
>
> *The difficulty of working within
> the constraints of field theory
> has led to few emulators among
> contemporary architects. Faculty
> still complain about the physical
> separation of offices, classrooms, and
> lecture centers, arguing that Netsch's
> grand plan prevents conversation
> between faculty and students instead
> of promoting it.* (p. 14)
> …
> *Walter Netsch was quoted as saying
> of the Circle Campus, "I hope this is
> the last nineteenth-century campus
> we ever design. Next time I hope to
> approach a campus as a single system,
> not a group of objects." Without our
> knowing how he would approach a
> 21st century campus, we will surely
> agree that Netsch's original intent
> of promoting conversation, debate,
> and learning between students and
> faculty are still goals worth pursuing,
> and, based on the record, have to a
> satisfying degree been achieved.*
> (pp. 15–16)

Copy from author in University
Archives, Northwestern University.

Kamin, Blair. "Marked for Demolition, Kenilworth House Is Worth Saving." *Chicago Tribune,* August 25, 2005.

Item (at the end of an article on a Daniel Burnham house in Kenilworth) mentions the purchase by architect Frank Gehry of the Inland Steel Building. Credits Netsch with being one of the building's early designers. Gehry states his intention to throw a party at the building this fall and invite "all the old Skidmore guys."

Olson, Janet. "Deconstructing Library (Re)construction: A Plaza-ble Tale, or, More Is Less." *Lantern* (Fall 2005): 2, 7. 1 illustration.

Article in Northwestern University Library's staff publication about rhetoric used to describe library building projects, with particular reference to the Library Plaza. "Walter Netsch kicked off the rhetoric-fest when he projected a structure that 'both inside and out becomes at times an object, at other times a continuous event.'" Notes that the 31,000-square-foot Library Plaza had unobstructed views of Lake Michigan until 1972, when the Norris University Center was constructed. Photo shows the Library Plaza, named for attorney and University trustee Kenneth Burgess, in 1969.

Schonwald, Josh. "University to Expand Library Collections to Prepare Next Generations of Scholars." *University of Chicago Chronicle* 24, no. 18 (June 9, 2005). 1 illustration.

Announces the addition to Regenstein Library, concentrating mostly on the impact of the library expansion on student and faculty research. Notes that "the building's architectural plan, which Walter Netsch designed, includes plans for an expansion. 'The foresight of the plan,' said Judith Nadler [director of the University Library], 'was crucial.'" Plans called for the addition to be connected to the west side of the existing building.

Schulze, Franz. *Illinois Institute of Technology: The Campus Guide; An Architectural Tour.* New York: Princeton Architectural Press, 2005. 111 pp. Illustrated.

Building-by-building history and guide to IIT's Chicago campus with photographs by Richard Barnes. Includes Netsch's Grover M. Hermann Hall (IIT's student union; pp. 42–43) and the Paul V. Galvin Library (pp. 46–47).

Waldheim, Charles, and Katrina Rüedi Ray. "Introduction: Chicago Is History." In *Chicago Architecture: Histories, Revisions, Alternatives,* edited by Charles Waldheim and Katrina Rüedi Ray, xix–xx. Chicago and London: University of Chicago Press, 2005.

This essay serves as an introduction to other writings — including those on Netsch (see Felsen and Dunn and Goodman, above) — included in the volume.

2006

Adams, Nicholas. *Skidmore, Owings & Merrill: SOM dal 1936.* Milan: Electa, 2006. 338 pp. Illustrated. In Italian.

First comprehensive history of SOM. The introduction provides an overview of the firm's history and growth, followed by sections on 27 major SOM commissions built between 1946 and 1990, including the Inland Steel Building (pp. 102–13, 17 photos, 1 elevation, and 1 floor plan) and the U.S. Air Force Academy (pp. 146–61, 13 photos). Reproduces black-and-white and color photographs, some full page and double spread. References to Netsch can be found throughout: pp. 9–10, 12, 15, 24, 30, 32–34 ["Il caso di Walter A. Netsch"], 36–37, 41, 47–49, 120, 124, 187, 195, and 203. Includes maps of New York City, Chicago, and San Francisco that pinpoint SOM projects (pp. 319–21), a bibliography of general sources, and a bibliography of primary and secondary works relating to the commissions presented in the book (pp. 322–31). The bibliography also lists awards and prizes for major buildings. Adams is a professor of the history of architecture at Vassar College.

Anderson, Maggie. "Space-shifting the Square." *Daily Iowan,* **January 31, 2006.**

Anecdotal article about a freshman who couldn't find her professor's office in the University of Iowa's Lindquist Center, a building designed by Netsch in 1972. The student was informed by Robert Bruegmann — who was on campus for a presentation entitled "Walter Netsch: Modernism at Mid-Century in Iowa" — that the building's complex geometry is based on Netsch's Field Theory.

Chartoff, Jacob, and Iker Gil Miguens. *When Campus Becomes City: UIC Masterplan.* **CD-ROM. Chicago: University of Illinois at Chicago, College of Architecture and the Arts, School of Architecture, Spring 2006. 287 pp. Illustrated.**

A compilation of materials collected and produced during an extensive study of the UIC campus. The report was accompanied by large-format panels, animations, and a model. The project was completed during the 2006 spring semester while the authors were pursuing their master of architecture degrees (p. 6).

Reproduces Netsch's original presentation diagrammatic drawings, campus plan, and construction photos (pp. 45–75 and 136–37). Includes no text beyond reprints of newspaper articles and brief captions.

Curry, Jessica. "Dawn Clark Netsch on Politics." *Chicago Life,* **November 2006, 34–36, 71. 1 illustration.**

Profile of and interview with Dawn Clark Netsch that reviews her groundbreaking career in Illinois state politics, her preferences for candidates in the upcoming local and state elections, and her social activism. She discusses her marriage to Walter Netsch and their love of the arts and the Chicago White Sox.

Cutler, Irving. *Chicago: Metropolis of the Mid-Continent.* **4th ed. Carbondale: Southern Illinois University Press, 2006. 447 pp. 1 illustration, maps.**

Historical and geographical introduction to the city of Chicago that charts its growth and urban development since the last Ice Age. Includes Netsch "among the most distinguished of the later-twentieth-century architects in the Second Chicago School" (p. 295). Also mentions Netsch's UIC campus, the Regenstein Library at the University of Chicago, and his early design for the Inland Steel Building, "which was the prototype of innovative structural features" (p. 289).

Nance, Kevin. "Building on Tradition." *Chicago Sun-Times,* **September 24, 2006.**

Lengthy newspaper article on SOM's past, present, and future. References Nicholas Adams's book (see above). Regards Netsch as an example of an SOM architect who "achieved a measure of individual fame." Mentions his initial design for the Inland Steel Building, Field Theory, and his "underappreciated Air Force Academy Chapel in Colorado." Includes Stanley Tigerman's recollections of interoffice rivalries in the 1960s and 1970s.

"United States Air Force Academy Cadet Chapel Restoration." *SOM Journal* **4 (2006): 92–105. 19 illustrations, 7 plans and diagrams.**

Report on SOM's restoration plan for the Cadet Chapel, completed in 2003. The restoration was intended to "fix problems of water filtration, repair any deteriorated components, remove any added elements, and restore the chapel to its original form and detailed profiles" (p. 93). The project was intended to "restore the interior space to its original visual brilliance and maintain its visceral spirituality" (p. 93). "The Cadet Chapel has become an icon of the Modern Age. The Chapel was designed to be provocative and iconic, and symbolic of the mission of the newly created Air Force" (p. 93).

Following one page of text, the article contains reproductions of color and black-and-white photographs of the chapel, some showing deterioration, and diagrams of the restoration work.

2007

Adams, Nicholas. *Skidmore, Owings & Merrill: SOM since 1936.* **London: Phaidon Press, 2007. 340 pp. Illustrated.**

English edition of *Skidmore, Owings & Merrill: SOM dal 1936,* published in Italy in 2006 (see above).

Chappell, Sally A. Kitt. *Chicago's Urban Nature: A Guide to the City's Architecture + Landscape.* **Chicago and London: University of Chicago Press, 2007. Illustrated.**

Credits Netsch, as a city park commissioner, with persuading the city of Chicago to try a landscape solution to beautifying North Lake Shore Drive. "The median planters with trees and flowers installed at this time have delighted everyone ever since" (p. 21). Also mentions Netsch's master plan for UIC (p. 110) and the Lake Meadows Shopping Center, an SOM project from the early 1950s. Quotes Netsch on Lake Meadows:

> It was not a sophisticated landscape design, but it turned out to have a nice aura. One of the reasons was the large scale. The idea was that it was a meadow by the lake. We were interested in openness. Owings did not want the closely packed quality of the near north side. (p. 221)

Knapp, Genevieve. "Examining the Legacy of NU's Most Iconic Architect." *North by Northwestern,* **October 18, 2007. www.northbynorthwestern.com /2007/10/4433. 3 pp. 3 illustrations.**

Article published online about Netsch's buildings at Northwestern University. Cites Field Theory and problems with navigation. Mentions the Francis Searle Building, Northwestern University

Library, and the Lindheimer Astronomical Research Center. Quotes Netsch about Lindheimer's demolition in September 1995:

> When they decided to take it down, I warned them that it was not a post and beam structure, and that it would come down with difficulty. I told them they'd have to separate parts, and they didn't do that. It made headlines and news films as it lay there sagging. It was quite a lesson in the means of structural form.

———. **"Tower Power: The History of NU's Sometimes-Purple Clock."** *North by Northwestern,* **October 18, 2007. www.northbynorthwestern.com /2007/10/4193. 2 pp. 1 illustration.**

Feature on Northwestern's clock tower, designed by Netsch for the plaza of the Rebecca Crown Center (1968). Quotes Netsch: "I thought it was important to have a symbol of entry to Northwestern." When asked how he would design it today, he answered, "I'm not sure how I'd do it, because I'm not thinking about it."

Higgins, Michael. "Architect Has Designs on Keeping License." *Chicago Tribune,* **May 21, 2007. 2 illustrations.**

Details Netsch's lawsuit to keep his Illinois state architect's license despite health problems that prevented him from fulfilling the state's continuing education requirement. Netsch filed suit on April 30, 2007, in Cook County Circuit Court, through his attorney Matthew Iverson. Quotes both Iverson and Dawn Clark Netsch about Netsch's resolve to qualify for a medical exemption, which was granted in 2005 but revoked in 2007.

Mitchell, William J. *Imagining MIT: Designing a Campus for the Twenty-First Century.* **Cambridge, MA: MIT Press, 2007. 142 pp.**

Brief mention of the U.S. Air Force Academy Cadet Chapel — "a soaring structure in aluminum by Walter Netsch … that would not be appropriate for MIT" (p. 5). Includes no references to MIT buildings designed and renovated by Netsch.

Pridmore, Jay. "A New Order." *Chicago,* **February 2007, 62–65, 98–104. 12 illustrations.**

Exposé on a "recent shakeup" at SOM that culminated in the departure of partner Adrian Smith in late 2006. Pridmore claims that SOM is "shrewdly remaking itself for the 21st century" by embracing modern designs by younger architects. Examines personalities, motives, and politics that are reshaping the firm, as well as current projects. Small photos show famous SOM commissions, including the Inland Steel Building (p. 64). Mentions conflicts between Netsch and Bruce Graham in the 1960s and 1970s (p. 101).

Contributors

Robert Bruegmann, historian and critic of the built environment, is professor of art history, architecture, and urban planning at the University of Illinois at Chicago. He is the author of numerous books and articles, including the award-winning volume *The Architects and the City: Holabird & Roche of Chicago, 1880–1918* (University of Chicago Press) and *Sprawl: A Compact History* (University of Chicago Press), a work that received worldwide attention. He is finishing a monograph on Chicago architect Harry Weese.

Russell Clement is head of the Art Collection at Northwestern University Library. The author of a series of research guides on fin-de-siècle French artists, he contributes reviews of architecture and design books to *Library Journal* and *Choice Magazine*.

Martin Felsen and **Sarah Dunn** are cofounders of UrbanLab in Chicago, a collaborative office practicing architecture and urbanism. Felsen and Dunn were recently named the next director and research director, respectively, of Archeworks, Chicago's alternative design school, where students create multidisciplinary design solutions for social, cultural, and environmental concerns. Felsen teaches city design and theory as an associate studio professor in the College of Architecture at the Illinois Institute of Technology. Dunn teaches architectural design and theory as an assistant professor in the School of Architecture at the University of Illinois at Chicago.

David Goodman is a visiting assistant professor of architecture in the College of Architecture at the Illinois Institute of Technology, where he teaches architectural design and theory. He is also cofounder of r+d studio, a Chicago-based architecture and urban design office.

Robert Allen Nauman teaches the history of art and architecture in the Department of Art and Art History at the University of Colorado at Boulder. He is the author of *On the Wings of Modernism: The United States Air Force Academy* (University of Illinois Press) and contributed to *Modernism at Mid-Century: The United States Air Force Academy* (University of Chicago Press).

Index

General Index

Photographs and drawings are indicated by page numbers in italics. Names followed by page numbers in bold type indicate authored or edited works, interviews (either interviewer or person interviewed), and photographers cited in the bibliography.

For the purposes of economy and because of the preponderance of short entries there, page ranges in the bibliographies have been treated as continuous whereas they usually are not.

Community Pediatric and Adolescent
Medicine (Netsch), 1978 (Baldwin
Building), Mayo Clinic, Rochester,
Minnesota, 18, 172
*Complexity and Contradiction in
Architecture* (Venturi), 90
Compostela (Spain), 92
computer technology, 9, 57, 128, 135, 174,
176
Concrete Contractors Association of
Greater Chicago, 17
Condit, Carl, 176–77
contextual architecture, 89–95, 102, 153,
178
Convent of La Tourette (Le Corbusier)
Eveux-sur-Arbresle, France, 55, 115
Cook, Sterling, 177
Corbusier. *See* Le Corbusier
Craig, Louis, **172**
Cross, Robert, **180**
Crowley, Susan, **195**
Crown-Zellerbach Headquarters
Building plans (Netsch), 1954, San
Francisco, 15, 16, 35, 142, 148, 182, 184
Crump, Joseph, **184**
Crystal House (Keck) Chicago Century
of Progress World's Fair, 29
Currie, Leonard, 155–56
Curry, Jessica, **198**
Cutler, Irving, **198**

Dailey, Gardner, 166
Daley, Richard J., 43–44
Danz, Ernest, **152**
Dart, Edward, 155–56, 176–77
Dartmouth College, Hanover, New
Hampshire, 27, 29
Davidson, Cameron, **194**
Davidson, Cynthia Chapin, **183**
Davidson, Donald C., 149
Davis, Gene, 112
*The Death and Life of Great American
Cities* (Jacobs), 90
Deering Library, Northwestern
University, Evanston, Illinois, 9, 11,
81–82, 90, 91, 170, 177
Delap, Tony, 112, 124
Del Monte Lodge (Owings) Monterey,
California, 166
Del Monte Shopping Center (Netsch),
1950, Del Monte, California, 15, 49, 139

democratic architecture, 112, 115
Deno House (Yost) Highland Park,
Illinois, 180
Department of Music, 1979, University of
Chicago, 18
Design and Craftsmanship Medal
(AIA), 16
Dessau (Germany), *87*, 89
Dickson, William R, **195**
Diedrich, John, **192**
Dixon, John Morris, **154**, **157**, **159**
Doms, Keith, **149**
Dooley, Edwin, 63
Dornbusch, Charles, 165–66
Douglas, James, 64, 166–67
Douglas Valley (Colorado), 51
Drexler, Arthur, **172**
Dreyfuss, Stuart, **173**
Dubuffet, Jean, 108
Dueholm, Ben, 13
Dunlap, William, 99
Dunn, Sarah, 13, **73–78**, **196**, 201
Dupré, Judith, **191**
Dutch architects, 111
Dymaxion House, 52, 72n61

Edelmann, Frédéric, **178**
860–880 Lake Shore Drive (Mies van der
Rohe, Chicago), 109, 126
Einstein, Albert, 24
Eisenhower, Dwight D., 47, 179
Eisenman, Peter, 86, 183
Electrical Engineering and Electronics
Complex. *See* Sherman Fairchild
Electrical Engineering and Electronics
Complex
Ellman, Richard, 5, 45n17
Elmendorf Air Force Base Hospital
(Netsch), 1952, Anchorage, Alaska, 15,
35
Elmslie, George Grant, 111
Elsen, Patricia, **162**
English Gothic architecture, 60
Entenza, John, 125
environmental concerns. *See* nature,
man-made forms; Netsch, Walter,
environmental concerns of; Netsch,
Walter, social consciousness of
Erler, Leo J., 50, 70
existence-will, 110, 114, 134
expressionist architecture, 93–95

Morton, David, **170**
Motherwell, Robert, 38, 112, 119, 124, 185
Mudd Library for Science and
Engineering. *See* Seeley G. Mudd
Library for Science and Engineering
Murphy, James A., **165, 168**
Murphy Jahn Associates, 181
Murray Matthew House (Netsch), c.
1954, Monterey, California, 34
Musée-Galerie de la SEITA (Paris), 19
Museum of Contemporary Art (Chicago)
*Late Entries to the Chicago Tribune
Tower Competition* exhibition, 18, 42,
115–16, 135, 173–74, 176
open forum on, 124–25
Museum of Modern Art (MOMA) New
York City
aesthetic change and, 111
Buildings for Business and Government
exhibition, 16, 143, 144
*Recent Buildings by Skidmore, Owings
& Merrill* exhibition, 15, 139
*Transformations in American
Architecture* exhibition, 18
Museum of Science and Industry
(Chicago), 19, 32, 44, 178–79
Muslims/Muslim Culture, 68, 135–36
Mussolini Moderne architecture, 110

Nadler, Judith, 197
Nagle, James, 173
Naha (Japan), 34
Nakassis, Magda, **194**
Nance, Kevin, **198**
Nashua (New Hampshire), 27
Nasland, Ken, 37
National Council of Churches, 64, 68
National Historic Landmark Districts,
47, 69, 194
National Register of Historic Places, 19,
188
NATO Headquarters (SOM) Brussels,
192
natural forms
abstractions of, 54
early interest in, 27
as influence, 10
man-made forms and, 49, 60, 100,
101, 106
order brought to, 55
U.S. Naval Postgraduate School and,
49–50, 52, 100–01

natural forms (*continued*)
See also chrysanthemum field
geometry; gingko leaves/trees
Nauman, Robert Allan, 13, **45n9, 47–69,
194**
Naval Postgraduate School. *See* U.S.
Naval Postgraduate School
Navy Pier (Chicago), 180
Neal, Steve, **191**
Nereim, Anders, **183**
Nervi, Pier Luigi, 111
Netsch, Anna Calista Smith, 27, *27*, 30, *31*
Netsch, Dawn Clark
as art donor, 11, 41, 162
on Goldsmith, 138
homage to, 10
at home, *2*
law practice of, 39
Netsch home and, 168
Netsches' art collection and, 158, 160,
186, 187, 190, 195
on Northwestern School of Law
faculty, 39
Owings and, 121
political career of, 39, 43, 119, 124, 170,
185–87, 190, 198
Walter and, 10, 11, 16, 38–39, *39*, 185,
189–90, 195, 198
Netsch, Walter
in the 1980s, *76*
Aalto and, 28, 48, 111
Air Force Academy and. *See* U.S.
Air Force Academy; U.S. Air Force
Academy Cadet Chapel
on architects' roles, 104, 187
on architectural education, 131, 136, 146
archives of, 45
art collection of, 24, 38, 158, 160, 161,
177, 186, 190, 195. *See also Living with
Art* exhibitions
as art donor, 11, 41, 162
Art Institute of Chicago, enrolled
in, 28
artwork by, 19, 42, 174, 183
awards received by. *See* awards
received by Netsch
biography of, 27–45
with Bruegmann, *25*
Bunshaft and. *See under* Bunshaft,
Gordon
career overview of, 196
on changing social patterns, 103

Netsch home and studio, 1974, Chicago
  in AIA Guide, 186, 194
  Chicago architecture and, 178
  Cohen on, 169
  Dawn Clark's role in planning, 168
  descriptions of, 24, 39
  Field Theory and, 168, 170–71, 195
  interior spaces of, 190, 195
  mentioned, 163
  modernism and, 191
  Moore on, 168
  in Netsch chronology, 17
  Netsch on, 108, 114, 119–20, 170, 187
  Netsches' art collection in, 120, 160,
    190
  photo of, 2
  See also Netsch, Walter, Chicago
    residences of
Neutra, Richard, 126
Nevel, Robert, 178
New Brutalism, 154
New Haven Fire Station (Carlin)
  Connecticut, 150
New Town (Netsch, master plan), 1973,
  Poinciana, Florida, 17
New Town-in-Town (Netsch, master
  plan), 1970, Newark, New Jersey, 17
Nexus World housing (Koolhaas), 83
Noel, Tom, **189**
Noland, Ken, 108, 112, 124
Norris University Center, Northwestern
  University, Evanston, Illinois, 177, 197
Northwestern University, Evanston,
  Illinois, 18, 150, 176
Northwestern University Deering
  Library, Evanston, Illinois, 9, 11, 81–82,
  90, 91, 170, 177
Northwestern University Francis Searle
  Building (Netsch), 1972, Evanston,
  Illinois, 17, 40, 169, 194
Northwestern University Lakefill
  Expansion Project (Netsch), 1962,
  Evanston, Illinois, 9, 12, 16, 40, 150, 153,
  157
Northwestern University Library
  (Netsch), 1964–70, Evanston, Illinois
    Air Force Academy Cadet Chapel
      and, 94
    in architectural history context, 79–95
    budget considerations of, 157, 158, 161,
      162–63
    Burchard on, 153

Northwestern University Library
  (continued)
    Chicago architecture and, 178
    computer facilities in, 9, 159
    construction of, 158, 161, 163
    contextual architecture and, 89–95,
      153, 154
    Core library, 9, 153, 159
    dedication of, 161
    Deering Library and, 9, 11, 81–82, 91
    design goals of, 161
    development plans of, 155
    dissenting views of, 162, 177
    expressionist architecture and, 93–95
    Field Theory and, 9–10, 76–77, 87, 159,
      161–62, 183
    in historical context, 170
    human program of, 160
    IIT libraries and, 9
    Joseph Regenstein Library and, 163
    Kleinschmidt on, 158
    Lakefill expansion project and, 157
    as machine, 87–95
    materials of, 91, 94
    mentioned, 173–74
    Netsch as Board of Governors' first
      life member, 12, 20, 194–95
    in Netsch chronology, 16, 17
    Netsch in, *44*
    Netsch on, 40, 128, 152, 159
    as Netsch/SOM project, 156
    Northwestern University Library
      Deering Family Award, 20
    Northwestern University Lakefill
      Expansion Project and, 9, 12, 153
    objectives of, 89–90, 133
    opening date of, scheduled, 158
    operative architecture and, 83–87
    overview of, 192, 194–95
    photos of, *80, 84, 85, 90, 93*
    as photo subject, 184
    Planning and Building Committee,
      40, 77, 85, 128, 161
    planning of, 9
    plans of, approved, 153
    plaza of, 80, 91, 161, 197
    sculptural forms of, 94, 161
    Seagram Building and, 86
    stacks, 77, 80–82, 85, 154, 159, 161
    Superior Craftsman Award for, 17
    as system, 80–83
    University Archives, 12

Index of Works by Walter Netsch

Photographs and drawings are indicated by page numbers in italics. Entries below correspond to the main index, where entries with numerous references appear individually in subentries under main headings.

Index of Locations with Works by Walter Netsch

Photographs and drawings are indicated by page numbers in italics. Entries below correspond to the main index, where entries with numerous references appear individually in subentries under main headings.

Inscription to Walter Netsch from his mentor, Nat Owings, in the 1974 SOM partners report